James Ulmer's
HOLLYWOOD
HOT LIST

James Ulmer's
HOLLYWOOD
HOT LIST

The Complete Guide
to Star Ranking

St. Martin's Griffin 🐾 New York

JAMES ULMER'S HOLLYWOOD HOT LIST. Copyright © 2000 by James Ulmer. All rights reserved. Printed in the United States of America. No part of this book may be used or reproduced in any manner whatsoever without written permission except in the case of brief quotations embodied in critical articles or reviews. For information, address St. Martin's Press, 175 Fifth Avenue, New York, N.Y. 10010.

www.stmartins.com
www.ulmerscale.com

Designed by Michael Mendelsohn at MM Design 2000, Inc.

Library of Congress Cataloging-in-Publication Data

Ulmer, James.
    James Ulmer's Hollywood hot list / by James Ulmer.
       p. cm.
    ISBN 0-312-25395-8
     1. Motion picture actors and actresses—United States—Biography.   2. Motion picture actors and actresses—Rating of—United States.   I. Title: Hollywood hot list.
II. Title.

PN1998.2 .U44 2000
791.43'028'092273—dc21
[B]

00-027965

First Edition: September 2000

10 9 8 7 6 5 4 3 2 1

Contents

The A+ List

The A List

The B+ List

The B List

The C List

Acknowledgments

This is a book that measures actors, yet I received immeasurable help from some less visible stars.

I thank my trusted webmaster, Craig Colbert, and my brilliant co-workers, Jim Herold and Brenda Berini, all of whom have been as dedicated as they have been undercompensated; the superb team at Exhibitor Relations Company, Inc.—Paul Dergarabedian, Randy Sanchez, Bryce Currence, and especially leading lady Julia Berggren; the generous Scott Downie and Ron Rodriguez at Celebrity Photo for coming to the rescue with a digital trove of images; my agent, Katherine Cowles, and my editor, Elizabeth Beier; Duane Byrge for his faith, humor, and free lodging while I wrote; Gabrielle Kelly for her many imaginations, inspirations, and helpful dinner parties; Jonathan Handel for his sharp pen and even sharper wit; Jim Korris, Stan Coleman, and Verna Flexon for their expertise and support early on; Rebekah Hirschler and her team at Creative Planet; Suki Medencevic; Rick Rosenthal; Shaun Redick at the William Morris Agency; Yoram Kahana and David John Basilio at Shooting Star; Debra Hill, Michael Hagemeyer, and Claude Hurwicz; and Hortense Powdermaker, for sounding the tribal drums.

Deep gratitude also must go to the Wisdom Keepers: the dozens of anonymous and invaluable industry experts in Hollywood and around the world, without whom The Ulmer Scale could not exist. Throughout the years, they have suffered through countless interviews and grading sessions for nothing but my thanks.

Finally, to my parents and Hugo, who long ago scaled the summit of any "list" in my life.

Introduction

 Star power is a little like real estate: If you're Julia Roberts or one of the two Toms, you own Hollywood. If you're John Travolta or Brad Pitt or anyone else on the A list, you've bought a hefty chunk. Everyone else is just renting.

In Hollywood, a star's value rises or falls depending on where he or she is in the pecking order of power. It's all about location, location, location.

It's a small tribe that makes up the top ranks of this pecking order—about two hundred elite, powerful stars. For the past several years, that tribe has been pegged to a comprehensive power list provided annually for Hollywood powerbrokers by my company, The Ulmer Scale (*www.ulmer-scale.com*). Ranking the star power of the world's top actors, the lineup tracks the meteoric rise of a Leo or a Matt as closely as it flaunts the decline of an aging action guy like Sly or a cooling screen-steamer like Demi.

The buzz starts early in the year: Who's on the list and who's off? Did Bruce Willis squeeze onto the coveted A+ roster this year? (Just barely.) Has Julia Roberts reclaimed her turf as the world's most bankable actress? (Definitely.) Did Will Smith beat out Eddie Murphy as the world's most powerful black star? (By a hefty eight points.)

Even the stars check their own rankings. After leafing through a recent list, one Oscar-winner quipped, "How much do I have to bribe you to get bumped up 20 points?"

Action star Dolph Lundgren once claimed in an on-camera interview that he "never pays attention to lists"—only to be seen, off camera, poring over these rankings to see if he really *did* rate the same score as Madonna (he did—that year).

Beginning a decade ago, in entertainment publications like *Premiere, Variety, The Hollywood Reporter* and *The Los Angeles Times,* these star rankings have become something of an institution in Hollywood, used by agents, actors, directors, producer, bankers, and studio executives whenever they cast or finance a film.

Tom Cruise and John Travolta's agents use the list, not to mention Jack Valenti, president of the Motion Picture Association of America—the organization that knows a few things about ratings, since it hands down those all-important PG, R, and NC-17 advisories.

Now, with the publication of this book, consumers can get a one-of-a-kind look at the same "cheat sheet" that Hollywood uses daily. It's the most complete power database ever published on Hollywood's top 200 stars, including hundreds of scores never before released.

But this book is much more than a list of scores. It also provides movie lovers with an "insider" context to help them appreciate the numbers. Like a camera with multiple lenses, the following chapters examine the complex, crazed and often comic world of star power—making it, faking it, maintaining it and, inevitably, the waning of it—from the perspectives of die-hard Hollywood professionals. Crewmembers, studio executives, bankers, producers, publicists, directors, agents and assorted hangers-on—all have had plenty of stories and opinions to share, and have faithfully "downloaded" them onto my notepads. (If only more of them had "downloaded" their dollars to help pay for those lunches.)

One chapter burrows into the outrageous world of star perks, where passions get indulged as ludicrously as pocketbooks. Another travels through the perils and profitability of promoting pictures abroad. Still others examine the youth market's "makeover" of Hollywood; the current casting crunch for hundreds of mid-level stars; techniques for giving a fading career a fast facelift; and the magical, shamanistic force that binds all Hollywood insiders together—"tribal power."

And who could resist the spell of another seductive power—industry gossip? "Hollywood Vine" disentangles the wiles and wherefores of its unique chokehold on a community obsessed with power, and with fear.

From there, it's a quick jump to "The Hollywood Hot List," where readers can find plenty of gossip on each of its 200 pages, dished out by some of the most authoritative (and wisely anonymous) sources in Hollywood and around the world.

But what really is behind this passion for pinpointing, this rage for ratings, anyway?

We are a society mesmerized by celebrities and their market power. America enjoys—or endures, depending on your outlook—the world's most sustained, pandemic, media-saturated, cash-generating fascination with movie stars on the planet. And why not, since we've created nearly all of them?

Movie stars are this country's pampered and privileged royalty. Or, more to the point, our favorite rare and exotic creatures. Their habitats, plumage, feeding habits, and mating rituals are scrutinized and commented on daily by hundreds of print, radio, TV, and Internet venues as avidly as any critter in Dr. Doolittle's menagerie. We are, quite simply, obsessed.

If you think this book will be any different, ask for your money back now.

Hollywood's business affairs are almost as appetizing to the consumer marketplace as its celebrity affairs. Who would have thought, a decade ago, that Hollywood's box office reports would be graphed and tracked in virtually every major newspaper and media outlet from Seattle to Secaucus?

From Capetown to Copenhagen, American movies have become to the world what Vasco Nuñez de Balboa was to only a portion of it: a relentless conquistador of local markets. More than half of Hollywood's total movie revenues, in fact, hail from abroad.

Seek out the cineplex in Singapore and meet—Travolta. Hop a moped in Mombasa and hear—Madonna. These creatures stalk the screens, media outlets, and Web sites of nearly every habitable country, and these countries are, in turn, just as happy as America is to report on, gossip about, fawn over, and generally beatify these highly exotic profit centers. Every detail of success or failure in their public or private lives is now global fair game.

A New Kind of Horse Race

In short, watching the rise and fall of American celebrities has become a global spectator sport, as popular as anything on *American Gladiators*.

Yet for all our fervor in following celebrities' careers, there has never been an adequate system to analyze and track those careers. We have a fine tracking system for the stock market, but not for the star market.

The sports world is far ahead of the entertainment industry in this regard. Sports scoring and risk assessment is often extremely sophisticated. A prime example is the racing form, used to handicap horses at the racetrack. It's a valuable betting tool for a game that risks financial sums far less than the cost of a major star's salary on a single feature film. Still, there's no similar methodology for handicapping the performances of some equally competitive human creatures—our movie stars.

To be fair, actors are hardly horses. They are creatures of artistic inspiration and expression, and their performances cannot be measured by speed or stamina or any other equine criteria. (However, if movie premieres and festivals are any indicators, they can certainly trot themselves around show grounds pretty impressively.)

The kind of scoring needed isn't primarily for the performances millions of moviegoers see in the cinemas. It is for those "performances" given by the stars off screen and witnessed by only a few hundred professionals. These include stars' abilities to trigger financing, promote their films, manage their careers, and conduct themselves professionally on and off the set. A star's acting talent is another criterion, but less critical to his or her ultimate market success.

Together, these factors track the "speed" and "stamina" of actors in the global marketplace—whether, indeed, they have "legs." It is a race that begs to be handicapped. Add some spicy, professional commentary and gossip about these stallionlike screen creatures, and you have a crib sheet as reliable and valuable as any used at The Kentucky Derby.

Using the Ulmer Scale

How are these movie star "racing forms" developed? The methodologies for scoring and indexing the 200 actors in this book are part of a proprietary system called The Ulmer Scale. This scale was developed over the past ten years through my relationships, as an entertainment journalist, with some of the world's leading producers, distributors, buyers, sellers, executives, agents, directors—and stars, too. Trekking the globe to film festivals and markets from Cannes to Cairo and beyond—*way* beyond: Greenland and Kathmandu come to mind—didn't hurt the scope of this research, either.

Dozens of industry professionals were polled and interviewed on one or more of the five star power ranking categories found in this book. (To maximize objectivity, actors were not polled.) Their scores for each actor were compiled into a 100-point index, and those tallies then ranked into The Ulmer Scale's proprietary A+, A, B+, B, and C lists—and the ever-popular "Bottom of the Heap." The final star power scores are listed at the top of each star's data page.

What is the critical factor that movie power brokers use in determining who they want to headline their films? Bankability, or "star power." Unlike box office numbers—end-game statistics that indicate an actor's market clout after a film is released—star power scores are pre-game numbers used to assess risk *before* the cameras roll. In this survey, these scores are determined by the graders' answers to the following question: To what extent is an actor's name alone able to raise 100 percent financing to make a major feature film?

Star power is not the same as box office. Measured by ticket sales alone, the roster of star power would look drastically different. For instance, who do you suppose would nab the number-one spot as the most powerful actress in the world: Julia Roberts? Meg Ryan? Demi Moore?

Carrie Fisher. Yes, by box office standards, Fisher is the highest-grossing female star on the planet. Her fourteen movies collectively have pulled in $1.4 billion, according to *Entertainment Weekly,* with most of that hailing from the *Star Wars* series. But Fisher's presence in that series was hardly responsible for its phenomenal success; that was the work of George Lucas's storytelling and the special effects. They were the Force with the real star power.

Nor, for that matter, was another A+ star at the box office, Jeff Goldblum, the main draw for those mega-grossers *Independence Day* and *Jurassic Park.* (He's a B on our list.) But don't try telling Goldblum that. "Jeff wants $3 million a movie now, and when people tell him that's ridiculous, he keeps reminding them he was in *Jurassic Park,*" related an agent last year. "But on that basis the fucking dinosaurs should be getting $5 million."

Other than dinosaurs, real A+ stars are the ones whose marquee value alone can trigger financing for a film, even if there is no script, director, or costars attached. They also can virtually guarantee strong ticket sales for the movie's opening weekend—the Holy Grail of feature film distribution.

An example: With a near-perfect score of 99, A+ star Tom Hanks could stand on his head in the middle of Santa Monica Boulevard and read the obituaries out loud—in Turkish—for the sequel to *Dead Again* and somebody would pay $80 million to make that movie. And millions would go see it. Ditto for Tom Cruise.

Everyone else's bankable value is measured against this gold standard. An actor's star power decreases as more packaging elements than name value alone are required to convince financiers to greenlight a film.

A star like Nic Cage may not trigger an automatic up-front sale, but like all other actors on the A list, he's a sure bet if the director and budget is right and the material is consistent with his past successful films.

Demi Moore's seat on the B+ list means that elements in her film package will weigh a bit heavier than for an A star—elements like budget, costars, and, in Moore's case, serious diva behavior.

By the time you hit the C-list stars—and there are busloads of them—an actor has about as much chance to trigger a big-budget studio deal as Yasser Arafat. Occasionally, though, the actor's name might help foreign sales in the ancillary markets, such as video and pay TV.

Since all power in Hollywood is relative, the value of these star power scores lies in their relativity. They allow every star in Hollywood to compete in the power game against every other star. Each star's score must therefore be analyzed *in comparison to* the scores of fellow actors. The fact that Mel Gibson scores 98 to Anjelica Huston's 44 means only that her name has less than half the chance to snag studio-level financing as Gibson's does. That's providing, of course, that Ms. Huston is not playing the lead in a transgendered musical version of *The Birdman of Alcatraz*. One presumes the film's material is consistent with her past fine work.

Some caveats: These scores are not meant to imply any dollar amount associated with a star's financial risk. They have nothing to do with defining a star's salary level, and certainly do not imply whether an actor should be hired or fired from a shoot. Nor are they meant to indicate the box-office bounty an actor will reap on his next feature film; the day any crib sheet tells you that is the day pigs fly.

Finally, a word on origins. The rankings in this book have been compiled from The Ulmer Scale's annually published database for movie industry professionals, *The Hot List*. This list is the Hollywood professional community's most complete reference guide on the star power of over 1,800 actors and directors worldwide. It has been featured in my past columns and articles for *Premiere* magazine, the *Los Angeles Times,* and *Weekly Variety,* as well as on TV shows such as *Entertainment Tonight, Fox Entertainment News, CNN Business Report,* and on the CBS and BBC networks. Internet cruisers can now find The Hot List at Creative Planet's family of business-to-business entertainment websites by visiting *www.ulmerscale.com* or *www.creative-planet.com*

With the publication of this new consumer version, readers can finally get a one-of-a-kind look at the same scorecard that Hollywood's top deal-makers use daily—and for a lot less money. In fact, the great majority of the information is published here for the first time. This includes rarely found listings of the stars' current agents and managers; rankings on their promotional willingness, career management, professionalism, and acting talent; their top five box-office movies; and their career trajectories.

Think of this new racing form as the film industry's Janitor in a Drum: an industrial-strength resource available for the first time for use in any film buff's home.

Legend

Name

If applicable, the star's real name is given underneath the star's screen name.

> Example: Demi Moore
>
> Real Name: Demetria Guynes

Hollywood Hot List Score

This score denotes the actor's global bankability for the year 2000, out of a possible 100 points. Bankability is defined as the power of an actor's name alone to raise 100 percent financing for a studio film.

Ranking

This number denotes the ranking order of the star compared to all other stars in the Hollywood Hot List's Top 200. An "8," for example, signifies the actor ranks eighth out of 200 in worldwide bankability.

D.O.B. and Birthplace

The date and location of the actor's birth.

Contacts

Key business contacts for the stars are listed here. These include the star's agent (A) and agency and, when available or applicable, the star's manager (M), attorney (Atty) and/or publicist (P).

The Inside Dirt

What Hollywood insiders are saying—off the record—about the world's top stars. These anonymous quotes are compiled from interviews with top producers, executives, agents, distributors, bankers, on-the-set professionals, and critics.

Other Scores

This quartet of scores highlights a star's additional power rankings in four categories affecting his or her overall bankability, or star power. Each score is based on a 100-point index. The categories are:

Legend

 Willingness to Travel & Promote: How cooperative is the actor in promoting his films to the U.S. and global media?

 Career Management: How well has the star chosen his roles to maximize his career potential?

 Professionalism: How reliable is the actor to work with, both on and off the set?

 Talent: Based solely on acting ability, how talented is this actor?

Box Office Bait

This section lists the domestic box office numbers for the star's top five grossing films tracked until mid-August of 1999, as reported by Exhibitor Relations Company.

Star Power

This graph compares the star's bankability scores for the past three years, from 1997 through 1999.

Career Trajectory

 The position of this arrow estimates the current direction of the star's career.

THE
A+
LIST

Julia Roberts Rank **1**   Bankability **100**

Real Name   Julie Fiona Roberts
D.O.B.   10/28/67
Place of Birth Smyrna, Georgia, USA
Contact   (A) Elaine Goldsmith-Thomas, ICM (NY)

Willingness to Travel/Promote	Professionalism	Career Mgmt	Talent
69	**74**	**86**	**71**

INSIDE DIRT

The only woman guaranteed to open a movie on her name alone.

♦ After *Erin Brockovich,* that makes four home runs in a row.

♦ Audiences still want her to do the *Pretty Woman.* They want that kilowatt smile. They won't acknowledge her serious side.

♦ With *Mary Reilly* and *Michael Collins* she rooted around the depths and found the depths weren't there.

♦ She's too contemporary-looking for period films.

♦ She's the ultimate ingenue victim.

♦ There are very few sexy, romantic heroines who are genuinely funny like Julia. Her counterpart in the '40s would be Carole Lombard or Jean Harlow.

♦ Her face reveals suffering well.

♦ She's vulnerable, and that appeals to men's protective instincts. They want to take care of her and take charge of her.

♦ You could put a sack on her face and she'd still be gorgeous.

Star Power

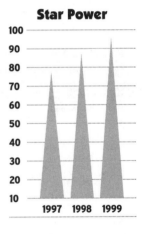

| | 1997 | 1998 | 1999 |

Box Office Bait

MOVIE	STUDIO	N.AMERICAN GROSS	RELEASE
Pretty Woman	BV	$178,406,268	3/23/90
My Best Friends Wedding	Sony/TS	$127,120,029	6/20/97
Hook	Tri-Star	$119,654,823	12/11/91
Notting Hill	Univ	$112,658,155 *	5/28/99
Sleeping With The Enemy	Fox	$101,599,005	2/8/91

Career Trajectory

Tom Hanks   Rank **2**   Bankability **99**

Real Name   Thomas J. Hanks
D.O.B.   7/9/56
Place of Birth   Concord, California, USA
Contact   (A) Richard Lovett CAA

Willingness to Travel/Promote	Professionalism	Career Mgmt	Talent
83	95	97	88

INSIDE DIRT

He's planned his career extremely carefully.

◆ He has great respect for his audiences and really reaches out to them.

◆ Tom's great with the press. And unlike Cruise or Pitt, he'll allow TV crews on his sets.

◆ His appeal? He's not stunningly good-looking, so he doesn't threaten men. And women want to nurture him.

◆ Tom Hanks is to actors what McDonald's is to hamburgers: bland, easy on the tastebuds, and not offensive to anyone.

◆ He has an amazing memory. Several years later, he remembered our interview in complete detail.

◆ He made the documentary *The Celluloid Closet* with us. His lawyer wanted him to do less gay stuff after *Philadelphia*. But Tom said yes, drove himself to the set, and didn't want any hair or makeup. He even said thank you to the crew.

◆ Tom's the coolest guy ever.

Star Power

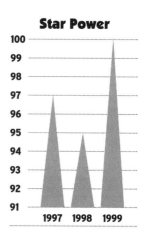

100
99
98
97
96
95
94
93
92
91
    1997 1998 1999

Box Office Bait			
MOVIE	STUDIO	N.AMERICAN GROSS	RELEASE
Forrest Gump	Para	$329,690,974	7/6/94
Saving Private Ryan	Dreamworks	$230,900,365	7/24/98
Toy Story (voice)	BV	$191,780,865	11/22/95
Apollo 13	Univ	$172,036,360	6/30/95
Sleepless in Seattle	Tri-Star	$126,007,337	6/25/93

Career Trajectory

Tom Cruise   Rank **3**

Real Name	Thomas Cruise Mapother IV
D.O.B.	7/3/62
Place of Birth	Syracuse, New York, USA
Contact	(A) Rick Nicita, CAA (P) Pat Kingsley, PMK

Willingness to Travel/Promote	Professionalism	Career Mgmt	Talent
82	**84**	**95**	**77**

INSIDE DIRT

Who is Tom Cruise? Rick Nicita and Pat Kingsley *are* Tom Cruise.

♦ He's worth every penny. He has never had a bad performance. And he promotes his films.

♦ He's unfortunately become an icon like Chevrolet, and he spends 100 percent of his time polishing that façade.

♦ Tom really has figured out what smile to use. In reality, he's a geeky band member stuck in a quarterback body.

♦ He's very cold and unsociable on the set. A real bag of hammers.

♦ Tom never tells the press, "Don't talk to me about Scientology." But he'll take legal steps if you make claims in print that he's gay.

♦ His charisma is so amazing it's kind of intimidating.

♦ He's sloppy. He may need ten takes before he gets it right and he rarely hits his marks. He's so earnest, people mistake it for acting.

♦ Anyone who could make a hit out of *Cocktail* deserves his success.

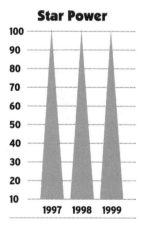

Star Power

(Vertical axis: 100, 90, 80, 70, 60, 50, 40, 30, 20, 10)
1997 1998 1999

Box Office Bait

MOVIE	STUDIO	N.AMERICAN GROSS	RELEASE
Mission: Impossible	Para	$180,981,866	5/22/96
Top Gun	Para	$176,781,728	5/16/86
Rain Man	MGM	$172,825,435	12/16/88
The Firm	Para	$158,308,178	6/30/93
Jerry MaGuire	Sony/TS	$153,620,822	12/13/96

Career Trajectory

Mel Gibson   Rank **4**   Bankability **98**

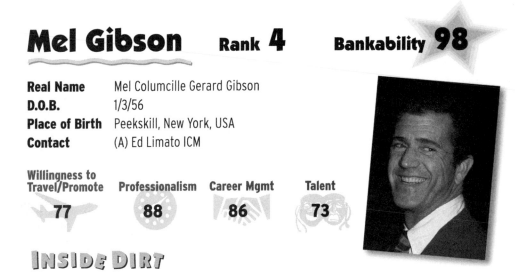

Real Name   Mel Columcille Gerard Gibson
D.O.B.   1/3/56
Place of Birth Peekskill, New York, USA
Contact   (A) Ed Limato ICM

Willingness to Travel/Promote	Professionalism	Career Mgmt	Talent
77	88	86	73

INSIDE DIRT

He can still reel in the young-woman demographic.

♦ He's a consummate professional and a gentleman, completely able to deal with his success.

♦ He's a guy you want to hang out with. There's not a bad thing to say about him.

♦ He'll cross over into smaller movies. He desperately wanted Robin Williams's role in *Good Will Hunting*.

♦ Mel needs to keep focusing on choosing the right roles. How he ever made *Bird on a Wire* escapes me.

♦ Like Sean Connery, he has that sexuality that doesn't seem to vaporize with age. It keeps him in the market longer.

♦ He's losing his leading-man appeal. He ain't that cute anymore. Can we say "co-lead" and "support-ing role" please?

Star Power

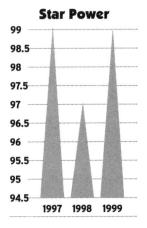

Chart showing values for 1997, 1998, 1999 on a scale from 94.5 to 99.

Box Office Bait

MOVIE	STUDIO	N.AMERICAN GROSS	RELEASE
Lethal Weapon 2	WB	$147,253,986	7/7/89
Lethal Weapon 3	WB	$144,731,527	5/15/92
Pocahontas (voice)	BV	$141,579,773	6/16/95
Ransom	BV	$136,485,602	11/8/96
Lethal Weapon 4	WB	$129,734,803	7/10/98

Career Trajectory

Bruce Willis   Rank 5   Bankability 97

Real Name   Walter Bruce Willis
D.O.B.   3/19/55
Place of Birth   Idar-Oberstein, West Germany
Contact   (A) Arnold Rifkin Cheyenne Enterprises

Willingness to Travel/Promote	Professionalism	Career Mgmt	Talent
80	72	85	65

INSIDE DIRT

He's still the strongest international action star.

- He walked off the *Broadway Brother* set, which made backers suspicious because he shot a film down. But they'll go along with him because they always want his next big movie.

- Both *The Fifth Element* and *Die Hard 3* did two to three times more business overseas than domestically.

- Women today want their heroes more vulnerable, and Willis delivers that.

- One of the few guys who'll cut his rate to do a film he likes.

- He's emotionally inaccessible on a set. He'll spin some discs and have everyone dance so they don't actually have to relate to him.

- He was great with the crew, but he needs adoration. He has these sycophantic guys who hang around with him.

Star Power

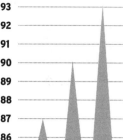

	1997	1998	1999

Box Office Bait			
MOVIE	STUDIO	N.AMERICAN GROSS	RELEASE
Armageddon	BV	$201,578,182	7/1/98
Look Who's Talking (voice)	Tri-Star	$140,088,813	10/13/89
Die Hard 2	Fox	$115,288,665	7/4/90
Pulp Fiction	Miramax	$107,921,755	10/14/94
Die Hard With a Vengeance	Fox	$100,003,359	5/19/95

Career Trajectory

2

Pork Bellies in Hollywood

Some people have asked why the film industry has become so obsessed with measuring and quantifying its actors, poking around into their "bankability" and "financial viability" and "global saleability." Aren't there any other "abilities" that those philistine bean counters out in Hollywood care about—such as, say, *acting* ability? Can't they just loosen up and realize that *this* is what an artist's true "power" is really about?

No, they can't. The town doesn't work that way.

Hollywood is an industry that mass-markets dreams. Those dreams may be the stuff of sublime emotional catharsis or truly tacky toilet humor, but they are inevitably very expensive to cast, produce and market—currently about $78 million per studio film, according to *Daily Variety*.

Because the costs are high, the risks are high. In this business, the best way to amortize that risk is to cast movies using known quantities—movie stars. And the best way to understand and exploit those quantities is to measure them, track them, price them, and compare them. Not much different than soup cans, really.

"This is not art, this is business, and business is about supply and demand," notes Diana Berman, a film marketing executive from Australia. "It's about product buy cycles."

In other words, stars are mass-marketing tools designed to provide product consistency to as big a buyer base as possible, hence lessening investment risk.

"So a commodity like Tom Hanks is going to underpin that risk the most

effectively," Berman continues. "After all, Tom Hanks is to actors what Mc-
Donald's is to hamburgers: bland, easy on the tastebuds, and not offensive
to anyone. A perfect marketing tool."

So much for actors as artists.

If that's not a sobering enough weltanschauung for you, here's another
meat metaphor from an anonymous, but equally unsentimental, source:
"Buying and selling stars is like trading futures in pork bellies. It's all about
future investments."

3

The Year in Review

Who are the best future investments for the film industry today? As usual, the candidates are almost exclusively male—although this year there's a distaff twist. In Hollywood, it's usually the men who win the battle of the sexes at the box office, proving that star power is rarely politically correct.

The reason is that men traditionally "drive the train" of Hollywood's storylines. This is particularly true of action-adventure films, still the most exportable Hollywood genre worldwide. It's so durable and forgiving a form that five of the world's top action-adventure stars are now over fifty, and two are practically geriatric: Clint Eastwood and Sean Connery are both seventy and *still* trying to kiss the girls. (Just try and see if a woman at that age could get away with smooching a young buck.)

The twist this year? A woman has finally beaten the boys at their own star-power game. For the first time, Julia Roberts nests alone at the top of the Hollywood heap. Thanks to five films in a row that each grossed over $100 million in the United States alone, Roberts has outperformed previous top runners Tom Cruise and Tom Hanks, vaulting from twelfth place to first as the only actor to boast a perfect score of 100. Industry watchers credit The Return of the Megawatt Smile Part I (*My Best Friend's Wedding*), Part II (*Notting Hill*) and Part III (*Runaway Bride*) for her renewed fortunes. In *Stepmom* and *Erin Brockovich* she smiled intermittently—call them Part III-1/2.

Roberts's rise plays into the growing importance of female audiences at the global turnstiles as they assert their decision-making and spending power. London-based marketing consultant Hy Smith hails Roberts for "making real women's movies, which have made her a bigger star than ever."

Roberts is not alone among women in seeing her bankability grow. Screen-steamer Catherine Zeta-Jones harnessed the biggest power surge this year in the wake of *Entrapment*, while Meg Ryan saw her fortunes rise from sixteenth place to eighth place. And Jodie Foster, who back in the late '80s and early '90s crowned the women's list as the most bankable actress in the world, watched her rank and scores fall for a second consecutive year to eighth place among actresses, thanks to her low output of films. But she boasted the highest score in professionalism of any star in this book. Her whopping 96 points on that scale edged out Meryl Streep and Tom Hanks by a single point each.

Among the men, the leaders of the Hollywood pack were once again the two Toms, both of whom narrowly missed perfect scores. For Hanks, it was the first time that he had met Cruise at the summit, and both have a habit of delivering domestic box office of over $100 million per film to a broad demographic. Considering their bountiful ability to deliver global audiences, they have become Hollywood's ultimate McActors: billions and billions served.

Although the A+ list this year shrunk by nearly half—from nine to five actors—there was a growth spurt in the A list, from twenty-seven actors last year to thirty-six. This boost is largely caused by Hollywood's ever-increasing appetite for hiring stars who can unconditionally guarantee full feature financing. More and more, these big name draws are becoming increasingly valuable in a world where many of the once-flush overseas markets—Hollywood's biggest revenue generator—are still recovering from economic turmoil and are pickier than ever about buying movie rights.

While A-lister Keanu Reeves accessed the matrix of global bankability to jump 23 points, for several leading men the data was less favorable. Leonardo DiCaprio proved that even rising from the *Titanic* doesn't stop a young leading man from washing up on *The Beach;* many wonder if Leo's career isn't treading water. And while Will Smith last year became the first black actor to join the elite dudes on the A+ list, this year he dropped 5 points from eighth to tenth place, only narrowly beating Arnold Schwarzenegger and Jim Carrey. He'll end up being the not-so-fresh Prince of Hollywood if he suffers another critical fizzle like the not-so-*Wild Wild West*.

Female Trouble

With the exception of Roberts's smiling fortunes, however, there is plenty for women to frown about. They still suffer the telltale three strikes against them at the global box office.

First, they're generally more bankable when acting collectively in ensembles (*The First Wives Club, Waiting to Exhale*) than when holding forth in leading roles.

Second, their greatest bankable value lies in the domestic and not the overseas market, from where more than half of Hollywood's feature revenues hail.

And third, they suffer shorter shelf lives as marquee stars than men do, often retreating after age 40 to the kinder pastures of TV movies to find their best roles.

"Because women's movies involve more comedic and dramatic elements," says Miramax L.A. president Mark Gill, "they're unfortunately held to a higher standard than men's films. Action and adventure films basically offer vicarious release, whereas women's films have to be really good to work. It's a real dilemma for women."

Still another dilemma is the skewed odds women suffer in working the Hollywood career game.

"For a woman to get ahead in this business is a very different thing than for a man," says Jana Sue Memel, president of Chanticleer Films. "Men can bully their way through the doors single-handedly to get what they want. For women, it's all about rallying twenty guys at your back to work the system. Actresses like Sally Field can do that. Sally knows how to play the games she needs to play to get what she wants. She knows how to get the gatekeepers to support her. She understands power."

Presumably so does Roberts, who is the first actress to win payday parity with the world's most bankable male stars. Her salary has now spiked so high she's joined Hollywood's heady "20/20 Club" ($20 million per film and 20 percent of the back end). But whereas it took Jim Carrey only a couple of years playing lead Hollywood roles to nab this brass ring, it took Roberts over eight years to fetch the same prize. So much for equal opportunity in Hollywood.

THE

A

LIST

John Travolta Rank 6

Bankability 94

Real Name	John Travolta
D.O.B.	2/18/54
Place of Birth	Englewood, New Jersey, USA
Contact	(A) Fred Westheimer, WMA

Willingness to Travel/Promote	Professionalism	Career Mgmt	Talent
50	65	82	60

INSIDE DIRT

His star can only rise in the action genre.

♦ The characters he plays are all a little subversive.

♦ I hate that Scientologists like him and Cruise are winning the ratings game. It really makes me barf.

♦ In Germany and France, he's not a star like he is here. But in an action movie, he's fine overseas.

♦ Like other actors, he leads a double life and goes to extreme lengths to keep it private. It's an ongoing factor in his career.

♦ He adores the press.

♦ His perk package for *Standing Room Only* was over $2 million—and around $1 million of that was just for the entourage.

♦ He's a lightweight as an actor. I look at him and think, I can't believe he's fooling all these people. And it's all because of Quentin.

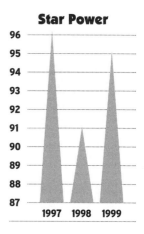

Star Power

96
95
94
93
92
91
90
89
88
87

1997 1998 1999

Box Office Bait

MOVIE	STUDIO	N.AMERICAN GROSS	RELEASE
Grease	Para	$153,112,093	6/16/78
Look Who's Talking	Tri-Star	$140,088,813	10/13/89
Face Off	Para	$112,273,211	6/27/97
Pulp Fiction	Miramax	$107,921,755	10/14/94
Phenomenon	BV	$104,632,573	7/3/96

Career Trajectory

Brad Pitt

Rank *7*   **Bankability** *94*

Real Name	William Bradley Pitt
D.O.B.	12/18/63
Place of Birth	Shawnee, Oklahoma, USA
Contact	(A) Kevin Huvane, CAA (M) Cynthia TK.

Willingness to Travel/Promote	Professionalism	Career Mgmt	Talent
50	**77**	**70**	**65**

INSIDE DIRT

Why did he drop in 1999? Because not enough moviegoers wanted to meet Joe Black. And *Fight Club* was too offbeat.

♦ *Sleepers* was a bigger hit in Japan than the United States because of Pitt's huge appeal there.

♦ Brad Pitt is an absolute doll.

♦ Straight men resent his pretty-boy appeal to women.

♦ He's generous, kind, and always remembers everyone's name on the set. He's easy to deal with and never a problem. He's not manipulative, and he doesn't have an icky staff to deal with. There's nothing wrong with that boy.

♦ Nice guy. Not a diva. Very polite, very deferential and cool. He's always very committed to the role.

♦ He could use a strongly drawn lead role in a major action film. Soon.

Star Power

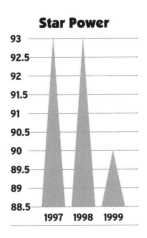

Box Office Bait			
MOVIE	STUDIO	N.AMERICAN GROSS	RELEASE
Interview with the Vampire	WB	$105,248,316	11/11/94
Seven	NL	$100,123,974	9/22/95
Legends of the Fall	Tri-Star	$66,492,292	12/25/94
Twelve Monkeys	Univ	$57,097,229	12/27/95
Sleepers	WB	$53,300,852	10/18/96

Career Trajectory

Meg Ryan

Rank 8

Bankability 93

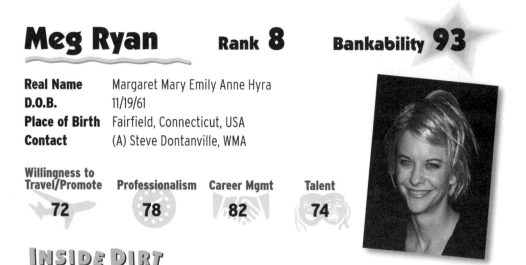

Real Name	Margaret Mary Emily Anne Hyra
D.O.B.	11/19/61
Place of Birth	Fairfield, Connecticut, USA
Contact	(A) Steve Dontanville, WMA

Willingness to Travel/Promote	Professionalism	Career Mgmt	Talent
72	78	82	74

INSIDE DIRT

You can't play cute and perky forever.

- *A Man and a Woman* proved she doesn't have the resources to do heavy drama.
- You put her in the right role and you'll laugh all the way to the bank.
- *City of Angels* proved she has trouble opening a movie on her own.
- Her value is slightly stronger overseas.
- She's big in Japan and Asia, where huge numbers of women go see romantic comedies.
- *Courage Under Fire* misfired. Why? She's just too cute for action films. With those doe eyes, every villain would melt away instead of shooting her off the screen.
- For promoting her films, I give a "10" in Germany.
- My patrons would love to see Meg Ryan naked.

Star Power

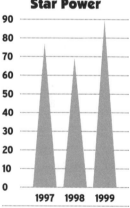

Graph showing values for 1997, 1998, 1999 (y-axis 0–90).

Box Office Bait

MOVIE	STUDIO	N.AMERICAN GROSS	RELEASE
Top Gun	Para	$176,781,728	5/16/86
Sleepless in Seattle	Tri-Star	$126,007,337	6/25/93
You've Got Mail	WB	$115,731,542	12/18/98
When Harry Met Sally	Columbia	$92,247,887	7/12/89
City of Angels	WB	$78,647,175	4/10/98

Career Trajectory

Leonardo DiCaprio

Rank 9 **Bankability 91**

Real Name	Leonardo Wilhelm DiCaprio
D.O.B.	11/11/74
Place of Birth	Hollywood, California, USA
Contact	(M) Rick Yorn AMG

Willingness to Travel/Promote	Professionalism	Career Mgmt	Talent
60	73	72	80

INSIDE DIRT

He still can't decide if he wants to be a star.

- He's a born screen idol.

- *Titanic* was the gutsiest choice of his career. Instead of playing another oddball role, he gambled on something much tougher: a traditional hero.

- He doesn't give a damn about promoting his movies. He'll say okay, I'll do the premiere but nothing else.

- No more period roles, Leo! You just can't carry a broadsword well.

- His appeal is in danger of falling into a pretty-boy groove. If he doesn't become a man soon, all bets are off.

- That's the way audiences want to see Leo—as a leading *boy*.

- He still sends scripts home for his mom to read. How lovely.

- Leo looks like his farts don't smell.

Star Power

100
90
80
70
60
50
40
30
20
10

1997 1998 1999

Box Office Bait

MOVIE	STUDIO	N.AMERICAN GROSS	RELEASE
Titanic	Para	$600,788,188	12/19/97
The Man in the Iron Mask	MGM	$56,968,169	3/13/98
Romeo and Juliet	Fox	$46,338,728	11/1/96
The Quick and the Dead	Sony/TS	$18,543,150	2/10/95
Marvin's Room	Miramax	$12,782,508	12/18/96

Career Trajectory

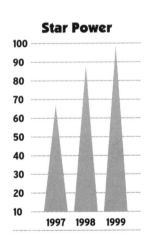

Will Smith

Rank 10 **Bankability 90**

Real Name	Willard Christopher Smith, Jr.
D.O.B.	9/25/68
Place of Birth	Philadelphia, Pennsylvania, USA
Contact	(A) Ken Stovitz CAA

Willingness to Travel/Promote	Professionalism	Career Mgmt	Talent
75	**90**	**90**	**86**

INSIDE DIRT

He's the new and improved Denzel Washington.

- He's the white man's black man. He's never been threatening to the power structure.

- No one has managed his career better than Will. He took his Quincy Jones contacts in TV and film and broke into the business. The rest is history.

- With *Independence Day,* he finally broke through big in Japan. That's almost unheard of for black actors.

- His appeal crosses ethnic groups and age demographics.

- He's locked himself into action comedies. Audiences could tire of that genre in a few years.

- The fact that *Wild Wild West* underperformed won't affect Will's bankability. He's too big.

- Will people really see him as a romantic lead? Every woman I know would love to go to bed with him.

- A dude with 'tude.

Star Power

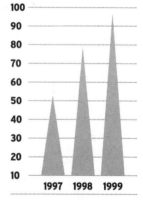

1997	1998	1999

Box Office Bait			
MOVIE	**STUDIO**	**N.AMERICAN GROSS**	**RELEASE**
Independence Day	Fox	$306,169,255	7/3/96
Men in Black	Sony/C	$250,690,539	7/2/97
Enemy of The State	BV	$111,544,445	11/20/98
Wild Wild West	WB	$110,726,211 *	6/30/99
Bad Boys	Sony/C	$66,491,850	4/7/95

Career Trajectory

Arnold Schwarzenegger

Rank 11

Bankability 89

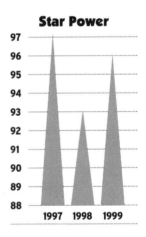

Real Name	Arnold Schwarzenegger
D.O.B.	7/30/47
Place of Birth	Graz, Austria
Contact	(A) Robert Stein, WMA

Willingness to Travel/Promote	Professionalism	Career Mgmt	Talent
92	87	80	45

INSIDE DIRT

He desperately needs a comeback.

♦ He's a big question mark. He isn't a superstar anymore. He won't disappear, but his value has dropped a bit recently.

♦ If you hire him, you have to provide a gym.

♦ Unlike Stallone, he can also do comedy.

♦ He's got a problem: He's wooden. Even if you have a top script like *True Lies,* it doesn't work for him. *Jingle All the Way* was a joke—on Arnold.

♦ One reason he's paid so much is that he promotes and markets his heart out. And he travels and does publicity in other languages, too.

♦ He's been very wise in managing his career.

♦ He's no Jack Nicholson.

Star Power

97
96
95
94
93
92
91
90
89
88

1997 1998 1999

Box Office Bait

MOVIE	STUDIO	N.AMERICAN GROSS	RELEASE
Terminator 2: Judgement Day	Tri-Star	$204,446,562	7/3/91
True Lies	Fox	$146,273,950	7/15/94
Total Recall	Tri-Star	$118,272,498	6/1/90
Twins	Univ	$111,784,821	12/9/88
Batman and Robin	WB	$107,285,004	6/20/97

Career Trajectory

Jim Carrey   Rank **12**   Bankability **89**

Real Name	James Eugene Carrey
D.O.B.	1/17/62
Place of Birth	Newmarket, Ontario, Canada
Contact	(A) Nick Stevens, UTA (M) Gold Miller Atlas

Willingness to Travel/Promote	Professionalism	Career Mgmt	Talent
73	84	83	79

INSIDE DIRT

He plays to an audience that doesn't demand nearly enough from him.

♦ He's smart. He'll do a smaller film, then a big one for the studios. It's the Clint Eastwood strategy of keeping your brand awareness high.

♦ The chance of *Man in the Moon* making money abroad is zilch. Who's heard of Andy Kaufman overseas?

♦ With strong directors who can channel all of Jim's energy, he could have a career forever.

♦ The French took a long time to warm up to him. We thought the success of *The Mask* had less to do with Carrey and more with the special effects.

♦ Hollywood won't support him in anything serious. Hence, no Oscar nomination for *The Truman Show*. They just want to see him act the clown.

♦ He's a complete pro on the set.

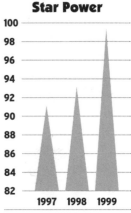

Star Power

100 / 98 / 96 / 94 / 92 / 90 / 88 / 86 / 84 / 82

1997   1998   1999

Box Office Bait			
MOVIE	**STUDIO**	**N.AMERICAN GROSS**	**RELEASE**
Batman Forever	WB	$183,997,904	6/16/95
Liar Liar	Univ	$181,395,380	3/21/97
Dumb and Dumber	NL	$127,140,750	12/16/94
The Truman Show	Para	$125,618,201	6/5/98
The Mask	NL	$119,936,108	7/29/94

Career Trajectory

Harrison Ford

Rank 13 **Bankability 88**

Real Name	Harrison Ford
D.O.B.	7/13/42
Place of Birth	Chicago, Illinois, USA
Contact	(M) Pat McQueeney

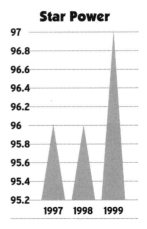

Willingness to Travel/Promote	Professionalism	Career Mgmt	Talent
71	87	89	70

INSIDE DIRT

Of the older action stars, he's aging the most gracefully.

- He's not a bad actor, just one of limited scope, like Clark Gable.

- Aside from *Sabrina,* he hasn't done anything that shows off his real talent.

- He was born for franchise films, just like Mel Gibson. But he could never do Indiana Jones again—he's too old now.

- *Air Force One* hurt him overseas, despite its box office. In the U.K., people were chuckling at this huffing and puffing middle-aged action star. But in Japan, they swallowed it whole.

- He demands a high level of professionalism and takes a direct hand in the script and production process. He promotes his movies overseas. Total pro.

- He's got the best career in the business. Will it keep going? Absolutely.

- Harrison Ford is over. *Over.*

Star Power

	1997	1998	1999

(Y-axis: 95.2, 95.4, 95.6, 95.8, 96, 96.2, 96.4, 96.6, 96.8, 97)

Box Office Bait

MOVIE	STUDIO	N.AMERICAN GROSS	RELEASE
Star Wars	Fox	$460,998,007	5/25/77
Return of the Jedi	Fox	$309,205,079	5/25/83
The Empire Strikes Back	Fox	$290,271,960	5/21/80
Raiders of the Lost Ark	Para	$245,034,358	6/12/81
Indiana Jones and the Last Crusade	Para	$197,171,806	5/27/89

Career Trajectory

Keanu Reeves Rank 14 Bankability 87

Real Name Keanu Charles Reeves
D.O.B. 9/2/64
Place of Birth Beirut, Lebanon
Contact (A) Kevin Huvane CAA (M) Erwin Stoff 3 Arts

Willingness to Travel/Promote	Professionalism	Career Mgmt	Talent
55	59	72	54

INSIDE DIRT

He's gorgeous first, an actor second.

◆ I think *Matrix* saved Keanu Reeves. Now he's become the action god for the new millennium.

◆ He's getting $30 million for his next two *Matrix* flicks plus up to $100 million back end. This boy knows his market.

◆ He had the courage to say no to *Speed 2* because he wanted to perform with his band instead. That was gutsy—and considering that movie, a wise career choice.

◆ On *Point Break* he always seemed really out of it and high. Then again, he was really young.

◆ His acting was so bad in *Little Buddha* that whole scenes of dialogue ended up on the cutting room floor. What was left was him bouncing around on horseback a lot.

◆ He's huge in Japan.

Star Power

| | 1997 | 1998 | 1999 |

(values: 72, 70, 68, 66, 64, 62, 60, 58, 56, 54)

Box Office Bait

MOVIE	STUDIO	N.AMERICAN GROSS	RELEASE
The Matrix	WB	$169,731,136 *	3/31/99
Speed	Fox	$121,221,490	6/10/94
Parenthood	Univ	$100,047,830	8/2/89
Bram Stoker's Drakula	Columbia	$82,416,928	11/13/92
Devil's Advocate	WB	$60,899,443	10/17/97

Career Trajectory

Adam Sandler Rank 15 Bankability 87

Real Name	Adam Sandler
D.O.B.	9/9/66
Place of Birth	Brooklyn, New York, USA
Contact	(A) Adam Venit, Endeavor (M) Brillstein/Grey

Willingness to Travel/Promote	Professionalism	Career Mgmt	Talent
47	67	90	45

INSIDE DIRT

As a member of the $20 million club, he's a guaranteed return on your investment.

- *The Waterboy* surprised everyone, most of all him.

- The Hollywood machine has anointed him to be the next Tom Hanks, and now they've had to go about creating the next self-fulfilling prophecy.

- He's very generous and very smart. He's very involved in the approval and disapproval of the writers and directors of his films. He reads the script and goes to see their movies.

- He's handling success very well. And he's conscious of his Jewishness. He's not ashamed of it. He's a good boy. He's real.

- He's getting nervous about how to handle his booming career. He's nervous with the press, too.

- He just got a check for $9 million on Friday, from his back-end participation in *Waterboy*.

Star Power

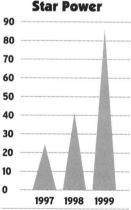

	Box Office Bait		
MOVIE	STUDIO	N.AMERICAN GROSS	RELEASE
The Waterboy	BV	$161,491,646	11/6/98
Big Daddy	Sony	$156,066,951	6/25/99
The Wedding Singer	NL	$80,224,502	2/13/98
Happy Gilmore	Univ	$38,648,864	2/16/96
Billy Madison	Univ	$25,441,250	2/10/95

Career Trajectory

Jack Nicholson Rank 16 Bankability 87

Real Name	John Joseph Nicholson
D.O.B.	4/22/37
Place of Birth	Neptune, New Jersey, USA
Contact	(A) Bressler Kelly & Associates

Willingness to Travel/Promote
79

Professionalism
74

Career Mgmt
83

Talent
89

INSIDE DIRT

Jack's pure rock 'n roll—and that never ages.

- He can always rely on comedy as he ages. His sexiness has been given longevity because of that.

- When he was younger, he had pure animal magnetism. Now he's turning into the Charlie Weaver of sex appeal.

- What a delicious screen persona.

- Forget about him. He doesn't let TV press onto his sets.

- During *The Crossing Guard* he was competely professional and really pushed Sean as the writer and director.

- He's an icon of the baby boomer geneation.

- He's very approachable at parties. And he'll talk to you forever if you talk about basketball.

- Jack still has a twinkle. But could I buy him making out on screen with a twenty-eight-year-old? Certainly not.

- He'll always be an old, aging rebel.

Star Power

88
87
86
85
84
83
82
81
80
79
         1997 1998 1999

Box Office Bait

MOVIE	STUDIO	N.AMERICAN GROSS	RELEASE
Batman	WB	$251,188,924	6/23/89
As Good As It Gets	Sony/TS	$148,478,011	12/24/97
A Few Good Men	Columbia	$141,340,178	12/11/92
One Flew Over the Cuckoo's Nest	MGM	$112,000,000 E	11/19/75
Terms of Endearment	Para	$108,423,489	11/23/83

Career Trajectory

Mike Myers Rank **17**   Bankability **86**

Real Name	Mike Myers
D.O.B.	5/23/63
Place of Birth	Scarborough, Ontario, Canada
Contact	(A) David O'Connor/Michael Davis, CAA

Willingness to Travel/Promote	Professionalism	Career Mgmt	Talent
78	**73**	 **81**	**70**

INSIDE DIRT

He's a red-hot commodity.

- His type of comedy travels very well.

- On *54*, he was obsessed with not having it be sold as a Mike Myers movie because he didn't think the movie was very good. And he was right, it wasn't. But he went off the deep end by having his friends act as watchdogs with him over the film's promotion. They'd phone Mike's reps and say, "I saw this poster and you can't say this or do that!"

- He's the ultimate control freak—worse than Tom Cruise.

- He was lots of fun on the *Wayne's World* set. Not difficult at all.

- He can definitely break out of the *Austin Powers* mold. But it would be a big risk for him to do something dark.

- People want to see him as a buffoonish and lovable guy.

Star Power

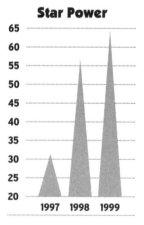

65	
60	
55	
50	
45	
40	
35	
30	
25	
20	

1997 1998 1999

Box Office Bait

MOVIE	STUDIO	N.AMERICAN GROSS	RELEASE
Austin Powers: The Spy Who Shagged Me	NL	$199,647,588	6/11/99
Wayne's World	Para	$121,697,323	2/15/92
Austin Powers: Int'l Man of Mystery	NL	$53,882,132	5/2/97
Wayne's World 2	Para	$46,637,382	12/10/93
54	Miramax	$16,757,163	8/28/98

Career Trajectory

Michael Douglas

Rank 18 **Bankability 85**

Real Name	Michael Douglas
D.O.B.	9/25/44
Place of Birth	New Brunswick, New Jersey, USA
Contact	(A) Richard Lovett, CAA

Willingness to Travel/Promote	Professionalism	Career Mgmt	Talent
75	87	80	62

INSIDE DIRT

He shouldn't be playing opposite women in their twenties. It's embarrassing.

♦ He's a damn good actor, and *Wonder Boys* was the perfect role for his transition to an older leading man.

♦ He tells you want he wants, and if you give it to him he's perfectly happy. In interviews, he wants to know the name and outlet of each journalist so he can say something personal to each.

♦ Michael is one of the brightest people walking around in Hollywood, bar none. He's incredibly street smart.

♦ Michael's pride in being a movie star has a lot to do with his childhood and who is father is. If he were anybody else, he would have chucked it a long time ago and become a director. In many senses he's a true filmmaker.

Star Power

A bar chart showing values for 1997, 1998, and 1999 on a scale from 77 to 86.

Box Office Bait			
MOVIE	STUDIO	N.AMERICAN GROSS	RELEASE
Fatal Attraction	Para	$156,587,582	9/18/87
One Flew Over the Cuckoo's Nest	MGM	$133,199,336 E	11/19/75
Basic Instinct	Tri-Star	$117,717,433	3/20/92
War of the Roses	Fox	$84,241,510	12/8/89
Disclosure	WB	$82,976,682	12/9/94

Career Trajectory

Kevin Spacey Rank 19   Bankability 85

Real Name	Kevin Matthew Fowler
D.O.B.	7/26/59
Place of Birth	South Orange, New Jersey, USA
Contact	(A) John Fogelman, WMA

Willingness to Travel/Promote	Professionalism	Career Mgmt	Talent
74	72	76	81

INSIDE DIRT

He can't decide if he wants to be an indie star or a movie star.

♦ Probably the finest actor in America today. He can do no wrong in my book.

♦ Even with his Oscars, he can't carry a studio film.

♦ He's really a character actor, but he's perceived as a leading man. That's largely because he promotes himself and his films and is seen everywhere.

♦ He's very difficult to work with. He makes Dustin Hoffman look easy.

♦ You get the feeling you're never really seeing everything he's got on-screen. He's kind of enigmatic.

♦ He's what you call "indie bait": an art-house actor who attracts more powerful stars to his projects.

♦ Kevin Spacey has charisma oozing out of his little finger. Just look at *American Beauty*.

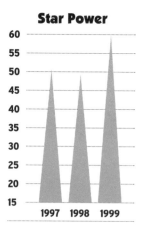

Star Power

60
55
50
45
40
35
30
25
20
15

1997 1998 1999

Box Office Bait

MOVIE	STUDIO	N.AMERICAN GROSS	RELEASE
A Bug's Life (voice)	BV	$162,798,565	11/20/98
A Time to Kill	WB	$108,766,007	7/24/96
Seven	NL	$100,123,974	9/22/95
Outbreak	WB	$67,598,303	3/10/95
L.A. Confidential	WB	$64,616,940	9/19/97

Career Trajectory

Sean Connery Rank 20   Bankability 85

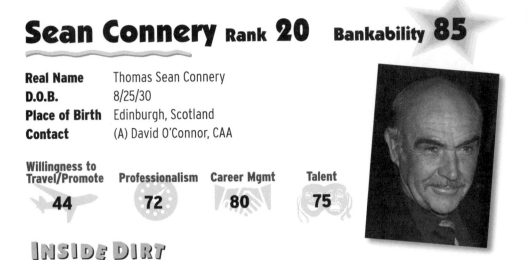

Real Name Thomas Sean Connery
D.O.B. 8/25/30
Place of Birth Edinburgh, Scotland
Contact (A) David O'Connor, CAA

Willingness to Travel/Promote	Professionalism	Career Mgmt	Talent
44	72	80	75

INSIDE DIRT

One of the few stars with a genuinely heroic presence.

- He's the most enduring movie star alive. His age has become an asset to his parts. His presence in a film completely defines everyone else in a way no other actor's does.

- He doesn't do shit for any of his movies. He doesn't travel or support them nearly enough.

- If he didn't have a great voice and a Scottish accent, we would have called him a dirty old bald man by now.

- In France, there's no sense Connery is getting too old.

- Fairly early on he just said fuck it with the hairpiece.

- He's more bankable in drama than action.

- He's best as the evil or wise sage.

- If there's a golf course in the city of his movie's release, chances are he'll be there.

Star Power

85
84.5
84
83.5
83
82.5
82
81.5
81
80.5

1997 1998 1999

Box Office Bait

MOVIE	STUDIO	N.AMERICAN GROSS	RELEASE
Indiana Jones and The Last Crusade	Para	$197,171,806	5/27/89
The Rock	BV	$134,069,511	6/7/96
Hunt for Red October	Para	$120,702,326	3/2/90
Entrapment	Fox	$84,425,156	4/30/99
Thunderball	MGM	$63,603,187	1965

Career Trajectory

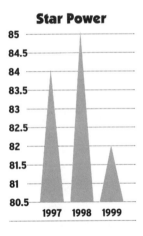

Robert Redford

Rank 21 **Bankability 84**

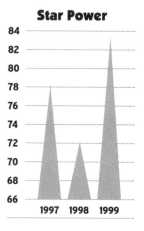

Real Name	Charles Robert Redford, Jr.
D.O.B.	8/13/37
Place of Birth	Santa Monica, California, USA
Contact	(A) David O'Connor, CAA

Willingness to Travel/Promote	Professionalism	Career Mgmt	Talent
28	50	66	61

INSIDE DIRT

He's a prima donna. And he won't travel to promote.

♦ *Up Close and Personal* was a mistake, but *The Horse Whisperer* edged up his score.

♦ He has real charisma in Japan.

♦ He's hopelessly goofy. He wears pink ski boots just to throw people off. His hobby is playing practical jokes on people.

♦ His reputation is that he has no sense of time, so scheduling is very difficult with him.

♦ Don't ever wait for Bob on the sunny side of the street—you'll get sunburned.

♦ Sundance has helped his credibility and means he's still taken seriously by critics.

♦ He's the male Loretta Young: an aging actor who is still wearing gowns and perfect makeup. He has to control everything.

♦ You know those love scenes for *Up Close and Personal*? It was like watching Michelle Pfeiffer make out with Grandpa.

Star Power

	1997	1998	1999
	78	67	84

(Chart axis values: 84, 82, 80, 78, 76, 74, 72, 70, 68, 66)

Box Office Bait

MOVIE	STUDIO	N.AMERICAN GROSS	RELEASE
The Sting	Univ	$159,616,327	12/25/73
Indecent Proposal	Para	$105,544,089	4/9/93
Butch Cassidy & The Sundance Kid	Fox	$102,308,889	1969
Out of Africa	Univ	$88,081,296	12/18/85
The Horse Whisperer	BV	$75,383,563	5/15/98

Career Trajectory

Robin Williams Rank **22** Bankability **84**

Real Name Robin McLaurim Williams
D.O.B. 7/21/52
Place of Birth Chicago, Illinois, USA
Contact (M) Mike Menchel AMG

Willingness to Travel/Promote	Professionalism	Career Mgmt	Talent
69	85	85	92

INSIDE DIRT

He's lost his subversive edge as a comedian.

- He's very valuable in Germany because he travels and gives a terrific performance to the press.

- In the movie I worked on, he had horrifically bad body odor. He was always extremely conscious of it, always borrowing people's shirts and sniffing himself. The grips head for the hills when Robin comes on the set.

- He'll always have a long career in France.

- He supports his fellow actors. He'll come to the set when he's not called just to give another actor someone to play off during a close-up.

- He's a perfectionist. On *The Fisher King* he offered to pay for extra takes himself to get it right.

- He made *Birdcage* a hit overseas.

- Unfortunately, Williams's talent has now retreated into kid comedy like *Jack* and schmaltz like *Good Will Hunting* and *What Dreams May Come*.

Star Power

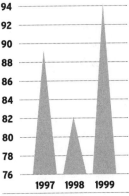

94
92
90
88
86
84
82
80
78
76

1997 1998 1999

Box Office Bait			
MOVIE	STUDIO	N.AMERICAN GROSS	RELEASE
Mrs. Doubtfire	Fox	$219,194,773	11/24/93
Aladdin (voice)	BV	$217,350,219	11/11/92
Good Will Hunting	Miramax	$138,339,411	12/5/97
Patch Adams	Univ	$135,014,968	12/25/98
The Birdcage	MGM	$124,060,553	3/8/96

Career Trajectory

Matt Damon Rank **23**   Bankability **83**

Real Name	Matthew Paige Damon
D.O.B.	10/8/70
Place of Birth	Cambridge, Massachusetts, USA
Contact	(A) Patrick Whitesell CAA

Willingness to Travel/Promote	Professionalism	Career Mgmt	Talent
55	**77**	**72**	**74**

INSIDE DIRT

Now he's got Ben Affleck to compete against.

- Matt has finally learned to do production stories so people won't forget about him. Ben Affleck did back-to-back movies and lots of press, and it served him well.

- I think he's afraid to make a commitment for fear it won't work. He's still not making enough movies.

- Matt is a much better actor than Ben Affleck. It's just that Matt is a little choosier in his roles. And *The Talented Mr. Ripley* was a great choice.

- He's done a terrific job building up his career and he supports his films.

- It's Ben Affleck they're all betting on.

Star Power

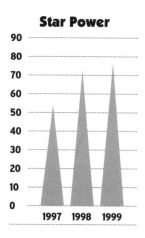

90		
80		
70		
60		
50		
40		
30		
20		
10		
0		
1997	1998	1999

Box Office Bait

MOVIE	STUDIO	N.AMERICAN GROSS	RELEASE
Saving Private Ryan (with re-issue)	Dreamworks	$230,900,365	7/24/98
Good Will Hunting	Miramax	$138,339,411	12/5/97
Courage Under Fire	Fox	$59,031,057	7/12/96
The Rainmaker	Para	$45,911,897	11/21/97
Rounders	Miramax	$22,921,898	9/11/98

Career Trajectory

Denzel Washington

Rank 24

Bankability 83

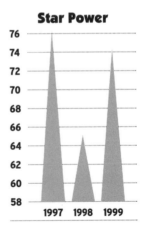

Real Name	Denzel Washington, Jr.
D.O.B.	12/28/54
Place of Birth	Mount Vernon, New York, USA
Contact	(A) Ed Limato, ICM

Willingness to Travel/Promote	Professionalism	Career Mgmt	Talent
59	**69**	**80**	**70**

INSIDE DIRT

I have a feeling Denzel might have peaked.

♦ I thought Denzel was bulletproof, but then came *The Preacher's Wife*.

♦ He likes clean, antiseptic roles.

♦ His rule is usually not to have sex or to be naked on screen.

♦ He brings a lot of star syndrome to the set.

♦ The way a scene is shot has to be designed around the way he's being shot. He has a huge influence on what a director can or can't do.

♦ His choices haven't been black characters, just characters who happen to be black.

♦ Even in Asia, Denzel is perceived more as a white actor.

♦ *The Bone Collector* could have buried him, but then *Hurricane* blew you away.

Star Power

76
74
72
70
68
66
64
62
60
58

1997 1998 1999

Box Office Bait

MOVIE	STUDIO	N.AMERICAN GROSS	RELEASE
The Pelican Brief	WB	$100,650,595	12/17/93
Crimson Tide	BV	$91,381,194	5/12/95
Philadelphia	Tri-Star	$77,324,422	12/22/93
Courage Under Fire	Fox	$59,031,057	7/12/96
Malcolm X	WB	$48,140,491	11/18/92

Career Trajectory

Nicolas Cage Rank 25   Bankability 82

Real Name	Nicholas Kim Coppola
D.O.B.	1/7/64
Place of Birth	Long Beach, California, USA
Contact	(A) Richard Lovett, CAA (M) Brillstein/Grey

Willingness to Travel/Promote	Professionalism	Career Mgmt	Talent
55	62	78	68

INSIDE DIRT

He's too quirky to be a franchise star.

◆ He made a very rapid transition from C list to A list with *Leaving Las Vegas*.

◆ Cage isn't a slam-dunk when you try to sell him worldwide. He may be over-priced.

◆ He's a decent enough actor but he's no looker, so whatever he does has to be based on some other appeal. And for the life of me, I don't know what that is.

◆ His type of action hero goes beyond beef and brawn to a more sensitive and fallible kind of guy.

◆ The French see Cage as more fragile and accessible, and they identify with that.

◆ A few years ago he was a ten for action adventure, now he's about a six.

◆ He's showing his age.

Star Power

Bar chart with y-axis from 10 to 100. Bars for 1997, 1998, 1999.

Box Office Bait			
MOVIE	**STUDIO**	**N.AMERICAN GROSS**	**RELEASE**
The Rock	BV	$134,069,511	6/7/96
Face Off	Para	$112,273,211	6/27/97
Con Air	BV	$100,927,613	6/6/97
Moonstruck	MGM	$79,765,241	12/16/87
City of Angels	WB	$78,647,175	4/10/98

Career Trajectory

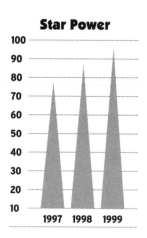

Eddie Murphy Rank **26**   Bankability **82**

Real Name	Edward Regan Murphy
D.O.B.	4/3/61
Place of Birth	Brooklyn, New York, USA
Contact	(A) Jim Wiatt, WMA

Willingness to Travel/Promote	Professionalism	Career Mgmt	Talent
52	**50**	**75**	**71**

INSIDE DIRT

Eddie is still not fireproof.

- He's back in form after *The Nutty Professor*.

- He tried to do drama with *Metro*—it was an express train to disaster.

- Eddie is surrounded by members of his family who I think are incompetent parasites. His entourage is huge.

- He demands no more than plenty of white stars demand, but he gets different reactions for it because he's black.

- Murphy is an amazing talent.

- His problem is his audiences. Their expectations are so straitjacketed that he doesn't have to reach that much.

- He's not good when choosing or developing his own stuff. He's always best with a strong producer like Brian Grazer.

- Overseas, he's most popular in Europe, Australia, and Japan.

- Don't put him in a ghetto movie. It would crash and burn abroad.

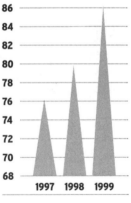

Star Power

86, 84, 82, 80, 78, 76, 74, 72, 70, 68

1997 1998 1999

Box Office Bait

MOVIE	STUDIO	N.AMERICAN GROSS	RELEASE
Beverly Hills Cop	Para	$234,760,478	12/5/84
Beverly Hills Cop 2	Para	$153,665,036	5/20/87
Doctor Dolittle	Fox	$144,156,464	6/26/98
The Nutty Professor	Univ	$128,814,019	6/28/96
Coming to America	Para	$128,152,301	6/29/88

Career Trajectory

Michelle Pfeiffer

Rank 27 **Bankability 81**

Real Name	Michelle Pfeiffer
D.O.B.	4/29/57
Place of Birth	Santa Ana, California, USA
Contact	(A) Ed Limato ICM

Willingness to Travel/Promote 43 **Professionalism** 75 **Career Mgmt** 73 **Talent** 70

INSIDE DIRT

I think she's underrated as an actress.

- All people see is a gorgeous woman and they don't remember how talented she truly is.

- She doesn't do a helluva lot of promotion and traveling. At the moment I think it's more because of her children.

- One of the few actresses who can play any part and get away with it. Before she did *Dangerous Minds,* who could have imagined her as a schoolteacher and a former Marine? You have to be a helluva good actress to get away with that.

- She isn't getting any younger, so she's starting to do more challenging roles.

- She's smart and she's easy to work with.

- She holes up in her Winnebago. She doesn't hang with the crew. But she doesn't have any attitude. A very nice girl.

Star Power

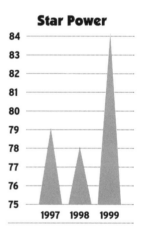

Values: 84, 83, 82, 81, 80, 79, 78, 77, 76, 75 — 1997 1998 1999

Box Office Bait

MOVIE	STUDIO	N.AMERICAN GROSS	RELEASE
Batman Returns	WB	$162,831,698	6/19/92
The Prince of Egypt (voice)	Dreamworks	$101,217,900	12/18/98
Dangerous Minds	BV	$84,916,677	8/11/95
Wolf	Columbia	$65,002,597	6/17/94
The Witches of Eastwick	WB	$63,749,955	6/12/87

Career Trajectory

Kevin Costner Rank 28 Bankability 81

Real Name Kevin Michael Costner
D.O.B. 1/18/55
Place of Birth Lynwood, California, USA
Contact Tig Productions, Warner Bros.

Willingness to Travel/Promote	Professionalism	Career Mgmt	Talent
82	56	39	51

INSIDE DIRT

Put that cowboy out to pasture.

♦ As I said after *Postman,* neither rain nor sleet nor snow will make him a Top 10 star. He's exhausted.

♦ Clint has learned when to put himself in a movie and when not to. Kevin hasn't.

♦ He hasn't been a hyphenate to his advantage, and he's about the only star who hasn't. His ego is just too damn big.

♦ He has lousy taste in projects.

♦ Germans love him, but only in the right movie.

♦ I wish he would fall in love with the script the way he falls in love with himself. I don't think he takes enough care in preparing the script, as both a director and an actor.

♦ Talk about bad career management. The problem is he doesn't have anyone advising him anymore.

♦ He's *so* over.

Star Power

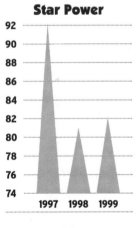

92
90
88
86
84
82
80
78
76
74

1997 1998 1999

Box Office Bait

MOVIE	STUDIO	N.AMERICAN GROSS	RELEASE
Dances With Wolves	OR	$184,010,809	11/9/90
Robin Hood: Prince of Thieves	WB	$165,493,908	6/14/91
The Bodyguard	WB	$121,936,132	11/25/92
Waterworld	Univ	$88,214,660	7/28/95
The Untouchables	Para	$76,254,308	6/3/87

Career Trajectory

George Clooney

Rank 29   **Bankability 81**

Real Name	George Timothy Clooney
D.O.B.	5/6/61
Place of Birth	Lexington, Kentucky, USA
Contact	(A) Bryan Lourd, CAA

Willingness to Travel/Promote	Professionalism	Career Mgmt	Talent
62	78	81	70

INSIDE DIRT

He's a reconstituted Harrison Ford.

- He has a certain movie-star quality that insulates him from being identified only as a doctor on *E.R.*

- He had four chances in four genres, and none of those movies worked. Then came *Out of Sight* and *Three Kings*.

- In Europe, we'll see a Pierce Brosnan film because of Pierce, but we still won't see a George Clooney because of George.

- His films have done better overseas than in North America.

- He killed the *Batman* franchise. But he's good at traveling for and supporting his films.

- Joel Schumacher should exorcise his demons: Put those Batmen in bed together or stop making this franchise. I'm tired of seeing these guys staring at each other's rubber nipples.

Star Power

Chart values: 73, 72, 71, 70, 69, 68, 67, 66, 65, 64 across 1997, 1998, 1999

Box Office Bait

MOVIE	STUDIO	N.AMERICAN GROSS	RELEASE
Batman and Robin	WB	$107,285,004	6/20/97
South Park: Bigger, (voice) Longer & Uncut	Para	$50,587,886	6/30/99
One Fine Day	Fox	$46,112,540	12/20/96
The Peacemaker	Dreamworks	$41,103,850	9/26/97
Out of Sight	Univ	$37,562,568	6/26/98

Career Trajectory

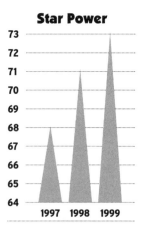

Pierce Brosnan Rank **30** Bankability **80**

Real Name	Pierce Brosnan
D.O.B.	5/16/53
Place of Birth	Drogheda, Ireland
Contact	(A) Fred Specktor, CAA

Willingness to Travel/Promote	Professionalism	Career Mgmt	Talent
70	**80**	**76**	**55**

INSIDE DIRT

If he stops doing James Bond, he'll have no long-term career.

♦ His sex scenes with Rene Russo in *The Thomas Crown Affair* are dynamite. Very believable. He's gone beyond Bond, finally.

♦ When he does romance, nothing happens. In both *The Mirror Has Two Faces* or *Mrs. Doubtfire,* no one spoke of him in any of the reviews. He simply doesn't have the heft of a Cary Grant.

♦ Everybody loves working with him. I've never heard anyone say a bad thing about Pierce.

♦ He gets roles he doesn't deserve because people like him so much.

♦ He's not the best actor in the known universe. He has a pretty stiff delivery.

♦ I've never worked with him, but he's an environmentalist so I love him.

Star Power

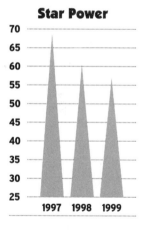

70
65
60
55
50
45
40
35
30
25

1997 1998 1999

Box Office Bait

MOVIE	STUDIO	N.AMERICAN GROSS	RELEASE
Mrs. Doubtfire	Fox	$219,194,773	11/24/93
Tomorrow Never Dies	MGM	$125,210,295	12/19/97
Goldeneye	MGM	$106,429,941	11/17/95
Dante's Peak	Univ	$67,090,725	2/7/97
The Mirror Has Two Faces	Sony/TS	$40,845,152	11/15/96

Career Trajectory

Gwyneth Paltrow

Rank 31   **Bankability 80**

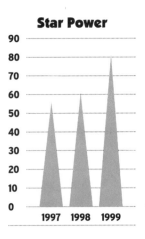

Real Name	Gwyneth Kate Paltrow
D.O.B.	9/28/73
Place of Birth	Los Angeles, California, USA
Contact	(A) Rick Kurtzman, CAA

Willingness to Travel/Promote	Professionalism	Career Mgmt	Talent
62	47	85	70

INSIDE DIRT

She's hardly the princess Hollywood makes her out to be.

♦ She was a prima donna on the set of *Shakespeare in Love*.

♦ Crew members can't stand her. She can be abusive and use people.

♦ Whoever is advising her on her career is doing a terrific job.

♦ It's easy for celebs to take the price tags off their heads and become too available to the paparazzi. But Gwyneth would arrive at events separately from her then-boyfriend Ben Affleck, because it makes photos of the two of them more valuable.

♦ She's so starved for attention and affection.

♦ She's gained a lot of her power from whom she was dating: Brad Pitt.

♦ She's gone to nice schools in the East, comes from a wealthy family—yet she sounds like a dodo on talk shows.

♦ I'll give this to her—she's a good actress.

Star Power

Bar chart showing values for 1997, 1998, 1999 with y-axis from 0 to 90.

Box Office Bait			
MOVIE	STUDIO	N.AMERICAN GROSS	RELEASE
Hook	Tri-Star	$119,654,823	12/11/91
Shakespeare in Love	Miramax	$100,241,322 *	12/11/98
Seven	NL	$100,123,974	9/22/95
A Perfect Murder	WB	$67,629,105	6/5/98
Malice	Columbia	$46,038,636	10/1/93

Career Trajectory

Cameron Diaz Rank **32** Bankability **79**

Real Name	Cameron Diaz
D.O.B.	8/30/72
Place of Birth	San Diego, California, USA
Contact	(A) Nick Styne, ICM (M) AMG

Willingness to Travel/Promote	Professionalism	Career Mgmt	Talent
58	**75**	**73**	**65**

INSIDE DIRT

She'll have sticking power, big time.

◆ In *My Best Friend's Wedding*, she almost stole the show from Julia.

◆ *Being John Malkovich* was unbelievably risky. People will be talking about it for years.

◆ She's far too beautiful to be as widely liked as she is. She's also really thin and that usually alienates a majority of females. But she's the exception that proves the rule.

◆ She has a face that the camera loves. For her limited gifts, she's done very well.

◆ With the right project and director, you can really get Cameron to lower her price.

◆ She speaks Spanish, so to stay hot she should go out and travel to Latin America and Spain, even France and Italy.

◆ I've heard she's just the sweetest thing around. Crew members adore her.

Star Power

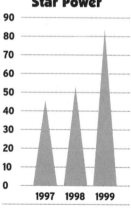

Values shown: 90, 80, 70, 60, 50, 40, 30, 20, 10, 0 — years 1997, 1998, 1999

Box Office Bait

MOVIE	STUDIO	N.AMERICAN GROSS	RELEASE
There's Something About Mary	Fox	$176,472,910	7/15/98
My Best Friend's Wedding	Sony/TS	$127,120,029	6/20/97
The Mask	NL	$119,936,108	7/29/94
Fear and Loathing in Las Vegas	Univ	$10,672,165	5/22/98
Very Bad Things	POLY	$9,801,782	11/25/98

Career Trajectory

Catherine Zeta-Jones

Rank 33   **Bankability 79**

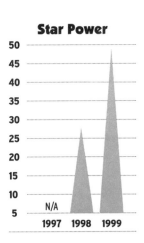

Real Name	Catherine Zeta-Jones
D.O.B.	9/25/69
Place of Birth	Swansea, Wales, UK
Contact	(A) Aleen Keshishian, ICM (M) John Crosby

Willingness to Travel/Promote	Professionalism	Career Mgmt	Talent
70	72	78	58

INSIDE DIRT

She's much bigger in the States than in her home country, Britain.

- She's made the right moves in the roles she's taken. And like Sharon Stone, she knows that at least 75 percent of her appeal is the way she looks. So she makes sure that she always looks like a star whenever she's seen.

- On *Zorro* she broke a crew member's heart. She had a big love affair with him. When they got back to Los Angeles she booted him out of the limousine on the way to the Oscars and told him to get lost forever.

- She was fine on the set, a regular gal.

- She's a real sizzler. Who says the Brits don't know how to cook?

Star Power

Chart values: 50, 45, 40, 35, 30, 25, 20, 15, 10, 5

1997	1998	1999
N/A		

Box Office Bait

MOVIE	STUDIO	N.AMERICAN GROSS	RELEASE
The Mask of Zorro	Sony	$93,771,072	7/17/98
Entrapment	Fox	$87,055,043 *	4/30/99
The Haunting	Dreamworks	$77,340,946 *	7/23/99
The Phantom	Para	$17,323,216	6/7/96
Christopher Columbus	WB	$8,203,138	8/21/92

Career Trajectory

Ben Affleck   Rank **34**   Bankability **79**

Real Name	Benjamin Geza Affleck
D.O.B.	8/16/72
Place of Birth	Berkeley, California, USA
Contact	(A) Patrick Whitesell, CAA

Willingness to Travel/Promote	Professionalism	Career Mgmt	Talent
45	**74**	**82**	**68**

INSIDE DIRT

They're betting on him being a big star. But he's not there yet.

♦ He's becoming the new leading man. When Cruise, Hanks, Pitt, and Clooney aren't available, Ben Affleck is next on the list.

♦ He's in a lot of movies, sometimes as the co-lead, like *Armageddon,* and sometimes as a bit part, like *Shakespeare in Love.* That's smart. His career harks back to the old studio system.

♦ They're marketed as a couple. I think Damon is playing the star of the two but there's a strength to Affleck. He could turn into a Clint Eastwood quiet-man type.

♦ Those two boys together raise suspicion.

♦ I just don't think he has the talent to make it. I think he's the president of the FL Club: the Fucking Lucky Club.

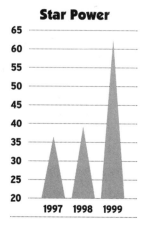

Star Power

65
60
55
50
45
40
35
30
25
20

1997 1998 1999

Box Office Bait			
MOVIE	STUDIO	N.AMERICAN GROSS	RELEASE
Armageddon	BV	$201,578,182	7/1/98
Good Will Hunting	Miramax	$138,339,411	12/5/97
Shakespeare in Love	Miramax	$100,241,322	12/11/98
Forces of Nature	Dreamworks	$52,900,680	3/19/99
School Ties	Para	$14,700,000	9/18/92

Career Trajectory

Anthony Hopkins

Rank 35   **Bankability 78**

Real Name Philip Anthony Hopkins
D.O.B. 12/31/37
Place of Birth Port Talbot, West Glamorgan, Wales
Contact (A) Rick Nicita, CAA

Willingness to Travel/Promote	Professionalism	Career Mgmt	Talent
58	70	72	88

INSIDE DIRT

He can be very testy to work with.

- He's such an incredible actor. And a perfect gentleman.
- He had a fit at the end of *Legends of the Fall* because Brad Pitt was being treated as a bigger star than he was. He was going to leave the movie early. He didn't, but he was rude the rest of the time he was on the film.
- He's always riding off to go to his AA meetings when the best thing he could possibly do would be to have a drink. He's a crew's nightmare.
- He felt the director on *Zorro* did too many takes, and that pissed him off.
- On *Legends of the Fall,* Tony actually paid the $15,000 salary upgrade for a crew member who was otherwise too expensive to keep. That was very generous.

Star Power

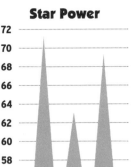

| | 1997 | 1998 | 1999 |

Box Office Bait

MOVIE	STUDIO	N.AMERICAN GROSS	RELEASE
Silence of the Lambs	Orion	$130,742,922	2/13/91
The Mask of Zorro	Sony	$93,771,072	7/17/98
Bram Stoker's Dracula	Columbia	$82,416,928	11/13/92
Legends of the Fall	Tri-Star	$66,492,292	12/25/94
Meet Joe Black	Univ	$44,606,335	11/13/98

Career Trajectory

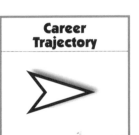

Richard Gere Rank 36   Bankability 78

Real Name	Richard Gere
D.O.B.	8/29/49
Place of Birth	Philadelphia, Pennsylvania, USA
Contact	(A) Ed Limato, ICM

Willingness to Travel/Promote	Professionalism	Career Mgmt	Talent
42	70	64	65

INSIDE DIRT

He'll slide fast if he doesn't find another hit soon.

- I've never seen him better than in *Runaway Bride*. He's just got more charisma and he's more likable and charming than ever.

- The man can't carry a movie anymore on his name alone.

- People seem to really like him. He's generous, collaborative, an all-round good guy.

- Richard manages to step back into the marketplace every now and again. But he's hanging on by a piece of string.

- I hear he drove Bruce Willis nuts on *The Jackal* because he had to meditate before each scene.

- I've known him since before he was a star. He takes himself very seriously but he's a great guy.

- He's not gay. And there's no such thing as a gerbil.

Star Power

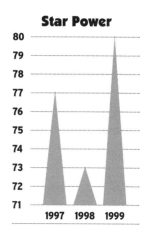

80
79
78
77
76
75
74
73
72
71

1997   1998   1999

Box Office Bait

MOVIE	STUDIO	N.AMERICAN GROSS	RELEASE
Pretty Woman	BV	$178,406,268	3/23/90
An Officer and A Gentleman	Para	$129,795,549	7/28/82
Runaway Bride	Para	$73,820,993	7/30/99
Primal Fear	Para	$56,116,183	4/3/96
The Jackal	Univ	$54,910,560	11/14/97

Career Trajectory

Nicole Kidman Rank **37** Bankability **78**

Real Name Nicole Kidman
D.O.B. 6/20/67
Place of Birth Honolulu, Hawaii, USA
Contact (A) Kevin Huvane, CAA (M) Marc Epstein

Willingness to Travel/Promote	Professionalism	Career Mgmt	Talent
52	87	86	68

INSIDE DIRT

Never underestimate that lady's abilities.

- She's picking really interesting roles. She has a great story sense. I think she'll be the next Julia Roberts.

- She's incredibly driven and smart. I'd fear Nicole more than I'd fear Tom, no question about it.

- She wears hair extensions and once before a press junket she lost them. So she just stuffed her hair under a baseball cap and went out. She's cool that way.

- The only thing where you can get her bristling is if you label her being a star because of Tom Cruise. People who do that never saw *Dead Calm*.

- She's completely anal. She's the decision maker in that household, not Tom. She determines every-thing. And it's the same with her career.

- She's a sweet and crazy ditz.

Star Power

| | 1997 | 1998 | 1999 |

Box Office Bait

MOVIE	STUDIO	N.AMERICAN GROSS	RELEASE
Batman Forever	WB	$183,997,904	6/16/95
Days of Thunder	Para	$82,663,996	6/27/90
Far and Away	Univ	$58,883,840	5/23/92
Eyes Wide Shut	WB	$52,135,879	7/16/99
Practical Magic	WB	$46,611,204	10/16/98

Career Trajectory

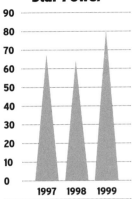

Jodie Foster Rank 38   Bankability 76

Real Name	Alicia Christian Foster
D.O.B.	11/19/62
Place of Birth	Los Angeles, California, USA
Contact	(A) Jim Wiatt, WMA

Willingness to Travel/Promote	Professionalism	Career Mgmt	Talent
77	96	83	87

INSIDE DIRT

The foreign market loves Jodie.

◆ She propelled *Contact* to over $100 million domestic. Only Julia Roberts had the same clout with *My Best Friend's Wedding*.

◆ When she tours in France, she speaks French to the distributors.

◆ Her directing hasn't helped her bankability in Europe.

◆ She proves you can control your life and give the press what they want if you know where to draw the line. She simply won't answer questions about sex or her sexual orientation.

◆ When she came to talk to our class, I never felt anyone to be so cold and impersonal.

◆ One of the best-prepared actresses ever. A wonderful co-worker.

◆ If she doesn't like the director and it isn't working for her, she can be difficult.

◆ At parties, you just hope that you're smart enough that she'll talk to you.

Star Power

Chart showing values for 1997, 1998, 1999 on a scale from 79.5 to 84.

Box Office Bait			
MOVIE	**STUDIO**	**N.AMERICAN GROSS**	**RELEASE**
Silence of the Lambs	Orion	$130,742,922	2/13/91
Maverick	WB	$101,619,662	5/20/94
Contact	WB	$100,769,177	7/11/97
Sommersby	WB	$50,052,806	2/5/93
Nell	Fox	$33,587,335	12/14/94

Career Trajectory

Sylvester Stallone

Rank 39 **Bankability 76**

Real Name	Sylvester Enzio Stallone
D.O.B.	7/6/46
Place of Birth	New York, New York, USA
Contact	(A) Jim Wiatt, WMA (M) Gerry Harrington

Willingness to Travel/Promote	Professionalism	Career Mgmt	Talent
80	**54**	**55**	**38**

INSIDE DIRT

He has a reputation for telling the director what to do.

- He's become a cliché of himself.

- Unlike Bruce Willis or Robin Williams, he can't cross over into smaller films. He tried to with *Cop Land* and failed. And forget comedy.

- Since *Judge Dred,* his international box-office numbers have been pretty poor.

- Buyers are telling me that in Germany, he's over. Too many films flopped there.

- At one point he was huge in Japan.

- He was totally professional and onboard for *Cop Land.*

- He very rarely works with a director of any clout because he wants to take over his movies.

- He still could have the career renaissance that Travolta had with *Pulp Fiction* if his management had the guts to put him into new parts.

- His entourage is ridiculous. He's over.

Star Power

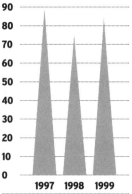

Vertical axis: 90, 80, 70, 60, 50, 40, 30, 20, 10, 0
Horizontal axis: 1997 1998 1999

Box Office Bait

MOVIE	STUDIO	N.AMERICAN GROSS	RELEASE
Rambo: First Blood Part 2	Tri-Star	$150,415,432	5/22/85
Rocky IV	MGM	$127,873,716	11/27/85
Rocky 3	MGM	$122,823,192	5/28/82
Rocky	MGM	$117,235,147	11/21/76
Antz (voice)	Dreamworks	$90,646,554	10/2/98

Career Trajectory

Robert De Niro Rank 40 Bankability 75

Real Name	Robert De Niro, Jr.
D.O.B.	8/17/43
Place of Birth	New York, New York, USA
Contact	(A) Bryan Lourd, CAA

Willingness to Travel/Promote	Professionalism	Career Mgmt	Talent
30	**80**	**63**	**89**

INSIDE DIRT

He sets the standard for entourage.

♦ He makes any movie that he's in brilliant. He's an actor other stars want to have in their movies.

♦ There are stars who always think they know better, that they could have chosen a better location. Not De Niro. He respects the crew.

♦ You have to budget about $250,000 a month just for his entourage. And he never remembers his lines.

♦ *Analyze This* really showed his range, and as a result he picked up a younger audience. Women loved it because they saw his softer side.

♦ Bobby's problem is he considers himself a leading man, so he shuns supporting roles. He could make a fortune playing number two to an A-list star.

♦ The greatest thing that ever walked the face of the earth.

Star Power

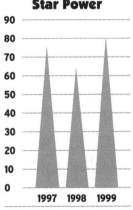

1997	1998	1999

Box Office Bait			
MOVIE	**STUDIO**	**N.AMERICAN GROSS**	**RELEASE**
Analyze This	WB	$106,694,016	3/5/99
Cape Fear	Univ	$79,118,315	11/13/91
Backdraft	Univ	$78,001,365	5/24/91
The Untouchables	Para	$76,254,308	6/3/87
Heat	WB	$66,802,342	12/15/95

Career Trajectory

Clint Eastwood Rank 41 Bankability 75

Real Name	Clinton Eastwood, Jr.
D.O.B.	5/31/30
Place of Birth	San Francisco, California, USA
Contact	(A) Leonard Hirschan, WMA

Willingness to Travel/Promote	Professionalism	Career Mgmt	Talent
82	**87**	**86**	**65**

INSIDE DIRT

Clint is like John Wayne: built to last forever.

♦ The only problem with Clint is that he's really starting to look old, craggy, and bald. He's out of the action beat now.

♦ He's huge in France and Germany. They respect longevity in age and career.

♦ He produces, directs, and acts, so he has the pick of anything he wants. And he can cast himself in it.

♦ Clint's weakness is romance and comedy. I refer to *Every Which Way But Loose,* where he played straight man to the orangutan.

♦ He has a short fuse about certain things. Somebody once took his parking space at Warner Bros., and Clint ended up taking a sledgehammer to the car.

♦ I think he'll be like John Huston. They'll take him off the set in a coffin.

Star Power

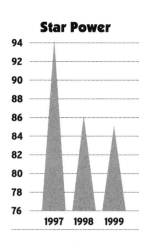

94
92
90
88
86
84
82
80
78
76

1997 1998 1999

Box Office Bait

MOVIE	STUDIO	N.AMERICAN GROSS	RELEASE
Every Which Way But Loose	WB	$115,333,336	1978
In The Line of Fire	Columbia	$102,238,862	7/9/93
Unforgiven	WB	$101,101,229	8/7/92
Any Which Way But Loose	WB	$90,000,000	1980
Sudden Impact	WB	$77,333,333	1983

Career Trajectory

4

Breakdowns on the Casting Highway

Casting call sixty years ago: Kate Hepburn and Cary Grant—perfect for *The Philadelphia Story* (1940). Humphrey Bogart and Ingrid Bergman—can't top 'em for *Casablanca* (1942).

Today's line-up? Tom Cruise and *Renée Zelwegger?* Julia Roberts and *Dermot Mulroney?*

Why don't our biggest stars pair up anymore? To paraphrase *Sunset Boulevard,* the pictures didn't get smaller—the casting did.

The reason we don't see Tom Cruise acting opposite many top stars (excepting his wife, Nicole Kidman) is that, at the going A+ prices, studios simply can't afford them. To put it another way, where Tom might once have been paired with a full-length femme, today all he'd get is a mini-driver.

That's the tough news for midrange stars: Hollywood is ditching them by the casting roadside.

The current collection of in-demand Hollywood actors is weighted to the extremes more than ever: a handful of A+ and A stars for marquee value, along with a huge group of C talent for affordability. Like a madam in a corset, it's the midsection that takes the squeeze.

What's causing this casting crunch in Hollywood?

With salaries skyrocketing, the only stars worth the price are the top-listers who can deliver the audience. There are too many B actors trying to hitch a ride on the Hollywood highway, and at fees of $10 to $15 million a film, no big-star vehicles are stopping to pick them up at that price. (Kurt Russell and Alec Baldwin, this means hitchers like you.) They'll stop for the C-listers, though. So new faces like Zelwegger get a clean shot a stardom in top-line Cruisers like *Jerry Maguire.*

That may be good news for the little guys, but here's the catch: There are fewer chances to thumb a ride. That highway has become so over-crowded that the studios have started to make fewer vehicles to drive on it. In fact, they're even making shorter roadways on which to put those cars. (Would that Los Angeles could have that problem.)

Translation: There are too many movies competing for too little screen time. The ones that do muscle into the good cinemas have to hit at the box office by the first weekend or risk getting yanked to make room for the next. For a star driver, that's not a lot of road to burn rubber on.

It's a hideously expensive drive, too. An orgy of spending is needed to market a movie for its opening weekend—enough to pay for a few smaller movies—in order for it even to squeak by to its second or third weekend.

Which brings us back to that casting squeeze. With more money spent on fewer films at greater risk, Hollywood is hiring bigger stars to leverage that risk. Now you see why Kurt and Alec and all the others are eating the big guys' dust—with hardly any *stardust* to show for it.

"The market in Hollywood is now for the thirty or so A+ and A players, or for a really good story," reports Peter Dekom, a business consultant and former Hollywood attorney. "And if you have both together, then you have a hit. Tom Hanks's and Adam Sandler's movies are proving that."

Easy for them, maybe. But the B guys are in a double bind: Getting into a movie with a bigger star is hard enough, but making sure it speeds to a hit immediately is almost too much to ask. No wonder the Bs suffer visions of ending up in Norma Desmondville—that dusty, deserted ghost town off the Hollywood highway, filled with more roadkill than a Texas barbecue pit.

But if you think the A guys are cruising merrily along without a hitch, check the highway again. They're fighting road rage.

Even for the most bankable stars, making movies is more aggravating than ever. With fewer pictures produced and higher budgets at risk, there's a more rapid failure rate for many stars' box-office performance.

No longer do star vehicles have the luxury of cruising along for weeks and months to find their audience. Now tow trucks are standing by to haul them off the road if they don't perform—fast.

Once top drivers like Bruce Willis and Sylvester Stallone were thought to be crash resistant at the box office. But then *Mercury Rising* and *Demolition Man* reminded everyone that—well, they'd better demolish those ideas.

Marquee names like Nic Cage, Brad Pitt, Will Smith, Harrison Ford, Jim Carrey, Robin Williams, and Julia Roberts all have had their share of fender-benders and collisions, too. Given today's massive movie costs, those smash-ups have put more than a few dents in the studios' confidence about big stars in star vehicles.

The remedy: Get a better roadside insurance policy.

To offset their star-driven concerns and to better answer to their stockholders, movie studios—fine, upstanding profit-seeking multinational corporations that they are—have been laying off some of the financial risk for their costlier films by taking outside partners. On *The Matrix* and *Analyze This,* for example, Warner Bros. hooked up with the independent company Village Roadshow. "They didn't feel that based on Keanu Reeves's and Robert DeNiro's last films, they were going to have a hit," says a sales agent.

You just can't trust good drivers these days.

For the studios, it's the buddy system all over again. Only this time, it's not about pairing the As with the Cs—it's all about getting enough Bs: bucks to protect your backside.

Back on the highway, the midrange stars are crowding the shoulder—thumbs out, hopes down, prices still up—as the big guys jostle for lanes. It may not be the Road to Wellville, but at least the SigAlerts are shorter than L.A.'s.

5

Perks of the Trade

Perks. An interesting word. It rhymes with jerks.

Perks are those outrageous "must haves" for any star: masseurs, private chefs, Learjets, and sometimes special "pets."

Designed by agents to be precisely as expensive as they are unnecessary, perks are what all stars want and what all producers fear. They are bribes. Most producers pay these bribes to get stars on their side before making a film.

Producers can be easily deluded sometimes.

Money doesn't always buy good behavior, as anyone who has worked with Gimme More—excuse me, Demi Moore—will tell you. Still, it may be worth shelling out the big bucks to avoid The Curse of the Pissed-Off Star. This is when the star terrorizes a set because his costar's most excellent and sexy Winnie is ten inches longer than his. ("Winnie" is a trailer, mind you.) Bribes can be useful that way.

When a producer bribes—excuse me, remunerates—a star $20 million to be in his film, you can figure an additional $2 to $3 million for perks. Excuse me, for Necessary and Justifiable Amenities to ensure that the Talent is in the Proper Emotional Mode to Channel the Performance that will Move the Hearts and Minds of Millions.

Oh, come off it. Whatever happened just to doing your job?

Herewith a crib sheet on some of the more popular Perks of the Trade that Hollywood serves up.

The Entourage

This one drives the studio suits nuts. Of all the expenses on a film, people cost the most. Star tag-alongs usually require renting extra trailers and hence extra Teamsters to service those trailers. For a sixty-day shoot, accommodating this multi-headed Hydra could easily be a six-digit budget booster.

Generally, the bigger the star, the bigger the entourage. Eddie Murphy has about fifteen tag-alongs in his. Sylvester Stalone, eleven. Sweet and lovely Demi Moore has been known to bring along nannies, gym trainers, hairdressers, and the like when she travels—enough so that, some years ago, she presented one indie company with a perk package costing around $900,000, most of which was for the entourage. Figuring Moore is less, the company passed.

Wesley Snipes's entourage isn't anything to invite home for Christmas dinner, either. An on-set professional bluntly called it "nasty." "They were like the enemy of the crew," our source told us. "We were just trying to keep Wesley away from them."

Some actors hardly have an entourage at all. Samuel Jackson had a total of one on *The Negotiator*. He was a fellow who doubled as both Jackson's assistant and stand-in while also being an actor in the film. That's excellent per-dollar value for your perk.

(On the questionable side, on other shoots Jackson has brought along two very pricey hairdressers —even though he has a shaved head.)

Sylvester Stallone's retinue of eleven servants is the stuff of legend—and some loathing—among Hollywood crews. For the shoot of *Demolition Man* in Rome, there were Tony his Teamster driver, a makeup person to make him look swarthy, a hairstylist to help him look less balding, a costumer to tend to his sartorial needs, four different assistants, a gym trainer, a publicist, and a golf pro. The golf pro's job was to supervise the crew as they built Sly an entire "Golf World" set on a separate soundstage for Sly's between-takes amusement. Included was a huge golf net, special lighting, a couch and a bar, and plenty of video equipment.

"One assistant's job was just to get Sly women for his movies," revealed a crew member. "On *Cliffhanger* the assistant had women helicoptered in.

On *Daylight* I remember some skanky Siberian hooker who would come to the set. She was so scary. Very ugly and manly."

Among non-Siberians, who rates inclusion in a star entourage? The worst culprit is a mealy-mouthed sycophant with a supremely exaggerated sense of self—in other words, the star's paid best friend. This person does zilch. This person is not a star's assistant or even the assistant's assistant, or even a "masseur" (or "masseuse)." But before long he (or she) is starting to behave around the set as if he really *were* the star.

Other excessive entourage billings include that personal chef who travels with the star and a paid staff person to walk the star's pets. Not to mention assorted extra hairdressers, and so on.

Then there are also the bodyguards, a.k.a. "the grease." Most high-profile stars avail themselves of this privilege, with the apparent glaring exception of Tom Cruise. "I think it was a fault with Tom—he never really had security or bodyguards," said a former member of his company. "I was shocked at the level he did *not* go to to make sure he was protected."

Producer Mike Medavoy wouldn't be shocked, however. Medavoy, the well-respected chairman and CEO of Phoenix Pictures and a former studio chief, disagrees that the "grease" is a necessary perk to safeguard the stars from possible attack.

"Let's face it," he concludes. "There is no such thing as a legitimate entourage. Period. I find these people with all the security and all that bullshit ridiculous. Because if somebody really wants to harass or kill any of these people, they will. They'll find them, they'll kill them. Nobody can prevent that. The President of the United States has been shot."

So much for entourages.

The Winnies

Winnebagos, or "Winnies," are those expensive oversized trailers that either are owned by the star (and rented out to the production at exorbitant rates) or are provided by the production itself. Most stars have been weaned on Winnies. Virtually all have some specific demands for customizing their trailers, some more outlandish than others.

These Winnie wanna-haves may include such critical items as a jet-propulsion steam Jacuzzi, a king-size water bed, a phalanx of phone lines, a computer with Internet access, and a satellite dish with widescreen TV to watch those Italian soft-porn channels. The Winnie's refrigerator may also need to be stocked at all times with specific kinds and amounts of manna for the star. Heaven forbid, for example, that Woody Harrelson's stash of fresh wheatgrass juice runs low.

Where an actor's Winnie is parked on location can be a status symbol and perk in itself—and not a welcome one to crew members. It's an unwritten law that the camera truck is always parked closest to the set because of all the heavy equipment that must be lugged to and from it. Right behind the camera truck are parked the actors' Winnies, even before other equipment trucks. "But on *Born on the Fourth of July,* Tom Cruise had his trailer parked *in front of* the camera truck, which everyone considered hideous," a crew member on the shoot recalled. "Like it really would have inconvenienced Tom to walk across the street with his Evian water instead of inconveniencing the whole camera and grip department." Make that the gripe department.

A clever star will put the exact size of trailer he wants into his contract. "It might say 27 feet, but there may be times when you're shooting on location where the best trailer available is 23.5 feet," Rhino Films president Stephen Nemeth sighs. "It's just absurd to discuss."

But being the fine producer he is, Nemeth does. "I tell the actor, 'If you can quantify the damages caused to you by a shorter trailer, I'll listen. But quite frankly, there aren't any. It's an ego thing and you've got the biggest one here.'"

Nice going, Steve.

Such territoriality over trailers can incite "Winnie wars" between the stars. During the filming of *Pacific Heights,* a crew member witnessed Michael Keaton—reportedly with measuring tape in hand—checking out how much bigger Melanie Griffith's Winnie was than his (she was using Don Johnson's camper from *Miami Vice*). Gripes soon sprouted that *hers* came equipped with a chef, too.

Likewise, Toby Maguire is reported to have taken the dreaded tape to measure costar Charlize Theron's trailer on the set of *The Ciderhouse Rules.*

Studio honchos don't exactly feel such behavior measures up. "It was outrageous that a twenty-one-year-old who isn't a star was behaving like that," said an executive close to the shoot. "Right away he got his wings clipped by [Miramax co-chief] Harvey Weinstein in a way that nobody would wish on their enemy. Now he's reformed."

Air Travel

Let it first be said that there are always a handful of stars who refuse to get too high-flying and just stick to the ground, for whatever reasons. Whoopi Goldberg travels in a custom-designed Greyhound bus. And when gravity-bound Billy Bob Thornton didn't get a train ticket in time to make his call for a shoot in the Midwest, Miramax ordered up a Town Car to drive him the thousand-plus miles to Missouri. A real deal on wheels.

When it comes to the most popular mode of transport, however, a studio can easily cough up tens of thousands of dollars on appeasing a star's air travel needs. It may have to shell out as many as twelve first-class round trip air tickets for the star's groupies and family alone.

Pricier still is hauling out the corporate jet for the star's use. Warner Bros. is notorious for commandeering them as star perks. But the actor must be a fairly heavy hitter at the box office to rate this kind of concession, primarily because of the supersonic expenses involved. These include fees for a pilot and a copilot as well as a flight attendant for anything bigger than a small Lear, and jet fuel by the truckload. Overnight accommodations in trendy hotels will also have to be divvied out to the plane's crew, not to mention landing fees and various incidentals. For one international round trip, the costs could soar to $150,000.

Sometimes hiring the star requires hiring his toys as well. John Travolta, an avid pilot, owns a 727 jet. Casting him often involves paying the actor to lease out his own plane (for a tidy six-figure fee) so that he can fly it to and from location. One agent dished: "John Travolta gets a million dollars for airplane fuel in his contracts. That's the rumor I heard."

Rumors tend to fly as high as 727's sometimes.

One of the more popular tales of star travel making the Hollywood rounds a few years back involved our beloved Demi Moore again, leading lady of Castle Rock's *A Few Good Men*.

The film's premiere was being held in Manhattan, and Castle Rock was desperate to have her attend. (Nicholson and Cruise were going, after all.) The problem was, Moore and her entourage were stuck out at her ranch in

Idaho. So against what a studio executive termed "everyone's better judgment," Castle Rock agreed to give her a private plane.

"The plane arrives in Sun Valley and Demi takes one look at it and says, 'Oh no, this plane won't do,'" an executive close to the picture relates. "She said it wasn't big enough for her nannies and all the rest of her entourage. More to the point, it wasn't big enough for all her luggage, which she didn't want to stack—it had to be laid out side by side. She also wanted her own private suite in the plane, to be able to stretch out and everything.

"So she called up and said, 'I'm not going to the premiere unless you send a bigger plane.'

"For that reason, Castle Rock caved. It sent the first plane home and ordered up a bigger private jet, which got there an hour and half later. And off Demi went to the premiere."

According to the executive, that bit of star toadying cost Castle Rock an extra $50,000 for the additional plane. Total tab for winging Demi and a few good airplanes to the one-night extravaganza: just south of $100,000.

If you think that's overly accommodating, how about a star insisting that his entire private gym be flown to his film's location? This is a mandatory perk for Arnold Schwarzenegger. Each of the many tailor-made pieces must be shipped to a room directly adjacent to where the star is staying, often requiring a film company to rent an extra suite next door to the star.

Oh yes, the personal trainer comes along for the ride, too.

Then there is the perk of arranging custom corporate jet flights solely to carry very small objects to a set or an office. These can be anything from a box of candy to a bowl of goldfish. A star may also demand that Mr. Pet fly on the corporate jet, an indulgence that Warners (a studio built on animated animals) has been known to grant. The studio puts the pet on the jet, flies the jet to the set where the pet and the jet are met by a vet, and—oh, zoots. It's about as appealing to studio suits as green eggs and ham.

Hotels

Ground Zero for Most Expensive Star Digs is the French Riviera's Hotel du Cap Eden Roc. A favorite playground for top stars and executives frolicking at the Cannes Film Festival, the hotel's standard suites can set you back two grand a night (payable in cash only). Robert DeNiro, one of the reigning kings of star perks, was there one year to promote *Guilty by Suspicion*, but he was guilty only of uncorking huge bills for his champagne-toting entourage. The final tally came to a budget-busting $36,000, of which $2,500 went toward a single bottle of brandy. Verdict: The insanity defense is in order.

Charlie (a.k.a. Charles) Sheen was staying at the du Cap while practicing for his role as Wild Thing, the pitcher who couldn't throw straight in *Major League 2*. From his shoreline suite, he tossed eighty Eden Roc ceramic ashtrays in the direction of a seaside boulder. At $25 an ashtray, that hurled a mere $2,000 onto his "extras" bill. He was right for the part, too—sources said he missed the rock every time.

Even in less exotic climes, a star's multiple-bedroom suite can set a film company back thousands of dollars a night. It's often cheaper for a film company to accommodate its top talent by renting a ritzy apartment or a house, which usually comes with maid service and a cook.

Some directors lay down the law. Stars in a Robert Altman film must forgo everything from their going rate to their personal makeup artists and hairdressers, in order to share in the common glory of working with a maestro. Not to mention the glory of cutting production costs.

David Levy, who has worked as a producer on several Altman films, insists that even with such "sacrifices," the director's casts are treated regally. For *Cookie's Fortune,* starring Glenn Close, Warren Beatty, and Bob Gutman, the production displaced over twenty homeowners in a small Mississippi town and put the cast and crew in private homes, many of them of the antebellum variety.

Why would any sane citizen pull up stakes and hand over his house keys to a bunch of Hollywood intruders?

"Actually, it was considered a good thing for the community," Levy says. "A lot of townspeople looked on it as their civic duty."

Duty? Might it also be—this was just a wild guess—that they were *paid handsomely* to do it?

"Well, it wouldn't be considered very hospitable or gracious to deny Ms. Close or Mr. Beatty or Mr. Gutman a private home if they wanted it."

So there you have it. Not only Hollywood handlers and moguls, even lowly townsfolk can't resist sucking up ever so graciously to Hollywood royalty. And who can resist a nip from the flask of Southern hospitality? That's a no-cost, ready-made perk right there.

Live Perks

Surprising as it may sound, some stars' perk lists even include other actors. Indie stalwarts like John Malkovich and Steve Buscemi "are like perks to the big movie stars, who like to have them in their films," notes Cassien Elwes, an executive at the William Morris Agency. Nic Cage reportedly wouldn't do *Con Air* unless both Malkovich and Buscemi were in the film. Sean Penn, Harvey Keitel, and Tim Roth are three other actors who serve nicely as perks.

Adds another agent: "Part of catering to the stars is casting the supporting actors they want and who will legitimize the rubbish that they're making." In other words, rubbish not repped by that particular agent.

Possum Tale

Of course, perks don't always need to be expensive to induce hemorrhoidal stress in studio executives. Take the bizarre case of Kirstie Ally, a noted animal lover.

During an out-of-town press junket for her film *Sibling Rivalry* the star had toted along one her favorite pets—a baby possum. She had tried bottle-feeding the bottle-nosed creature, but that apparently wasn't doing the job. So Ally phoned up a studio publicity honcho back in Hollywood and let loose her demand: send over one lactating human female who would be willing to wet-nurse this lovable cuddly thing. Pronto.

The executive on the line was dumbfounded. "You're kidding, right?"

But Ally insisted she wasn't. In fact, if she didn't get this positively necessary perk, she was going to junk the junket. No publicity for the picture, no media for the movie. Fly her home.

In a word, she was playing possum.

Not wishing to end up as road kill, the studio—for a mere $1,000 a day—found a woman willing to wet-nurse a baby possum to keep its star happy.

"I've dined out on that story for years," said our studio snitch with a proud, parental grin.

A very tasty tale, indeed.

6

Trains, Planes, and "Working It"

It's not just the magic of movies that audiences crave. They want to know more *about* the magic and about the business of that magic. At office watercoolers, in schools, on camping trips, and at dinner parties, news and views on Hollywood's movies, moguls, and machinations are traded as eagerly as hot shares in a bull market.

Stars today are a lot savvier about "the business." They know that deal-making and starmaking go hand in hand, so many of them have dug into their costume trunks and donned another hat—this time as businesspeople. In an unusual left-brain move, they've formed their own production companies and are earning a cut of their movies' profits.

In Hollywood parlance, that's the infamous "back end"—which means that a film can make over $100 million and still "officially" be losing money.

But the smart stars aren't just any kind of businesspeople—they're salespeople. Promoting a picture directly affects those profits, so a thesp's willingness to pack his bags, hop a plane, and press the flesh (and flush out the press) becomes critical. An actor's box office, after all, is only as strong as the audience's awareness of him and his movie. And those audiences need to see and hear their stars outside the confines of the big screen to keep their radar turned on and their interest high.

So take note, all you stars: Your fans are ready for your close-ups a lot more than you think.

"You have to keep yourself out there on a regular basis," says Sharlette Hambrick, a senior producer at *Entertainment Tonight.* "Fans want to see you in real life, too. So you do your charity baseball games. You make sure people know whom you're dating. You work it."

Are studio stars "working it" by traveling more to promote their "reel life," too? Are they flogging their films enough?

"Yes and no," says John Rentsch, vice president of international marketing for Paramount Pictures. "Yes, in that they want to exploit the opportunities. No, in that their schedules often don't give them the time needed to exploit them."

For movie stars, the pressure of promoting a major feature can be daunting. There are dozens, even hundreds, more media outlets to service than there were ten years ago. That means legions more journalists pestering them and their handlers to get more sound bites and word bites—any bites they can take out of them.

For two days they sit in the same hotel room reciting the same boring answers to the same boring questions from a different gooey-eyed penster every ten minutes. It's like rotating ducks in a shooting gallery—they just keep popping up.

Plus the the stuffy distributors' dinners. Plus the dizzying rounds of "round-robin" group interviews. Plus those sardine-packed press conferences with everyone dying to know (or see) the color of their BVDs.

And that's just the domestic publicity. The twelve-hour flights, jet-lag headaches, and Japanese junkets in a foreign tongue haven't even begun.

No wonder stars are just plain pooped by the time their movies premiere in the United States. They've also got a mild case of attention deficit disorder because they're thinking about their next project. They know that if they don't jump into a movie soon after their last one's release, they can end up like Cher just before those hair care commercials—out of sight of the public, and out of mind. (Some thought Cher was out of *her* mind to be flogging hairspray.) And maybe out of work, not to put too fine a sheen on it.

"Generally, stars want to be in a fairly decent movie every six months," says Rentsch, "and that doesn't leave much time to travel and promote. The minimum you need to go off on an international tour is one week, but a month is ideal. Yet there are very few stars who can afford to take a month off to do a proper international campaign."

But not doing overseas promotion would be like biting the hand that feeds them. Those overseas movie revenues, remember, often can save stars and their films from box-office oblivion. Their left brain sees it as maximizing their cost-benefit ratios and servicing their profit centers; the right brain says it's all in the service of Art—not to mention the service of that French "masseuse" waiting for them in their deluxe Paris suite. With both brains in agreement, they hop a Town Car to the Concorde and fly off to hawk their wares and "work it"—in the business sense, of course.

Pumping hands with the Germans, Japanese, French, Brits, and Aussies is especially recommended, since they're seven very profitable markets for those Hollywood wares and can nicely feed and pamper that "back end" (again, in the business sense).

Stars—left-brained or right-brained—can take a lesson from some of their peers who rank at the top of their class in their willingness to travel and promote their movies:

Sandra Bullock "works" the ladies' list best with 87 out of 100 points. She also wins hearts in Germany by speaking German, while the French *sont amoureux* with Jodie Foster (77 points) because she speaks French. Sharon Stone (78), Oprah Winfrey and Michael Jordan (tied at 84), and Tom Hanks and Leslie Nielsen (tied at 83) also keep their careers soaring by flying the globe.

Arnold Schwarzenegger pumps publicity iron the best of all, bench-pressing a hefty 92 points on The Ulmer Scale.

The worst salesmen? Marlon Brando (9), Woody Allen (17), and Robert Redford (28).

"Trying to get them to travel or promote is like asking China to free Tibet," says a publicist. "Don't count on it."

P.S. (*For stars' eyes only*): Those Japanese junkets where everyone was asking questions in a funny language? It was actually English, but you were too dazed and dog-eared to notice. Have your manager check the clipping services to find out what you really said about your sake-soaked dinner hosts that night.

THE

B+

LIST

Sandra Bullock Rank 42 Bankability 74

Real Name	Sandra Annette Bullock
D.O.B.	7/26/64
Place of Birth	Arlington, Virginia, USA
Contact	(A) Kevin Huvane, CAA

Willingness to Travel/Promote	Professionalism	Career Mgmt	Talent
87	**81**	**81**	**60**

INSIDE DIRT

She can't choose a role to save her life, unless it's in romantic comedy.

- Even Sandra needs a strong male lead in her big action pictures. She can't open a movie on her name alone.

- She suffered a lot of bad choices after *While You Were Sleeping*. And she's a bit ditsy.

- She's very professional. She understands the international market and the importance of getting out there to promote.

- In Germany she speaks German because she lived there as a child. That's why she's particularly popular there.

- Her career could use a boost, like being seen out in public with a date.

- The girl-next door thing is getting old. At this point people want her to move out of that neighborhood.

Star Power

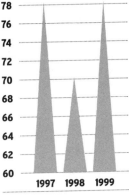

(Chart axis values: 78, 76, 74, 72, 70, 68, 66, 64, 62, 60 — years 1997, 1998, 1999)

Box Office Bait

MOVIE	STUDIO	N.AMERICAN GROSS	RELEASE
Speed	Fox	$121,221,490	6/10/94
A Time To Kill	WB	$108,766,007	7/24/96
The Prince of Egypt (voice)	Dreamworks	$101,217,900	12/18/98
While You Were Sleeping	BV	$81,052,361	4/21/95
Hope Floats	Fox	$60,033,780	5/29/98

Career Trajectory

Hugh Grant Rank **43**   Bankability **74**

Real Name	Hugh Grant
D.O.B.	9/9/60
Place of Birth	London, England, UK
Contact	(A) Beth Swofford, CAA

Willingness to Travel/Promote **67**

Professionalism **74**

Career Mgmt **77**

Talent **67**

INSIDE DIRT

There's still some negativity from the "incident."

♦ When you think of Hugh Grant what do you think of first? A movie, or Divine Brown? So if it's an even match between him and another actor for the same role, the other actor will get it.

♦ He's smart, he's a gentleman, he's great. He's completely self-deprecating and wonderful.

♦ In *Notting Hill* he was flopping his hair and Julia was smiling incessantly. It was like watching two one-trick ponies stuck in the same barn trying to kick themselves out.

♦ As long as they can write bumbling character parts for him, he'll work forever.

♦ He's definitely a favorite around Miramax. He's nicknamed any corporate jet that Harvey [Weinstein] flies on "the floating ashtray."

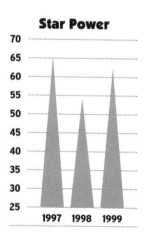

Star Power

(bar chart showing values for 1997, 1998, 1999 with y-axis from 25 to 70)

Box Office Bait

MOVIE	STUDIO	N.AMERICAN GROSS	RELEASE
Notting Hill	Univ	$112,658,155	5/28/99
Nine Months	Fox	$69,689,009	7/12/95
Four Weddings and A Funeral	GRAM	$52,636,671	3/9/94
Sense and Sensibility	Sony	$42,975,897	12/13/95
Remains of The Day	Columbia	$22,954,968	11/5/93

Career Trajectory

Wesley Snipes Rank **44** Bankability **74**

Real Name	Wesley Snipes
D.O.B.	7/31/62
Place of Birth	Orlando, Florida, USA
Contact	(A) Scott Lambert, WMA

Willingness to Travel/Promote **61**

Professionalism **62**

Career Mgmt **60**

Talent **65**

INSIDE DIRT

He invariably causes scheduling complications on his films.

- There's a big entourage factor with him.

- Wesley can be funny and sexy *and* dramatic.

- He's not as versatile as other action stars.

- There are delays due to his trying to take control of the movie, his discussions of how scenes should be covered, how shots should be composed.

- He was almost all set to star in *Shaft,* produced by Scott Rudin. So Wesley shows up at Rudin's office with a posse of about ten people and apparently won't take his shades off during the meeting. Immediately he insists on all these script changes or he won't do the film. Rudin gets so angry he throws Snipes out of his office and hires Sam Jackson instead. Who is much more pleasant.

- Now he's a B action star.

Star Power

66
64
62
60
58
56
54
52
50
48

1997 1998 1999

Box Office Bait

MOVIE	STUDIO	N.AMERICAN GROSS	RELEASE
White Men Can't Jump	Fox	$71,969,454	3/27/92
Blade	NL	$70,001,065	8/21/98
Waiting to Exhale	Fox	$67,001,595	12/22/95
Rising Sun	Fox	$61,202,789	7/30/93
Demolition Man	WB	$58,028,937	10/8/93

Career Trajectory

Sharon Stone Rank **45** Bankability **73**

Real Name Sharon Stone
D.O.B. 3/10/58
Place of Birth Meadville, Pennsylvania, USA
Contact (Atty) Chuck Binder (A) Ed Limato, ICM

Willingness to Travel/Promote
85

Professionalism
31

Career Mgmt
78

Talent
69

INSIDE DIRT

She's one mean cookie.

♦ She'll verbally destroy someone on a set, just because she can.

♦ She's horrible. She can be untrustworthy and betray people. Never again.

♦ For one of her films, there was this shower scene with a big tank filled with water above the set. The crew hated her so much that they stood in line to pee in the tank. And she actually showered.

♦ She's one of the most spankable—I mean bank-able—female stars internationally.

♦ *Casino* reinvented her. She's now perceived as an actress rather than a bimbo.

♦ She's very hot in France. They even gave her the bloody Legion of Honor.

♦ If she wants to be a star in ten years she has to keep playing meaty roles. Otherwise she'll get stuck playing faded sexpots—and Tennessee Williams isn't around to write roles for them anymore.

♦ *The Muse* was the first good thing she's done in years.

Star Power

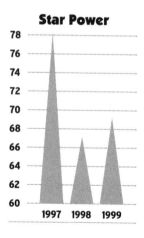

78 ···
76 ···
74 ···
72 ···
70 ···
68 ···
66 ···
64 ···
62 ···
60 ···
　1997　1998　1999

Box Office Bait

MOVIE	STUDIO	N.AMERICAN GROSS	RELEASE
The Flintstones	Univ	$130,512,915	5/27/94
Boomerang	Para	$70,052,444	7/1/92
The Last Boy Scout	WB	$58,926,549	12/13/91
Executive Decision	WB	$56,679,192	3/15/96
Jungle Fever	Univ	$32,550,172	6/7/91

Career Trajectory

Dustin Hoffman Rank 46 Bankability 72

Real Name	Dustin Hoffman
D.O.B.	8/8/37
Place of Birth	Los Angeles, California, USA
Contact	(A) Jeff Berg, ICM (M) AMG

Willingness to Travel/Promote	Professionalism	Career Mgmt	Talent
61	51	78	95

INSIDE DIRT

He has a reputation for obsessiveness and big-star stuff.

♦ He's a consummate actor. When you can get him to travel, he handles press better than anyone I know.

♦ His mind spins out in all directions at press junkets. He'll start with some theory about acting and then go on about aliens from Mars and then back to his kids and metaphysics. It's like watching a centrifuge.

♦ He's a perfectionist. Once he develops his character during production, he wants to go back and reshoot earlier scenes. It's a major problem with production schedules. On *Tootsie* this was the stuff of legend—the movie went something like ten weeks over schedule.

♦ Sometimes he's just plain nasty.

♦ Dustin should have done more comedy like *Tootsie*, which would have prepared him better for moving into older age.

♦ He's been dropping fast.

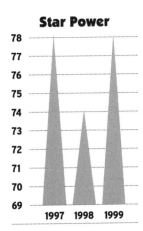

Star Power

1997 1998 1999

Box Office Bait			
MOVIE	STUDIO	N.AMERICAN GROSS	RELEASE
Tootsie	Columbia	$177,200,000	12/17/82
Rain Man	MGM	$172,825,435	12/16/88
Hook	Tri-Star	$119,654,823	12/11/91
Kramer vs. Kramer	Columbia	$106,260,000	12/19/79
Dick Tracy	BV	$103,738,726	6/15/90

Career Trajectory

Tommy Lee Jones

Rank 47   **Bankability 71**

Real Name	Tommy Lee Jones
D.O.B.	9/15/46
Place of Birth	San Saba, Texas, USA
Contact	(M) Michael Black, MBM Inc.

Willingness to Travel/Promote	Professionalism	Career Mgmt	Talent
55	**51**	**72**	**71**

INSIDE DIRT

An ornery old devil, but an excellent second lead.

- He considers himself an intellectual and thinks journalists in general are just incredibly stupid. And he'll tell you that. He can be very condescending.

- I worked with him on *Between Heaven and Earth* in Thailand. On a typical day, he'd come out of his trailer spewing venom at the crew.

- He was never unprofessional. He showed up on time, and when you'd knock on his door, he'd come to the set.

- When he was doing *Bull Durham* with director Ron Shelton and his wife, Lolita Davidovich, he was sitting outside his trailer when Lolita walks by and says, "Oh, hi, Tommy, how are you?" And Tommy says, "Well, I'm fine, but I'm not fuckin' the director, am I?"

- He has a strong following in Japan.

- If his ex-Harvard roomie, Al Gore, gets elected, then *this* Texas boy will be spending time in the White House.

Star Power

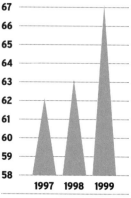

| | 1997 | 1998 | 1999 |

Box Office Bait

MOVIE	STUDIO	N.AMERICAN GROSS	RELEASE
Men in Black	Sony/C	$250,690,539	7/2/97
Batman Forever	WB	$183,997,904	6/16/95
The Fugitive	WB	$183,752,965	8/6/93
Love Story	Para	$108,222,222	1970
The Client	WB	$92,112,663	7/20/94

Career Trajectory

Jackie Chan   Rank **48**   Bankability **70**

Real Name	Kong-sang Chan
D.O.B.	4/7/54
Place of Birth	Hong Kong
Contact	(M) Brad Schenck, Blue Train Entertainment
	(A) Brian Gersh

Willingness to Travel/Promote	Professionalism	Career Mgmt	Talent
88	**87**	**85**	**63**

INSIDE DIRT

He's managed his career brilliantly.

♦ Jacke Chan can only do Jackie Chan movies. The only way he could do anything else is if he's paired with just the right actor.

♦ He brings a sense of humor that wasn't there in Bruce Lee's generation.

♦ I think he got lucky being with Chris Tucker in *Rush Hour*—"the fastest hands in the East, the fastest mouth in the West." That was genius casting.

♦ He's got Asia all wired, but his movies don't even get released theatrically in Europe.

♦ He's never had a chance to have a new career because all his old movies are being remarketed and re-sold as new Jackie Chan films. That's why he never seems to age.

♦ He's seen in Hollywood as an action novelty.

Star Power

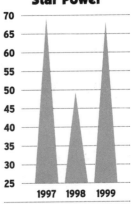

70
65
60
55
50
45
40
35
30
25

1997   1998   1999

Box Office Bait

MOVIE	STUDIO	N.AMERICAN GROSS	RELEASE
Rush Hour	NL	$141,153,686	9/18/98
Cannonball Run	Fox	$88,445,000	1981
Rumble in The Bronx	NL	$32,380,143	2/23/96
Cannonball Run II	WB	$28,078,073	6/29/84
Mr. Nice Guy	NL	$12,716,953	3/20/98

Career Trajectory

Meryl Streep Rank 49   Bankability 70

Real Name	Mary Louise Streep
D.O.B.	6/22/49
Place of Birth	Summit, New Jersey, USA
Contact	(A) Kevin Huvane, CAA

Willingness to Travel/Promote	Professionalism	Career Mgmt	Talent
42	95	63	96

INSIDE DIRT

She gives you 1,000 percent on the set.

◆ She nails a scene right away. She'll do two takes, and if the director says "again," she'll say, "What are you looking for here?" She's an absolute pro.

◆ She doesn't like to do interviews, but she's such a pro she'll do them.

◆ A sensational actress and a wonderful person.

◆ She likes to make movies in Connecticut and New York so she's close to her family.

◆ She always gives a great performance, but she doesn't deliver audience.

◆ She's incredibly strong in Germany. I'd buy a movie starring Meryl any day of the week.

◆ She's been nominated more than Tom Hanks and has won as many Oscars, but because she's a woman she's making less money than he is.

Star Power

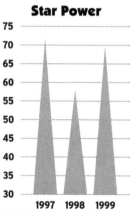

	1997	1998	1999

(values on axis: 75, 70, 65, 60, 55, 50, 45, 40, 35, 30)

Box Office Bait

MOVIE	STUDIO	N.AMERICAN GROSS	RELEASE
Kramer vs. Kramer	Columbia	$106,260,000	12/19/79
Out of Africa	Univ	$88,081,296	12/18/85
The Bridges of Madison County	WB	$70,953,946	6/2/95
Death Becomes Her	Univ	$58,448,072	7/31/92
The Deer Hunter	Univ	$50,432,174	1978

Career Trajectory

Antonio Banderas

Rank 50　　**Bankability 69**

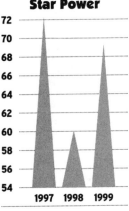

Real Name	José Antonio Domínguez Banderas
D.O.B.	10/10/60
Place of Birth	Málaga, Spain
Contact	(A) Emanuel Nunez, CAA

Willingness to Travel/Promote	Professionalism	Career Mgmt	Talent
70	73	79	68

INSIDE DIRT

A very good and very serious director.

♦ He's surprisingly down to earth for a guy with his vast success. He shows up, does his work. He has a star-size entourage but you can get to him, you can speak directly to him.

♦ Banderas will say yes to anything, but then when you try to nail him down on a deal suddenly he's nowhere to be found.

♦ He's a different kind of person when Melanie is around. When she's in town he's anxious, he'd get really pissed off if he'd have to be waiting too long in his trailer before shooting. When she's not in town, he's fine.

♦ He directed *Crazy in Alabama* for us. He was totally professional. He didn't treat Melanie differently than any other actor.

♦ He crosses over. He can even heat the Scandinavians up.

Star Power

72
70
68
66
64
62
60
58
56
54

1997　1998　1999

Box Office Bait			
MOVIE	STUDIO	N.AMERICAN GROSS	RELEASE
Interview with the Vampire	WB	$105,248,316	11/11/94
The Mask of Zorro	Sony	$93,771,072	7/17/98
Philadelphia	Tri-Star	$77,324,422	12/22/93
Evita	BV	$50,038,461	12/25/96
Assassins	WB	$28,787,744	10/6/95

Career Trajectory

Johnny Depp Rank **51**   Bankability **69**

Real Name	John Christopher Depp III
D.O.B.	6/9/63
Place of Birth	Owensboro, Kentucky, USA
Contact	(A) Tracey Jacobs, UTA

Willingness to Travel/Promote — **30**

Professionalism — **37**

Career Mgmt — **53**

Talent — **75**

INSIDE DIRT

A compelling actor who keeps making the wrong movie.

♦ He could have been a matinee idol like DiCaprio, but he's made too many specialty films.

♦ His name is worth more in Europe than the States.

♦ He's a chameleon. He gets completely inhabited by the director he's working with.

♦ He's as pleasant or as mean as the director sets him up to be. The rumor is that he pummeled an executive on the Roman Polanski movie he just shot.

♦ Every time his career goes into a lull, he beats up on somebody.

♦ He hates producers.

♦ The problems with *The Brave* weren't so much Depp's behavior as his lack of experience.

♦ At Cannes, he showed me one of his bad reviews and said, "I still have a lot to learn."

♦ He's going to be a big movie star.

Star Power

70
68
66
64
62
60
58
56
54
52

1997 1998 1999

Box Office Bait

MOVIE	STUDIO	N.AMERICAN GROSS	RELEASE
Platoon	Orion	$137,963,328	12/19/86
Edward Scissorhands	Fox	$54,155,571	12/7/90
Donnie Brasco	Sony/TS	$41,909,762	2/28/97
Freddy's Dead	NL	$34,015,591	9/13/91
A Nightmare On Elm Street	NL	$26,104,194	11/1/84

Career Trajectory

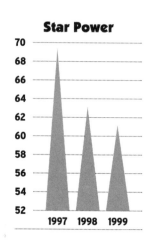

Ashley Judd Rank **52**   Bankability **68**

Real Name	Ashley Tyler Ciminella
D.O.B.	4/19/68
Place of Birth	Los Angeles, California, USA
Contact	(A) Mike Simpson, WMA

Willingness to Travel/Promote	Professionalism	Career Mgmt	Talent
60	**70**	**69**	**68**

INSIDE DIRT

She needs some new direction and new management.

♦ She is a very committed actress. When she's researching a role, she'll send you the book she thinks that character will have read.

♦ She's into mythology. She's the coolest chick around.

♦ I hear she's overpriced herself.

♦ Ashley's talented, but she has to watch her ego. In her mind she's a bigger star than she is, so she's stopped picking more interesting projects.

♦ She doesn't seem to know how to choose the right role in the right movie.

♦ And her Oscar dress! It was split up to the crotch— she was showing too much of her country roots. She came off more as white trash than glamour queen.

♦ That photo spread with Matthew McConaughey sure helped her visibility a lot.

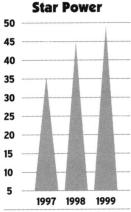

Star Power

50
45
40
35
30
25
20
15
10
5

1997 1998 1999

Box Office Bait

MOVIE	STUDIO	N.AMERICAN GROSS	RELEASE
A Time to Kill	WB	$108,766,007	7/24/96
Heat	WB	$66,802,342	12/15/95
Kiss The Girls	Para	$60,521,885	10/3/97
Natural Born Killers	WB	$50,271,653	8/26/94
Kuffs	Univ	$19,585,735	1/10/92

Career Trajectory

Annette Bening

Rank 53 **Bankability 67**

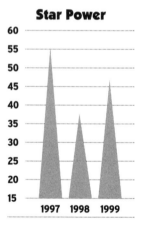

Real Name	Annette Bening
D.O.B.	5/29/58
Place of Birth	Topeka, Kansas, USA
Contact	(A) Kevin Huvane, CAA

Willingness to Travel/Promote	Professionalism	Career Mgmt	Talent
41	72	63	73

INSIDE DIRT

She's a regular gal in an irregular world.

♦ I don't agree that she's sacrificed her career to her family—she made her best career move with *American Beauty*.

♦ She's very friendly. She talks to people on the set. She considers herself one of the group.

♦ If her stage work in *Hedda Gabler* was any evidence, she should stick to making movies.

♦ Annette should sue Columbia for infringement—their screen logo looks just like her.

Star Power

Chart values (vertical axis): 60, 55, 50, 45, 40, 35, 30, 25, 20, 15

Years: 1997 1998 1999

Box Office Bait

MOVIE	STUDIO	N.AMERICAN GROSS	RELEASE
The American President	Sony	$60,009,496	11/17/95
Bugsy	Tri-Star	$49,091,562	12/13/91
Regarding Henry	Para	$43,001,500	7/10/91
The Great Outdoors	Univ	$41,455,230	6/17/88
The Siege	Fox	$40,932,372	11/6/98

Career Trajectory

Russell Crowe Rank **54** Bankability **66**

Real Name	Russell Ira Crowe
D.O.B.	4/7/64
Place of Birth	New Zealand
Contact	(A) George Freeman ICM

Willingness to Travel/Promote	Professionalism	Career Mgmt	Talent
56	**49**	**51**	**70**

INSIDE DIRT

He doesn't do enough publicity, and that's damaged his career.

♦ Russell Crowe is a real up-and-comer.

♦ The buzz is that he can be somewhat difficult. We worked with him on *Romper-Stomper,* and he was brilliant. But his star rose very quickly and that has affected his ego.

♦ He should do smaller indie movies from time to time. The big movies don't do much for him—*Gladiator* is just a Roman ruin.

♦ There are all these stories about how he threatens to get in fistfights with his directors. He's worse than Val Kilmer.

♦ He wants to change the script to his liking, and pouts if he doesn't get his way. But I'd work with him in a nanosecond, because he's good and has conviction.

♦ He's highly respected.

Star Power

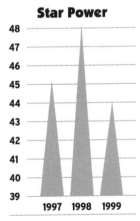

48
47
46
45
44
43
42
41
40
39

1997 1998 1999

Box Office Bait

MOVIE	STUDIO	N.AMERICAN GROSS	RELEASE
L.A. Confidential	WB	$64,616,940	9/19/97
Virtuosity	Para	$24,047,675	8/4/95
The Quick and the Dead	Sony/TS	$18,543,150	2/10/95
The Sum of Us	S Golwyn	$742,981	3/8/95

Career Trajectory

Sigourney Weaver

Rank 55 **Bankability 66**

Real Name	Susan Alexandra Weaver
D.O.B.	10/8/49
Place of Birth	New York, New York, USA
Contact	(A) Sam Cohn, ICM

Willingness to Travel/Promote	Professionalism	Career Mgmt	Talent
62	71	57	68

INSIDE DIRT

A talented actress who takes journeyman roles.

♦ She has the sole position in this town of being a woman who can consistently succeed in an action film. And she's very smart.

♦ I just don't see Sigourney being able to lead any franchise film I'd invest in.

♦ She was first perceived as a serious actress. Then when she did *Alien* she was seen as an action star. And now she's trying to prove how sexy she is, and it feels forced. She's tried on her different personae like coats, and when the coat's off you don't know what you're getting.

♦ Sigourney Weaver is cold. She's not right for romantic comedy. She's tall and has this big face.

♦ Amazon woman!

Star Power

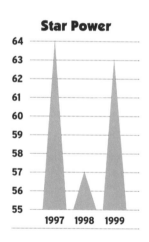

64
63
62
61
60
59
58
57
56
55

1997 1998 1999

Box Office Bait			
MOVIE	STUDIO	N.AMERICAN GROSS	RELEASE
Ghostbusters (with re-issue)	Columbia	$230,247,625	7/8/84
Ghostbusters II	Columbia	$112,494,738	6/16/89
Alien	Fox	$89,555,556	1979
Aliens	Fox	$81,843,793	7/18/86
Dave	WB	$63,193,194	5/7/93

Career Trajectory

Sean Penn   Rank **56**   Bankability **66**

Real Name Sean Penn
D.O.B. 8/17/60
Place of Birth Santa Monica, California, USA
Contact (A) John Burnham, WMA

Willingness to Travel/Promote	Professionalism	Career Mgmt	Talent
60	**50**	**46**	**87**

INSIDE DIRT

He'll have a long career arc because he also directs.

♦ He's punched a few people in his time, but I've heard he's professional on the set.

♦ He's thrown fits because he can't get the private jet for the weekend.

♦ We worked with him and found he was just the opposite of his reputation—incredibly gracious, well educated, and a real entertainer.

♦ He generates a lot of trust in other actors.

♦ He's a maniac when it comes to the artistic integrity of a contract. To get him to play a small role in one film, he insisted on having final cut for his friend the director.

♦ He always plays the *fleur du mal*—flower of evil.

♦ Because of the Madonna connection, he's well known in Asia.

♦ He hates the press.

♦ He's the most powerful actor of his generation.

Star Power

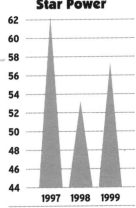

	1997	1998	1999

Box Office Bait

MOVIE	STUDIO	N.AMERICAN GROSS	RELEASE
Bad Boys	Sony	$66,491,850	4/7/95
The Game	POLY	$48,139,354	9/12/97
Colors	Orion	$46,124,752	4/15/88
Taps	Fox	$45,555,556	1981
Dead Man Walking	GRAM	$39,379,757	12/29/95

Career Trajectory

Demi Moore Rank 57 Bankability 66

Real Name	Demetria Guynes
D.O.B.	11/11/62
Place of Birth	Roswell, New Mexico, USA
Contact	(A) Kevin Huvane CAA

Willingness to Travel/Promote	Professionalism	Career Mgmt	Talent
71	60	68	52

INSIDE DIRT

She's a prima donna. She holds up productions.

◆ She assumes too much control of the decision-making process on a set, and her judgment doesn't justify that.

◆ *Striptease* was a major mistake. And it didn't make her sellable on her name alone.

◆ She has a cast-iron narcissism that doesn't allow for any audience sympathy.

◆ She's hottest in the rental markets overseas.

◆ She makes sex look like a weapon.

◆ What genre is she going to survive in? "Self-aggrandizing."

◆ Her expenses on a film are huge. They call her "Gimme More."

◆ She's a publicist's nightmare. But she can go out there and charm the pants off everyone.

◆ There are African countries that could live on what has been spent on her plastic surgery.

Star Power

Values on axis: 76, 74, 72, 70, 68, 66, 64, 62, 60, 58 — years 1997, 1998, 1999

Box Office Bait

MOVIE	STUDIO	N.AMERICAN GROSS	RELEASE
Ghost	Para	$217,534,330	7/13/90
A Few Good Men	Columbia	$141,340,178	12/11/92
Indecent Proposal	Para	$105,544,089	4/9/93
The Hunchback of Notre Dame (voice)	BV	$100,137,089	6/21/96
Disclosure	WB	$82,976,682	12/9/94

Career Trajectory

Kim Basinger Rank 58   Bankability 65

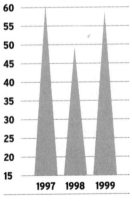

Real Name	Kim Basinger
D.O.B.	12/8/53
Place of Birth	Athens, Georgia, USA
Contact	(A) Josh Lieberman, CAA

Willingness to Travel/Promote	Professionalism	Career Mgmt	Talent
58	52	42	62

INSIDE DIRT

As a sex symbol, she's finished.

♦ For a while she was so difficult to work with that nobody would hire her. Then she sort of got religion and started to behave. She got *L.A. Confidential* and everyone knew she was okay again. That's a big reason why she was good enough and damn popular enough to win the Oscar.

♦ She's had a minor comeback. But where is she now?

♦ Her best move was not making *Boxing Helena*— even if it did mean legal troubles.

♦ During the shooting of *The Marrying Man,* she would order a case of Evian water to be delivered on the set every day so she could wash her hair in it.

♦ She was in a hotel in Dublin and asked for a papaya—and I mean "asked" as Marie Antoinette would "ask" her subjects to eat cake.

♦ She's milk and honey these days.

Star Power

Year	
60	
55	
50	
45	
40	
35	
30	
25	
20	
15	

1997 1998 1999

Box Office Bait

MOVIE	STUDIO	N.AMERICAN GROSS	RELEASE
Batman	WB	$251,188,924	6/23/89
L.A. Confidential	WB	$64,616,940	9/19/97
Never Say Never Again	WB	$62,666,667	1983
The Natural	Tri-Star	$47,951,979	5/11/84
Wayne's World 2	Para	$46,637,382	12/10/93

Career Trajectory

Michael Caine

Rank 59 **Bankability 64**

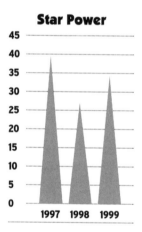

Real Name	Maurice Joseph Micklewhite
D.O.B.	3/15/33
Place of Birth	Bermondsey, London, England
Contact	(A) Toni Howard, ICM

Willingness to Travel/Promote **55**

Professionalism **73**

Career Mgmt **60**

Talent **71**

INSIDE DIRT

He's on the upswing, thanks to *Ciderhouse Rules*.

♦ A year ago I thought *Little Voice* was a lucky fluke, like *Boogie Nights* was for Burt Reynolds. Then came his Oscar.

♦ Often he seems on autopilot when he acts. He's far more talented than he's motivated to reveal.

♦ He's a hoot to hang with. He once suggested that Tuesday Weld marry Frederick March III so that she could become Tuesday March the Third.

♦ When he gets an offer, all he wants to know is: Where's it shooting, and how much?

♦ A gem on the set. During *Death Trap,* we had to order three different pairs of silk Gucci pajamas to accommodate his constant weight gain. Finally he suggested that we bring in his wife, that if he could fuck her he could lose weight. And it worked!

Star Power

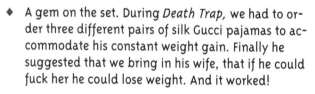

45
40
35
30
25
20
15
10
5
0
      1997 1998 1999

Box Office Bait

MOVIE	STUDIO	N.AMERICAN GROSS	RELEASE
California Suite	Columbia	$63,080,444	1978
Bridge Too Far	UA	$45,278,680	1977
Dirty Rotten Scoundrels	Orion	$41,412,820	12/14/88
Hannah & Her Sisters	Orion	$40,084,041	2/7/86
On Deadly Ground	WB	$38,572,114	2/18/94

Career Trajectory

Drew Barrymore

Rank 60

Bankability 64

Real Name Drew Blythe Barrymore
D.O.B. 2/22/75
Place of Birth Los Angeles, California, USA
Contact (A) Patrick Whitesell/Bryan Lourd, CAA

Willingness to Travel/Promote	Professionalism	Career Mgmt	Talent
76	68	65	70

INSIDE DIRT

She gets bigger and bigger with every movie she does.

♦ She appeals most to teenage boys and young men, which is a helluva big demographic.

♦ I think she's become a very accomplished actress. I think she does have range. I would take all kinds of chances with her.

♦ Strangely enough, she's not that attractive. But she carries off roles very well that are normally given to very attractive women.

♦ I think she'll be around for a long time. When her looks start going, she'll become a comedienne, a character actress.

♦ When she was a kid I loved her. When she was a teen I hated her. And now I'm back to loving her.

Star Power

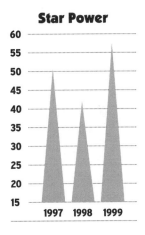

60
55
50
45
40
35
30
25
20
15

1997 1998 1999

Box Office Bait

MOVIE	STUDIO	N.AMERICAN GROSS	RELEASE
E.T. (with re-issue)	Univ	$399,804,539	6/11/82
Batman Forever	WB	$183,997,904	6/16/95
Scream	Miramax/Dimension	$103,001,286	12/20/96
The Wedding Singer	NL	$80,224,502	2/13/98
Ever After	Fox	$65,703,412	7/31/98

Career Trajectory

Ben Stiller   Rank **61**   Bankability **64**

Real Name   Ben Stiller
D.O.B.   11/30/65
Place of Birth   New York, New York, USA
Contact   (A) Nick Stevens, UTA (Atty) Larry Rose

Willingness to Travel/Promote	Professionalism	Career Mgmt	Talent
70	**64**	**52**	**65**

INSIDE DIRT

He's a nouveau Jerry Lewis minus the buffoon.

♦ He's sort of taken on the Dustin Hoffman roles for his generation. And he's very personable, very vulnerable.

♦ I think Ben is a bit of an egomaniac. He can dish out quite a bit of arrogance, but not on any tangible issue.

♦ He can be somewhat difficult to work with, but nothing that would make someone say I don't want to hire him.

♦ I may be one of the few who believe it, but I thought he did a brilliant job directing *The Cable Guy*.

♦ He's really smart about story and character. I think he's going to be a fine director.

♦ He's done very well with his career, considering that he looks like a monkey.

Star Power

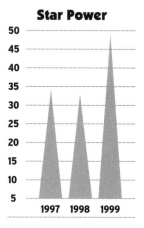

| | 1997 | 1998 | 1999 |

Box Office Bait

MOVIE	STUDIO	N.AMERICAN GROSS	RELEASE
There's Something About Mary	Fox	$176,472,910	7/15/98
The Cable Guy	Sony	$60,240,295	6/14/96
Happy Gilmore	Univ	$38,648,864	2/16/96
Empire of The Sun	WB	$22,224,737	12/9/87
Reality Bites	Univ	$20,982,557	2/18/94

Career Trajectory

Kate Winslet Rank 62

Bankability 64

Real Name Kate Winslet
D.O.B. 10/5/75
Place of Birth Reading, Berkshire, England, UK
Contact (A) Hylda Queally, WMA

Willingness to Travel/Promote	Professionalism	Career Mgmt	Talent
75	81	71	83

INSIDE DIRT

With *Titanic* she went from art-house ingenue to name above the title.

♦ Despite *Titanic,* I don't think she'll ever be a big star. She'll still take small parts in big movies and big parts in small movies because she comes out of the British repertory tradition.

♦ She was cast in the Minnie Driver role in *Good Will Hunting* but couldn't do it because *Titanic* went so far over schedule.

♦ I told her, "You took quite a chance in making *Hideous Kinky.*" And she replied, "Life is full of chances. I suppose I could have gotten a million dollars, maybe more, for making some other movie, but the people making it were my friends." This girl has her head screwed on right.

♦ She has exactly the career she wants.

♦ One charming and mature young lady.

Star Power

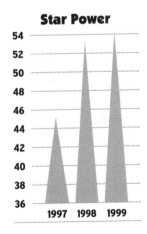

54
52
50
48
46
44
42
40
38
36

1997 1998 1999

Box Office Bait

MOVIE	STUDIO	N.AMERICAN GROSS	RELEASE
Titanic	Para	$600,788,188	12/19/97
Sense and Sensibility	Sony	$42,975,897	12/13/95
A Kid in King Arthur's Court	BV	$13,402,111	8/11/95
Hamlet	Sony	$4,450,546	12/25/96
Heavenly Creatures	Miramax	$3,129,018	11/16/94

Career Trajectory

Winona Ryder Rank 63 Bankability 63

Real Name Winona Laura Horowitz
D.O.B. 10/29/71
Place of Birth Winona, Minnesota, USA
Contact (A) Ed Limato, ICM (M) Carol Bodie

Willingness to Travel/Promote	Professionalism	Career Mgmt	Talent
52	67	54	69

INSIDE DIRT

Like [Antonio] Banderas, she's quick to say yes to projects and then reconsider.

♦ I think the community wants her to come back. They want her to succeed.

♦ She's an extraordinary talent.

♦ Her biggest problem is that she's known for being a brat. She doesn't return phone calls for days. Or she says yes to something and doesn't show up.

♦ She's just very moody and very difficult.

♦ She's sort of a ghostly creature who floats above the ether in a lot of her movies. She's the Kate Moss of the motion picture industry; she's the waif. But waifs don't age well. And that look doesn't engender star power.

♦ She should move into art films for a long-term career.

♦ She's so damn gamine.

Star Power

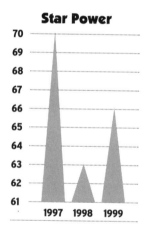

	1997	1998	1999

Box Office Bait

MOVIE	STUDIO	N.AMERICAN GROSS	RELEASE
Bram Stoker's Dracula	Columbia	$82,416,928	11/13/92
Beetlejuice	WB	$73,707,461	3/30/88
Edward Scissorhands	Fox	$54,155,571	12/7/90
Little Women	Columbia	$50,003,303	12/21/94
Alien Resurrection	Fox	$47,263,778	11/26/97

Career Trajectory

Samuel L. Jackson

Rank 64   **Bankability 63**

Real Name	Samuel Leroy Jackson
D.O.B.	12/21/48
Place of Birth	Washington D.C., USA
Contact	(A) Toni Howard, ICM

Willingness to Travel/Promote	Professionalism	Career Mgmt	Talent
82	**75**	**68**	**74**

INSIDE DIRT

The "black factor" is a problem with Jackson overseas.

♦ He's an interestingly dangerous actor—maybe too dangerous for people.

♦ He stars in those urban American adventures that don't perform well abroad.

♦ He travels and promotes everything. He's a nine out of ten in that regard.

♦ If he's on his own without anyone else in the package, we can't sell him.

♦ Every year he's involved in at least one independent film that would not get made without his participation. That shows character.

♦ He brings a positive spark to a set. There's no star attitude.

♦ He had some star attitude on *The Negotiator*.

♦ The guy brings along one or two extremely expensive hairdressers onto his picture, even though he has a *shaved head*. Talk about perks.

Star Power

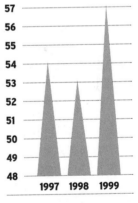

57
56
55
54
53
52
51
50
49
48

1997 1998 1999

Box Office Bait

MOVIE	STUDIO	N.AMERICAN GROSS	RELEASE
Star Wars Episode One: The Phantom Menace	Fox	$412,775,151	5/19/99
Jurassic Park	Univ	$357,067,947	6/11/93
Coming to America	Para	$128,152,301	6/29/88
A Time to Kill	WB	$108,766,007	7/24/96
Pulp Fiction	Miramax	$107,921,755	10/14/94

Career Trajectory

Cate Blanchett

Rank 65　　**Bankability 63**

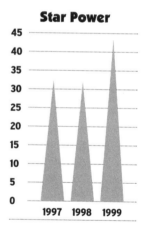

Real Name	Cate Blanchett
D.O.B.	5/14/69
Place of Birth	Melbourne, Australia
Contact	(A) Hylda Queally, WMA

Willingness to Travel/Promote	Professionalism	Career Mgmt	Talent
76	**80**	**70**	**74**

INSIDE DIRT

She's a high-budget art-film actress.

- She's very, very smart.

- She's everybody's darling because she's really well behaved and charming. She supports her films by promoting them, as she did on *Elizabeth*. And oh, by the way, she's a really good actress.

- She's a better screen actor than stage actor.

- Whether her talent will translate into long-term stardom, it's too early to tell. But she seems to make all the right moves in terms of doing publicity and attending award shows.

- She's brilliant because she can go from Elizabethan drama to *Pushing Tin,* where she was fabulous and unrecognizable as Billy Bob Thornton's wife, in an otherwise undistinguished movie.

- Like Emily Watson or Kristen Scott-Thomas, she lends legitimacy to any project.

Star Power

	1997	1998	1999

(chart showing values rising toward 40, 40, and 45 across 1997, 1998, 1999)

Box Office Bait

MOVIE	STUDIO	N.AMERICAN GROSS	RELEASE
Elizabeth	Gram	$30,012,990	11/6/98
An Ideal Husband	Miramax	$16,454,382 *	6/18/99
Pushing Tin	Fox	$8,408,835	4/23/99
Paradise Road	Fox/S	$1,921,471	4/11/97
Oscar & Lucinda	Fox/S	$1,508,689	12/31/97

Career Trajectory

Edward Norton Rank **66** Bankability **63**

Real Name	Edward Norton
D.O.B.	8/18/69
Place of Birth	Boston, Massachusetts, USA
Contact	(A) Brian Swardstrom, Endeavor

Willingness to Travel/Promote	Professionalism	Career Mgmt	Talent
67	**74**	**60**	**89**

INSIDE DIRT

One of the top-ten talents in the business.

♦ He's loved by the eighteen to twenty-nine-year-olds and somewhat feared by the over-thirties. *American History X* had them worried. They wondered whether he really was that bizarre character.

♦ After *American History X* and *Rounders,* he wasn't very bankable. And after *Fight Club,* he's still kind of on the ropes.

♦ He should have gotten the Oscar for *Primal Fear.*

♦ He's very smart. He got Nora Ephron to rewrite the script for the film he directed, *Keeping the Faith,* practically for nothing.

♦ I'm very happy he's directing—maybe it will help him accommodate his need to control everything.

♦ His career choices are brilliant. He's the one. Women are crazy about him.

♦ He's the Robert De Niro of his generation.

Star Power

1997	~42
1998	~43
1999	~57

(Chart axis: 15, 20, 25, 30, 35, 40, 45, 50, 55, 60)

Box Office Bait

MOVIE	STUDIO	N.AMERICAN GROSS	RELEASE
Primal Fear	Para	$56,116,183	4/3/96
Rounders	Miramax	$22,921,898	9/11/98
The People vs. Larry Flynt	Sony	$20,036,079	12/25/96
Everyone Says I Love You	Miramax	$9,714,482	12/6/96
American History X	NL	$6,712,241	10/28/98

Career Trajectory

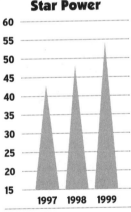

Goldie Hawn Rank 67   Bankability 62

Real Name	Goldie Studlendgehawn
D.O.B.	11/21/45
Place of Birth	Washington, D.C., USA
Contact	(A) Jim Wiatt, WMA

Willingness to Travel/Promote	Professionalism	Career Mgmt	Talent
74	85	64	72

INSIDE DIRT

She's got one of the longest and best-managed careers in Hollywood.

♦ She can't carry a film on her own. But with another star at her side, Goldie's as good as gold.

♦ She should work more. She's good even in bad movies. But she should forget dramatic roles.

♦ Lose the lip collagen!

♦ She has a wonderful body but sometimes she shows it off too much.

♦ In France, they feel like she overacts. They love her as a personality but they can rip her apart as an actress.

♦ A complete pro. She's a one-take Sally.

♦ She's been around since *Laugh-In* in the mid-'60s. That's more than a thirty-year career.

♦ She's a hit with the media overseas.

♦ At fifty-something she's still coquettish.

Star Power

(Bar chart, y-axis values: 44, 46, 48, 50, 52, 54, 56, 58, 60, 62; x-axis years: 1997, 1998, 1999)

Box Office Bait

MOVIE	STUDIO	N.AMERICAN GROSS	RELEASE
First Wives Club	Para	$105,475,862	9/20/96
Private Benjamin	WB	$76,444,444	10/10/80
Bird on a Wire	Univ	$70,978,012	5/18/90
Housesitter	Univ	$60,370,013	6/12/92
Death Becomes Her	Univ	$58,448,072	7/31/92

Career Trajectory

Al Pacino

Rank 68

Bankability 62

Real Name	Alfredo James Pacino
D.O.B.	4/25/40
Place of Birth	New York City, New York, USA
Contact	(A) Rick Nicita, CAA (M) Keith Addis Industry Entertainment

Willingness to Travel/Promote	Professionalism	Career Mgmt	Talent
60	**77**	**45**	**90**

INSIDE DIRT

Like Gere, he needs major marquee support.

◆ He can't carry a movie by himself anymore.

◆ He knows his future with mainstream audiences lies in pairing him opposite Gen X stars like Johnny Depp and Chris O'Donnell.

◆ Because of his theater pedigree, his career isn't hurt by the poor films he's in. Anyone else doing *Scent of a Woman* would have been laughed off the screen. Pacino got an Oscar for it.

◆ In some overseas territories, Pacino is a better name than DeNiro, who's had a lot of bombs.

◆ He's managed his career very wisely. Now he balances theater with big studio films, which is a better pedigree even than doing indie films.

◆ I don't know a bad thing to say about Al.

Star Power

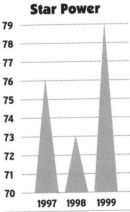

79
78
77
76
75
74
73
72
71
70

1997 1998 1999

Box Office Bait

MOVIE	STUDIO	N.AMERICAN GROSS	RELEASE
The Godfather (with re-issue)	Para	$136,228,625	3/15/72
Dick Tracy	BV	$103,738,726	6/15/90
Heat	WB	$66,802,342	12/15/95
The Godfather III	Para	$66,520,529	12/25/90
Scent of a Woman	Univ	$62,724,644	12/23/92

Career Trajectory

Barbra Streisand

Rank 69　　**Bankability 62**

Real Name	Barbara Joan Streisand
D.O.B.	4/24/42
Place of Birth	Brooklyn, New York, USA
Contact	(A) Jeff Berg, ICM

Willingness to Travel/Promote	Professionalism	Career Mgmt	Talent
62	50	36	87

INSIDE DIRT

She's impossible to control and she has no regard for budget.

- Why does she take five years between films? Because it takes so long for a crew to agree to work with her.

- The very thing she's criticized for—directing, producing, and starring in films—is the thing that's made her so successful.

- I wish she'd work more.

- She has no perspective on anything except the radius from the center of her head to the tip of her nose. I wouldn't bond her.

- During *The Mirror Has Two Faces,* she was firing hair and makeup people right and left. The crew kept a graveyard with little tombstones for all the people who bit the dust on the picture.

- Barbra is a zero in France. Zero! We don't care about her, we don't like her, and she's ugly.

Star Power

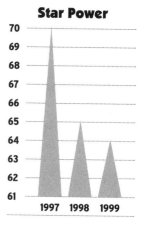

	1997	1998	1999

(y-axis: 61–70)

Box Office Bait

MOVIE	STUDIO	N.AMERICAN GROSS	RELEASE
A Star Is Born	WB	$82,444,444	1976
Prince of Tides	Columbia	$74,632,400	12/25/91
What's Up Doc	WB	$62,222,222	1972
The Main Event	WB	$58,666,667	1979
Funny Girl	Columbia	$58,500,000	1968

Career Trajectory

Julianne Moore

Rank 70 **Bankability 61**

Real Name	Julie Anne Smith
D.O.B.	12/3/61
Place of Birth	Fayetteville, North Carolina, USA
Contact	(A) Kevin Huvane, CAA

Willingness to Travel/Promote 58 **Professionalism** 68 **Career Mgmt** 70 **Talent** 77

INSIDE DIRT

A brilliant actress who hasn't found her breakout role yet.

◆ Her best quality is her discipline in servicing the story and not promoting a star persona. But that can be a liability for her bankability. She can't open a movie.

◆ She's gained respect by doing films with British directors.

◆ In terms of sellability, she's still not on the map internationally.

◆ She's trying to glam up her image, which will help.

◆ Starring in *Hannibal* will be her litmus test for commercial viability.

Star Power

38	
37	
36	
35	
34	
33	
32	
31	
30	
29	

1997 1998 1999

Box Office Bait

MOVIE	STUDIO	N.AMERICAN GROSS	RELEASE
Lost World: Jurassic Park	Universal	$229,086,679	5/23/97
The Fugitive	WB	$183,875,760	8/6/93
Hand That Rocks The Cradle	Buena Vista	$88,036,683	1/10/92
Nine Months	Fox	$69,689,009	7/12/95
Assassins	WB	$28,787,744	10/6/95

Career Trajectory

Helen Hunt Rank **71**   Bankability **61**

Real Name   Helen Elizabeth Hunt
D.O.B.   6/15/63
Place of Birth Los Angeles, California, USA
Contact   (A) Bryan Lourd CAA (M) Connie Tavel

Willingness to Travel/Promote	Professionalism	Career Mgmt	Talent
77	**75**	**62**	**70**

INSIDE DIRT

Even with her Oscar, she's not a bankable actress by any means.

- She was doing her TV series for so long that we simply haven't seen her in enough movies.

- Is Helen Hunt going to be an international star? No, it's the Renée Zelwegger thing: She's not cute enough. But that's the onus we put on women. Jack Nicholson certainly doesn't get saddled with it.

- I've only heard wonderful things from her camp about her. A kind, generous lady. Very genuine, down-to-earth, grounded.

- A very smart lady whose management does not have what can be construed as any sizable intellect.

- Trying to do Shakespeare was not a good idea in her case.

- Delicious to work with.

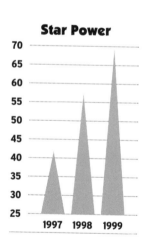

Star Power

70
65
60
55
50
45
40
35
30
25

1997 1998 1999

Box Office Bait

MOVIE	STUDIO	N.AMERICAN GROSS	RELEASE
Twister	WB	$241,721,524	5/10/96
As Good As It Gets	Sony/TS	$148,478,011	12/24/97
Peggy Sue Got Married	Tri-Star	$41,382,841	10/10/86
Only You	Tri-Star	$20,003,957	10/7/94
Rollercoaster	Univer	$19,321,707 E	1977

Career Trajectory

Jennifer Lopez Rank 72 Bankability 60

Real Name	Jennifer Lopez
D.O.B.	7/24/70
Place of Birth	The Bronx, New York, USA
Contact	(A) Risa Shapiro, ICM

Willingness to Travel/Promote	Professionalism	Career Mgmt	Talent
80	70	75	65

INSIDE DIRT

Like Salma Hayek, she's one of the few breakthrough Hispanic actresses.

♦ She's a saucy Latin bombshell whom Hollywood uses to exploit what it calls its Latin niche audience. Only in America can a group of 60 million people be called a niche.

♦ She's the highest-paid Latina performer in movies. She's had a big impact.

♦ She's had to conform to a Hollywood/American idea of beauty. She's lost all this weight. She used to be voluptuous, and now she's got this tiny waist and big boobs.

♦ They've packaged her as Hot Tamale Lite. That may be the only way to package her, of course.

♦ She's lucky she's got a music career, too.

♦ Gorgeous—what else matters?

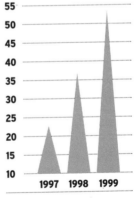

Star Power

55 · 50 · 45 · 40 · 35 · 30 · 25 · 20 · 15 · 10

1997 1998 1999

Box Office Bait

MOVIE	STUDIO	N.AMERICAN GROSS	RELEASE
Antz (voice)	Dreamworks	$90,646,554	10/2/98
Anaconda	Sony	$65,885,767	4/11/97
Jack	BV	$58,617,334	8/9/96
Out of Sight	Univ	$37,562,568	6/26/98
Money Train	Sony/C	$35,305,090	11/22/95

Career Trajectory

Glenn Close Rank 73 Bankability 60

Real Name	Glenn Close
D.O.B.	3/19/47
Place of Birth	Greenwich, Connecticut, USA
Contact	(A) Kevin Huvane, CAA

Willingness to Travel/Promote	Professionalism	Career Mgmt	Talent
57	**82**	**49**	**84**

INSIDE DIRT

She lives somewhat in the shadow of Meryl Streep.

♦ She's one classy dame—and a real powerhouse.

♦ She's doing more TV movies because the good roles for women over forty are in MOWs [movies of the week] or miniseries.

♦ Glenn doesn't disappear totally into her roles like Meryl does. She has a larger-than-life persona. She's got a bit of the Gloria Swanson in her.

♦ Glenn is full of opinions and ideas. Very much a collaborator. And she doesn't need a lot of takes.

♦ Every day while watching dailies with her, I thought, what a privilege to sit in the presence of such genius.

♦ She loves playing character roles. Glenn doesn't have the hang-ups about playing older women that Jessica [Lange] has.

♦ Her weak points? I'm still looking for them.

Star Power

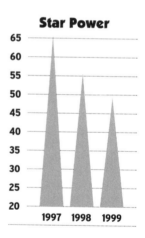

Box Office Bait			
MOVIE	**STUDIO**	**N.AMERICAN GROSS**	**RELEASE**
Air Force One	Sony	$172,956,409	7/25/97
Tarzan (voice)	BV	$161,851,795	6/15/99
Fatal Attraction	Para	$156,587,582	9/18/87
101 Dalmations (Live Action)	BV	$136,182,161	11/27/96
Hook	Tri-Star	$119,654,823	12/11/91

Career Trajectory

Natalie Portman

Rank 74   **Bankability 60**

Real Name	Natalie Portman
D.O.B.	6/9/81
Place of Birth	Jerusalem, Israel
Contact	(A) Joe Funicello, ICM (Atty) Ira Schreck

Willingness to Travel/Promote	Professionalism	Career Mgmt	Talent
68	74	79	85

INSIDE DIRT

Having very protective parents makes it tough for her to travel and promote.

♦ She has a very aggressive career arc. She's just going to get better and better.

♦ She's phenomenal in every way.

♦ We had her on her first big role, *The Professional,* and I said wow, there's one future star in the making.

♦ She's Israeli. Did you know that? She speaks Hebrew.

♦ She likes to defy her parents. How? She wants to party. The night of the premiere of *Beautiful Girls,* she wanted to go out with Ben and Matt and others, but her father was against it so she threw a tantrum and went anyway. It was a wild party, but she's a very responsible girl.

♦ She's taking some time off to go to Harvard. Now she'll be super-hot *and* super-smart.

Star Power

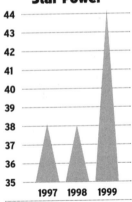

44
43
42
41
40
39
38
37
36
35

1997 1998 1999

Box Office Bait

MOVIE	STUDIO	N.AMERICAN GROSS	RELEASE
Star Wars Episode One: The Phantom Menace	Fox	$412,775,151	5/19/99
Heat	WB	$66,802,342	12/15/95
Mars Attacks!	WB	$37,754,208	12/13/96
The Professional	Columbia	$19,284,974	11/18/94
Beautiful Girls	Miramax	$10,601,348	2/9/96

Career Trajectory

Liam Neeson Rank **75**   Bankability **60**

Real Name   Liam Neeson
D.O.B.   6/7/52
Place of Birth Ballymena, Northern Ireland
Contact   (A) Sam Cohn/Ed Limato/Edward Yablans ICM

Willingness to Travel/Promote	Professionalism	Career Mgmt	Talent
64	**85**	**60**	**73**

INSIDE DIRT

Female audiences don't rush to see Neeson.

♦ His star quality isn't there.

♦ The kind of larger-than-life characters he plays aren't in vogue much anymore. So if he's not able to scale down his talent to fit more conventional roles, he'll become kind of a joke.

♦ He's like a chameleon. You never look at him in a film and say, that's Liam.

♦ He's more commercial than Fiennes or Day-Lewis.

♦ He's always picked good pictures, but they haven't been as successful as they should have.

♦ Liam tried to break out into action films with *Rob Roy,* but did anyone care?

♦ Liam is more like a guy's guy.

♦ He needs a big action hit.

♦ A thinking man's Errol Flynn.

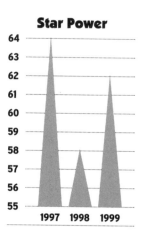

Star Power

1997 1998 1999

Box Office Bait

MOVIE	STUDIO	N.AMERICAN GROSS	RELEASE
Star Wars Episode One: The Phantom Menace	Fox	$412,775,151	5/19/99
Schindler'S List	Univ	$96,065,768	12/15/93
The Haunting	Dreamworks	$77,340,946	7/23/99
Excalibur	WB	$38,000,000	4/10/81
The Dead Pool	WB	$37,814,698	7/13/88

Career Trajectory

Rene Russo   Rank **76**   Bankability **60**

Real Name   Rene Russo
D.O.B.   2/17/54
Place of Birth   Burbank, California, USA
Contact   (A) Bernard Carneol, Progressive Arts

Willingness to Travel/Promote   **65**
Professionalism   **77**
Career Mgmt   **68**
Talent   **68**

INSIDE DIRT

There's a lease on a leading lady's screen life.

♦ She got a boost from *The Thomas Crown Affair*. But she's forty-six, and there's an imaginary barrier for women in romantic roles; Meryl Streep is playing mothers now.

♦ When she was a top model in the '70s, she was a wild girl in the fast lane. Now she's a saint.

♦ She's a born-again Christian. She gives a tenth of all her income to the church, and she prays before making all her big decisions—often in tongues. Then she does a steamy sexual role with Pierce Brosnan. That took guts.

♦ She's on a soapbox about actors who don't have to look young. Funny, that wasn't her concern ten years ago. Now she's middle-aged and still wants to be kissed by the leading man.

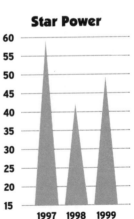

Star Power

| | 1997 | 1998 | 1999 |

Box Office Bait

MOVIE	STUDIO	N.AMERICAN GROSS	RELEASE
Lethal Weapon 3	WB	$144,731,527	5/15/92
Ransom	BV	$136,485,602	11/8/96
Lethal Weapon 4	WB	$129,734,803	7/10/98
In The Line of Fire	Columbia	$102,238,862	7/9/93
Get Shorty	MGM	$72,400,510	10/20/95

Career Trajectory

Jude Law Rank **77** Bankability **60**

Real Name	Jude Law
D.O.B.	12/29/72
Place of Birth	London, England
Contact	(A) Josh Lieberman, CAA

Willingness to Travel/Promote	Professionalism	Career Mgmt	Talent
81	76	77	74

INSIDE DIRT

He's the sexiest straight Brit that's come down the pike in quite a while.

♦ Jude Law? What's that? A new series on CBS?

♦ He's an absolutely brilliant actor.

♦ Of all the recent Brit pack, he's the one that's broken out. He's taken bigger American films and has a distinctive look.

♦ I don't see him crossing over into the mainstream.

♦ Like Rufus Sewell, he's another brooding Brit.

♦ *The Talented Mr. Ripley* proved the talent was there, but his talent is for the art film and not so much for the old-fashioned Hollywood star vehicle. He's more Lawrence Olivier than Cary Grant.

♦ Of course he likes to travel and promote! He's British, and they had all the colonies, after all.

Star Power

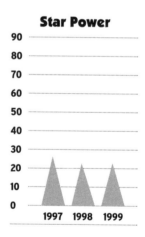

90
80
70
60
50
40
30
20
10
0
1997 1998 1999

Box Office Bait

MOVIE	STUDIO	N.AMERICAN GROSS	RELEASE
The Talented Mr. Ripley	Paramount	$91,292,135	12/25/99
Gattaca	Sony/Columbia	$12,532,777	10/24/97
eXistenZ	Miramax	$2,840,417	4/23/99
Wilde	SPC	$2,412,601	5/1/98
Bent	MGM	$496,059	11/26/97

Career Trajectory

Billy Crystal   Rank **78**   Bankability **60**

Real Name	Billy Crystal
D.O.B.	3/14/47
Place of Birth	Long Beach, New York, USA
Contact	(A) Jim Wiatt, WMA (M) MBST

Willingness to Travel/Promote	Professionalism	Career Mgmt	Talent
58	**72**	**52**	**73**

INSIDE DIRT

His 50 minutes were almost up before *Analyze This* saved him.

♦ He's suffered from the same curse as many other *Saturday Night Live* alumni: a very talented sketch comic who can't hold his own when he goes after a movie career.

♦ If *Analyze This* had bombed, it would have been over for him.

♦ *My Giant? City Slicker 2? Mr. Saturday Night?* Puhleeze. Thank god for his Oscar gig.

♦ He's made one appalling movie after another. Everyone in the business thinks *Analyze This* was a fluke, so he went six months without a movie offer.

♦ Billy is so desperate to be taken seriously that it has ruined his basic talent, which is being funny.

♦ The Oscar show? It's a negative for him. It just shows him off as a TV pitch man.

Star Power

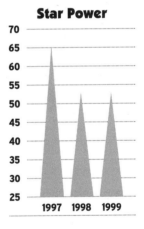

| 70 |
| 65 |
| 60 |
| 55 |
| 50 |
| 45 |
| 40 |
| 35 |
| 30 |
| 25 |

1997 1998 1999

Box Office Bait

MOVIE	STUDIO	N.AMERICAN GROSS	RELEASE
City Slickers	Columbia	$123,534,798	6/7/91
Analyze This	WB	$106,694,016	3/5/99
When Harry Met Sally	Columbia	$92,247,887	7/12/89
Throw Momma From the Train	Orion	$57,695,259	12/11/87
City Slickers 2	Columbia	$43,622,150	6/10/94

Career Trajectory

John Cusack Rank 79   Bankability 60

Real Name	John Paul Cusack
D.O.B.	6/28/66
Place of Birth	Evanston, Illinois, USA
Contact	(A) Gaby Morgerman, WMA

Willingness to Travel/Promote	Professionalism	Career Mgmt	Talent
65	73	70	78

INSIDE DIRT

He's never sold out in a movie. He never went for the huge bucks.

♦ He's a really attractive screen personality who also develops and produces films, such as *Grosse Pointe Blank* and *High Fidelity*. All actors say they want to take more control of their careers, but John's really doing it.

♦ A lot of his project choices are made on the basis of directors he'd like to work with. It's a short list.

♦ For the quality and scope of his talent and résumé, he should be a much bigger star.

♦ He can use an image booster in a big way. He should get a romance in his life. What happened to his dating Neve Campbell?

♦ He and [Tim] Robbins are supposed to be friends but they are extremely competitive around each other.

♦ What a smart guy.

Star Power

50	
48	
46	
44	
42	
40	
38	
36	
34	
32	

1997 1998 1999

Box Office Bait

MOVIE	STUDIO	N.AMERICAN GROSS	RELEASE
Con Air	BV	$100,927,613	6/6/97
Anastasia	Fox	$56,491,351	11/14/97
Stand By Me	Columbia	$51,914,208	8/8/86
Broadcast News	Fox	$49,154,886	12/16/87
The Thin Red Line	Fox	$36,393,442	12/23/98

Career Trajectory

Charlize Theron

Rank 80   **Bankability 60**

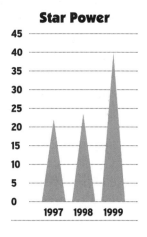

Real Name	Charlize Theron
D.O.B.	8/7/75
Place of Birth	Benoni, South Africa
Contact	(A) J.J. Harris, UTA

Willingness to Travel/Promote 60   **Professionalism** 55   **Career Mgmt** 64   **Talent** 62

INSIDE DIRT

She's walking a very fine line between sex symbol and actress.

♦ She's making the right moves to become known in popular films like *The Ciderhouse Rules,* and she's proved her acting chops in *Devil's Advocate* and *The Astronaut's Wife.*

♦ None of her films has broken out overseas.

♦ *The Astronaut's Wife* made her an international name. If it had failed, she would gone back to being just another mid-level actress. But she'll never be a Julia Roberts.

♦ She definitely has talent, presence, and beauty. Like Halle Berry, she's the icing on the cake—but you still need the cake.

♦ She's awfully sexy. She's hot. I'd keep my eye on her career, big time.

Star Power

```
45
40
35
30
25
20
15
10
5
0
    1997  1998  1999
```

Box Office Bait

MOVIE	STUDIO	N.AMERICAN GROSS	RELEASE
Devil's Advocate	WB	$60,899,443	10/17/97
Mighty Joe Young	BV	$50,628,009	12/25/98
That Thing You Do!	Fox	$25,731,918	10/4/96
Trial and Error	NL	$13,600,890	5/30/97
2 Days in The Valley	MGM	$11,127,959	9/27/96

Career Trajectory

Gene Hackman Rank 81 Bankability 60

Real Name	Eugene Alden Hackman
D.O.B.	1/30/30
Place of Birth	San Bernadino, California, USA
Contact	(A) Fred Specktor, CAA

Willingness to Travel/Promote	Professionalism	Career Mgmt	Talent
51	83	66	75

INSIDE DIRT

Great talent. Too many films.

- He's an incredibly great actor. He's very intense. He's not on the set for fun and games.

- You don't see the work that goes into his roles, he doesn't get the credit. Yet he's really well respected by his peers.

- Everyone says he's just in it for the paycheck.

- He started out as a leading man in *The French Connection.* He could carry it off in the '60s and '70s when movies took more chances. Now they don't, and he can't.

- Hackman in a love scene? Please. People would scream if he kissed somebody.

- In *The Firm,* you could see him contemplating an affair with Tom Cruise's wife and you wanted to shout at the screen, Okay, gramps, don't go there!

Star Power

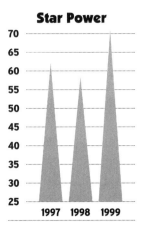

70		
65		
60		
55		
50		
45		
40		
35		
30		
25		
1997	1998	1999

Box Office Bait			
MOVIE	STUDIO	N.AMERICAN GROSS	RELEASE
The Firm	Para	$158,308,178	6/30/93
Super Man II	WB	$144,666,667	1981
Super Man	WB	$134,218,018	12/15/78
The Birdcage	MGM	$124,060,553	3/8/96
Enemy of the State	BV	$111,544,445	11/20/98

Career Trajectory

Warren Beatty Rank 82 Bankability 60

Real Name	Henry Warren Beatty
D.O.B.	3/30/37
Place of Birth	Richmond, Virginia, USA
Contact	(A) Josh Lieberman, CAA

Willingness to Travel/Promote **Professionalism** **Career Mgmt** **Talent**

56 **55** **58** **75**

INSIDE DIRT

He's a master manipulator in Hollywood

♦ He's got no conception of time on a set. His movies usually go over budget.

♦ I have the highest level of regard for Beatty. He's taken some real chances as an actor.

♦ In *Love Affair* he protected himself the way aging glamour queens do: soft focus, low lighting, Vaseline on the lens. It just drew attention to the aging problem.

♦ He should lie down on a slab next to King Tut; he's had as much work done on him. He's probably as well preserved.

♦ It's over for him as a romantic leading man.

♦ He's exceptionally knowledgeable about the business.

♦ He's obsessive. He'll call you in the middle of the night and pick your brains to smithereens about something.

♦ Warren for President? Wasn't the last womanizer in the White House enough?

Star Power

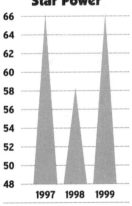

66	
64	
62	
60	
58	
56	
54	
52	
50	
48	
	1997 1998 1999

Box Office Bait

MOVIE	STUDIO	N.AMERICAN GROSS	RELEASE
Heaven Can Wait	Paramount	$109,777,778	1978
Dick Tracy	BV	$103,738,726	6/15/90
Shampoo	Columbia	$52,937,778	1975
Bonnie and Clyde	WB	$50,666,667	1967
Bugsy	Tri-Star	$49,091,562	12/13/91

Career Trajectory

Tim Robbins Rank 83 Bankability 60

Real Name	Timothy Francis Robbins
D.O.B.	10/16/58
Place of Birth	West Covina, California, USA
Contact	(A) Elaine Goldsmith-Thomas, ICM (NY)

Willingness to Travel/Promote	Professionalism	Career Mgmt	Talent
44	73	67	78

INSIDE DIRT

His mood swings on the set can be a little draining.

♦ Tim is a guy who considers his opinions to be empirical truth.

♦ I think Tim is a tremendous talent.

♦ He's two people. One day he'll show up on set and be this charming, delightful, good-hearted collaborative spirit. Then there's the other side of him, where nobody does their job as well as he does or cares about anything as much as he does. Then he's put-upon and sullen.

♦ Generous actors will run lines off-camera for another actor who's on-camera. Tim frequently chose not to extend that courtesy.

♦ An indie national treasure.

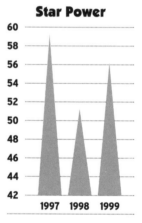

Star Power

60
58
56
54
52
50
48
46
44
42

1997 1998 1999

Box Office Bait			
MOVIE	**STUDIO**	**N.AMERICAN GROSS**	**RELEASE**
Top Gun	Para	$176,781,728	5/16/86
Bull Durham	Orion	$50,346,467	6/15/88
Nothing To Lose	BV	$44,477,235	7/18/97
Jungle Fever	Univ	$32,550,172	6/7/91
The Shawshank Redemption	Columbia	$28,233,104	9/23/94

Career Trajectory

Steve Martin Rank **84**

Bankability 60

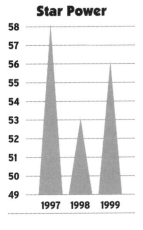

Real Name	Steve Martin
D.O.B.	8/14/45
Place of Birth	Waco, Texas, USA
Contact	(A) Ed Limato, ICM

Willingness to Travel/Promote	Professionalism	Career Mgmt	Talent
57	**82**	**62**	**77**

INSIDE DIRT

He'd rather be known as a writer than a comic.

♦ He's box-office poison overseas.

♦ He's so desperately earnest now that he's not funny anymore. Everyone feels sorry for him, being this little clown trying to be serious. His audiences are abandoning him.

♦ A really brilliant guy. He's a thoughtful connoisseur of art and a brilliant writer and satirist. Look at his articles in *The New Yorker,* his books, his plays—he's got a brilliant, cosmopolitan, eclectic mind that goes far beyond being a comedy actor.

♦ He has a weirdly European sensibility for Hollywood.

♦ On the set, he's gracious, interesting, thoughtful, and funny. But terribly shy. He's isolated by being so much more intelligent than most people he works with.

♦ He has a life that can sustain itself without making hit movies as a comedian. Lucky for him.

Star Power

	1997	1998	1999

(Chart values on axis: 58, 57, 56, 55, 54, 53, 52, 51, 50, 49)

Box Office Bait

MOVIE	STUDIO	N.AMERICAN GROSS	RELEASE
The Prince of Egypt (voice)	Dreamworks	$101,217,900	12/18/98
Parenthood	Univ	$100,047,830	8/2/89
The Soldier	Univ	$95,532,569	1979
Father of the Bride	BV	$89,325,780	12/20/91
Father of the Bride Part II	BV	$76,592,999	12/8/95

Career Trajectory

Jeff Bridges Rank **85** Bankability **59**

Real Name	Jeffrey Leon Bridges
D.O.B.	12/4/49
Place of Birth	Los Angeles, California, USA
Contact	(A) David Schiff, UTA

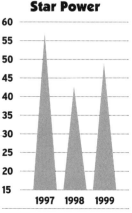

Willingness to Travel/Promote	Professionalism	Career Mgmt	Talent
62	**90**	**56**	**78**

INSIDE DIRT

Along with Hanks, Jeff has the best reputation in town.

♦ Just try to find anything bad to say about Jeff Bridges. You'd have to look under some pretty prehistoric rocks.

♦ He's one of America's finest actors. But he needs to do more down-to-earth projects.

♦ On each of his films he makes a beautiful book of black-and-white photos that he's taken of everybody on the set. Then he gives a copy to each person in the cast and crew. Everyone loves him.

♦ This is a man who was tortured by the romantic feelings Barbra Streisand had for him on *The Mirror Has Two Faces.* His family always comes first.

♦ He's tremendously respected. But he disappears off the map a lot.

♦ Oh, be still my heart! A total "10."

Star Power

60
55
50
45
40
35
30
25
20
15
1997 1998 1999

Box Office Bait

MOVIE	STUDIO	N.AMERICAN GROSS	RELEASE
The Fisher King	Tri-Star	$41,864,521	9/20/91
The Mirror Has Two Faces	Sony/TS	$40,845,152	11/15/96
Jagged Edge	Columbia	$36,896,147	10/4/85
Blown Away	MGM	$30,059,999	7/1/94
Last Picture Show	Columbia	$29,133,333	1971

Career Trajectory

Danny De Vito

Rank 86   **Bankability 59**

Real Name	Danny De Vito
D.O.B.	11/17/44
Place of Birth	Neptune, New Jersey, USA
Contact	(A) Kevin Huvane, CAA

Willingness to Travel/Promote   **Professionalism**   **Career Mgmt**   **Talent**

69   83   80   75

INSIDE DIRT

Brilliant, professional, charming, and short.

- I think he's a Renaissance man. He's played so many different kinds of parts—from *Taxi* to *One Flew Over the Cuckoo's Nest*. He was compelling and very moving in *Living Out Loud*.

- By Hollywood standards he's too short, too ugly, and too weird. And yet he's done astonishingly well because he's funny, he's smart, and he's talented.

- Because he also directs and produces, he's cast in parts that other stars with his same look and physique wouldn't get. Why? Because they're not the multitalented Danny DeVito.

- He's a true pro. It doesn't matter how long you have to keep him on the set, or how many takes you have to do—he'll go beyond that and then some.

- Talk about a brilliant career.

Star Power

65	
64	
63	
62	
61	
60	
59	
58	
57	
56	

1997 1998 1999

Box Office Bait

MOVIE	STUDIO	N.AMERICAN GROSS	RELEASE
Batman Returns	WB	$162,831,698	6/19/92
One Flew Over The Cuckoo's Nest	MGM	$112,000,000	11/19/75
Twins	Univ	$111,784,821	12/9/88
Terms of Endearment	Para	$108,423,489	11/23/83
Pulp Fiction	Miramax	$107,921,755	10/14/94

Career Trajectory

Kurt Russell   Rank **87**   Bankability **59**

Real Name	Kurt Vogel Russell
D.O.B.	3/17/51
Place of Birth	Springfield, Massachusetts, USA
Contact	(A) Rick Nicita, CAA

Willingness to Travel/Promote	Professionalism	Career Mgmt	Talent
63	72	60	52

INSIDE DIRT

He's completely amused by the outrageous success he's had.

♦ A journeyman actor who's so overpaid it's unbelievable.

♦ Women like him as an action hero. I've heard lots of them rhapsodize about his tight ass.

♦ He's gone through stardom and has come out of it well grounded. He's a very devoted family man who shows up on the set on time and is very professional. He doesn't bring an ego.

♦ He'll come to the set when he's not even scheduled, just to be with the other actors.

♦ For fun he'll fly one of his three planes up to his ranch and hunt game with bow and arrows. This, while Goldie is at home getting her fingernails done.

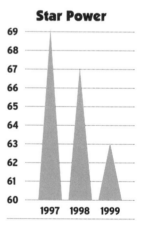

Star Power

69
68
67
66
65
64
63
62
61
60

1997 1998 1999

Box Office Bait

MOVIE	STUDIO	N.AMERICAN GROSS	RELEASE
The Fox and The Hound (voice)	BV	$87,013,956	1981
Backdraft	Univ	$78,001,365	5/24/91
Stargate	MGM	$71,434,689	10/28/94
Tango & Cash	WB	$63,399,930	12/22/89
Executive Decision	WB	$56,679,192	3/15/96

Career Trajectory

Paul Newman Rank 88   Bankability 59

Real Name Paul Leonard Newman
D.O.B. 1/26/25
Place of Birth Shaker Heights, Ohio, USA
Contact (A) Sam Cohn, ICM

Willingness to Travel/Promote	Professionalism	Career Mgmt	Talent
✈ 50	82	63	84

INSIDE DIRT

He was kind and professional, but a little hazy and vague.

♦ I worked with him on *Nobody's Fool*. He took a long time to respond to you. And he just kind of wandered. You'd have to lead him very specifically to the set. He wasn't really connected all the time. I felt that he was really aging, and I feel bad saying that.

♦ He is very present once the cameras are rolling. He knows his lines and everything.

♦ I saw him when he visited Tom [Cruise] on the set of *Mission Impossible*. He didn't seem all that sharp.

♦ What a brilliant career. He'll always be my hero.

Star Power

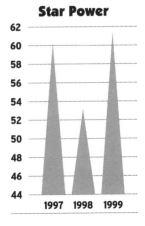

	1997	1998	1999

Box Office Bait

MOVIE	STUDIO	N.AMERICAN GROSS	RELEASE
The Sting	Univ	$159,616,327	12/25/73
The Towering Inferno	Fox	$116,000,000	12/17/74
Butch Cassidy and the Sundance Kid	Fox	$102,308,889	1969
The Verdict	Fox	$59,222,222	12/17/82
Message in a Bottle	WB	$52,799,004	2/12/99

Career Trajectory

Bill Murray   Rank **89**   Bankability **59**

Real Name	Bill Murray
D.O.B.	9/21/50
Place of Birth	Wilmette, Illinois, USA
Contact	(A) Jessica Tuchinsky, CAA

Willingness to Travel/Promote	Professionalism	Career Mgmt	Talent
51	55	42	64

INSIDE DIRT

Great talent. Never figured out how to use it.

◆ He made a shrewd career choice in making *Rushmore*. People could see he's a real actor and not just doing studio turns like *Stripes*.

◆ He's made such bad selections.

◆ I've heard from a production person that on *Groundhog Day* Bill was in such a fog on the set that literally he couldn't remember having filmed some of the scenes. You just had to kind of move him around and say, "You have to do this today, Bill," or "We did that yesterday." It's the way he still is.

◆ He's distracted and prone to fits of depression. His mind wanders a lot.

◆ Bill Murray is trying to play the *enfant terrible* when he's no longer an *enfant* and too often *terrible*.

Star Power

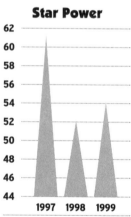

62
60
58
56
54
52
50
48
46
44

1997   1998   1999

Box Office Bait

MOVIE	STUDIO	N.AMERICAN GROSS	RELEASE
Ghostbusters (with re-issue)	Columbia	$230,247,625	7/8/84
Tootsie	Columbia	$177,200,000	12/17/82
Ghostbusters II	Columbia	$112,494,738	6/16/89
Stripes	Columbia	$90,859,087	1981
Space Jam	WB	$90,384,232	11/15/96

Career Trajectory

Emma Thompson

Rank 90　**Bankability 59**

Real Name	Emma Thompson
D.O.B.	4/15/59
Place of Birth	Paddington, London, England
Contact	(A) Nicole David, WMA

Willingness to Travel/Promote **65**　**Professionalism** **85**　**Career Mgmt** **66**　**Talent** **84**

INSIDE DIRT

The English Meryl Streep.

♦ She had all the elements come together at the right time. She did classy roles for major auteurs when those kind of independent films were becoming very popular.

♦ As an executive producer she's proving herself to be gracious tenfold in her willingness to call talent, executives, and cinematographers and say, "I really believe in this movie. Please come on board."

♦ She'd be the last person to ever ask for special perks.

♦ I think she's gotten a bit too comfortable with herself. She kind of plays the grande dame.

♦ I know people—practically Joes off the street—who've submitted material to her, and not only did she, in time, pay attention to it, she responded personally. This is rare.

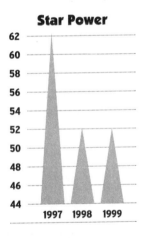

Star Power

	1997	1998	1999

Box Office Bait

MOVIE	STUDIO	N.AMERICAN GROSS	RELEASE
Sense and Sensibility	Sony/C	$42,975,897	12/13/95
Primary Colors	Univ	$39,017,984	3/20/98
Dead Again	Para	$37,378,123	8/23/91
Junior	Univ	$36,719,600	11/23/94
Howards End	SPC	$25,960,280	3/13/92

Career Trajectory

Val Kilmer   Rank **91**   Bankability **59**

Real Name	Val Edward Kilmer
D.O.B.	12/31/59
Place of Birth	Los Angeles, California, USA
Contact	(A) Rick Nicita, CAA

Willingness to Travel/Promote **46**   **Professionalism** **19**   **Career Mgmt** **45**   **Talent** **53**

INSIDE DIRT

An abusive man who has caused many, many delays.

- One of the meanest human beings the world has ever spawned. He's just an unhappy man.

- On some movies he's impossible, and on some movies he's just fine.

- He tries intellectually to challenge his producer and director to get control rather than to get what's best for the film. He's had at least one director fired, on *The Island of Dr. Moreau.*

- He's impetuous; he'll agree to something and then want to change it.

- As an actor, I like him.

- The few producers who can yell at him and keep him in line call him a pussycat. The rest call him a monster.

- He's a detriment when it comes to putting him on the road. You're better off saying, don't come.

- He has the charm of a snail.

Star Power

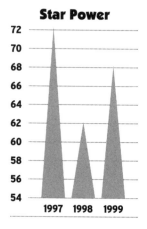

72
70
68
66
64
62
60
58
56
54

1997 1998 1999

Box Office Bait

MOVIE	STUDIO	N.AMERICAN GROSS	RELEASE
Batman Forever	WB	$183,997,904	6/16/95
Top Gun	Para	$176,781,728	5/16/86
The Prince of Egypt (voice)	Dreamworks	$101,217,900	12/18/98
Heat	WB	$66,802,342	12/15/95
The Saint	Para	$61,355,436	4/4/97

Career Trajectory

Uma Thurman Rank **92** Bankability **59**

Real Name Uma Karuna Thurman
D.O.B. 4/29/70
Place of Birth Boston, Massachusetts, USA
Contact (A) Bryan Lourd, CAA

Willingness to Travel/Promote	Professionalism	Career Mgmt	Talent
60	76	71	64

INSIDE DIRT

She's pure sexual provocation, and she sells it.

- Of all the sexpots, she has the best ratio of sex, human awareness, mystery, and acting talent.

- She's positioned herself to be an actress first, who happens to be drop-dead gorgeous. Unlike Demi, we'll still be seeing her around in ten years' time.

- She has the potential for a very long career.

- I found her incredibly intelligent and very pre-pared. And very enthusiastic.

- She's been especially good as an actress since she's had her baby.

- They love her in France.

- Because of *Pulp Fiction,* she's still sellable just about everywhere.

- If she ever did a full-on glamour part she'd blow the roof off the theater.

Star Power

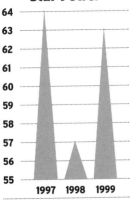

Chart values: 64, 63, 62, 61, 60, 59, 58, 57, 56, 55 — years 1997, 1998, 1999

Box Office Bait

MOVIE	STUDIO	N.AMERICAN GROSS	RELEASE
Pulp Fiction	Miramax	$107,921,755	10/14/94
Batman and Robin	WB	$107,285,004	6/20/97
The Truth About Cats and Dogs	Fox	$34,848,673	4/26/96
Dangerous Liaisons	WB	$32,663,833	12/21/88
Final Analysis	WB	$27,339,324	2/7/92

Career Trajectory

John Malkovich

Rank 93   **Bankability 58**

Real Name   John Gavin Malkovich
D.O.B.   12/9/53
Place of Birth   Christopher, Illinois, USA
Contact   (A) Hylda Queally, WMA

Willingness to Travel/Promote	Professionalism	Career Mgmt	Talent
64	83	55	78

INSIDE DIRT

He's extremely professional but overvalued.

- He's definitely worth something in the international marketplace—not for your big-budget action film but for a nice $10 to $20-million project.
- He's best for upscale subject matter, especially period films.
- His career? He's too intellectual. Too artsy.
- He was very diligent in promoting the project we worked on. Of course, it was his directing debut, so that may have made a difference.
- The fact that he decided to do *Being John Malkovich* tells you he takes risks. It's all about the world seen through the eyes of—John. Unreal.
- He needs strong directors to steer him away from becoming too self-indulgent as an actor.
- He's an amazing presence. He was brilliant as the psycho in *In the Line of Fire*.
- John's an enigmatic guy.

Star Power

50
48
46
44
42
40
38
36
34
32

1997 1998 1999

Box Office Bait

MOVIE	STUDIO	N.AMERICAN GROSS	RELEASE
In the Line of Fire	Columbia	$102,238,862	7/9/93
Con Air	BV	$100,927,613	6/6/97
The Man in the Iron Mask	MGM	$56,968,169	3/13/98
The Killing Fields	WB	$34,607,720	11/2/84
Places in the Heart	Tri-Star	$34,431,005	9/21/84

Career Trajectory

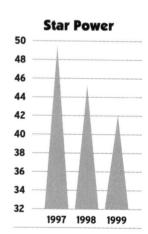

Whitney Houston

Rank 94   **Bankability 58**

Real Name	Whitney Elizabeth Houston
D.O.B.	8/9/63
Place of Birth	East Orange, New Jersey, USA
Contact	(A) Nicole David, WMA

Willingness to Travel/Promote	Professionalism	Career Mgmt	Talent
40	50	71	51

INSIDE DIRT

She's an average actress and a better singer.

- Her continued marriage to a criminal loser like Bobby Brown is hurting her in the minds of her public.

- *Waiting to Exhale* was a shrewd career choice.

- *The Bodyguard* proved she could act. At least she could hold her own against Kevin Costner's Steve McQueen haircut.

- For acting range, I'd give her a four out of ten.

- She looks like a doll and a sweetheart but she's really a nightmare to work with. During *The Preacher's Wife,* it became a pattern: She would just not show up for work on Mondays. Who knew why?

- The whitest black female star.

- I would have graded her lower in professionalism but she always shows up for those benefit parties.

Star Power

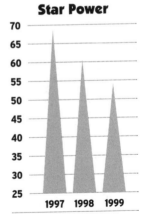

70
65
60
55
50
45
40
35
30
25

1997 1998 1999

Box Office Bait

MOVIE	STUDIO	N.AMERICAN GROSS	RELEASE
The Bodyguard	WB	$121,936,132	11/25/92
Waiting to Exhale	Fox	$67,001,595	12/22/95
The Preacher's Wife	BV	$48,093,211	12/13/96

Career Trajectory

Woody Harrelson

Rank 95   **Bankability 58**

Real Name	Woodrow Tracy Harrelson
D.O.B.	7/23/61
Place of Birth	Midland, Texas, USA
Contact	(A) Bryan Lourd, CAA

Willingness to Travel/Promote	Professionalism	Career Mgmt	Talent
63	58	58	71

INSIDE DIRT

His persona is too loopy for people to realize what a good actor he is.

♦ He's more of a big goofy kid than a leading man. He likes hemp and he's a tree-hugger.

♦ *Natural Born Killers* and *Larry Flynt* proved he has tremendous range.

♦ A homeopathic nut who won't take any antibiotics and nearly lost his leg in Costa Rica when he got an infection.

♦ On a set, you have to run interference on the wacko factor. Make sure he has his vegetarian food and wheatgrass concoctions at regular intervals. Remember, you are harnessing a powerful comedic presence on-screen. It could be worse.

♦ The rumors are that he likes to get stoned a lot. But nothing that's ever affected his work or bankable status. And now he can get high on O_2 with his oxygen bar.

Star Power

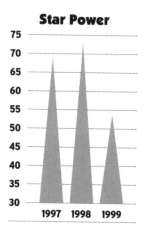

| | 1997 | 1998 | 1999 |

Box Office Bait

MOVIE	STUDIO	N.AMERICAN GROSS	RELEASE
Antz (voice)	Dreamworks	$90,646,554	10/2/98
Hannah & Her Sisters	Orion	$40,084,041	2/7/86
Manhattan	UA	$39,072,576	1979
Annie Hall	MGM	$27,324,847	1977
Casino Royale	Columbia	$22,666,667	1967

Career Trajectory

Angelina Jolie Rank 96 Bankability 57

Real Name Angelina Jolie Voight
D.O.B. 6/4/75
Place of Birth Los Angeles, California, USA
Contact (A) Geyer Kosinski, Industry Entertainment

Willingness to Travel/Promote
81

Professionalism
70

Career Mgmt
78

Talent
73

INSIDE DIRT

She's artistic and sensitive and also incredibly high-strung, like an Arabian steed.

♦ After her Oscar, she's at the pinnacle of "the flavor of the month" phenomenon. Audiences will have to decide whether it's 15 minutes or 15 years of fame.

♦ She has tremendous radiance mixed with a little craziness, which tends to overshadow her acting abilities and even limit her range.

♦ Angelina, stop trying to shock people and just try to make good films!

♦ She's coming up in *Tomb Raider,* (adapted from) one of the best-selling video games. But almost every movie from a video game has crashed and burned badly, so this could be potentially disastrous for her.

♦ Some of her best work was for HBO's *Gia*, which was never seen overseas.

♦ She's got to work on her award acceptance speeches.

Star Power

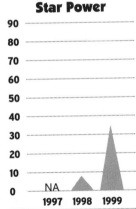

90
80
70
60
50
40
30
20
10
0   NA
    1997 1998 1999

Box Office Bait

MOVIE	STUDIO	N.AMERICAN GROSS	RELEASE
Gone in Sixty Seconds	Buena Vista	$93,577,259	6/9/00
The Bone Collector	Universal	$65,061,354	11/5/99
Girl, Interrupted	Sony	$28,871,190	12/21/99
Pushing Tin	Fox	$8,408,835	4/23/99
Playing God	Buena Vista	$4,166,918	10/17/97

Career Trajectory

Matthew McConaughey

Rank 97   **Bankability 57**

Real Name	Mathew David McConaughey
D.O.B.	11/4/69
Place of Birth	Uvalde, Texas, USA
Contact	(M) Beth Holden, AMG (A) Todd "Gus" Gustawes, AMG

Willingness to Travel/Promote	Professionalism	Career Mgmt	Talent
45	70	59	54

INSIDE DIRT

There's a high risk Matthew won't make it.

♦ He ought to be playing more down and dirty bad-ass roles. His best performance was in a sequel to *The Texas Chainsaw Massacre,* and I'm not kidding.

♦ When he's playing intellectuals in *Contact* or *Amistad,* he's totally unbelievable.

♦ Memo to Matthew: Stay out of period films.

♦ Older women like him.

♦ He was hyped too hard and too fast by the Hollywood publicity machine. That's good for three months of A-list parties and a couple of movies. Then you've got to prove yourself.

♦ He's not a good enough actor to take roles that aren't based on sex appeal and make them special.

♦ He's a complete professional.

♦ He's strong in the U.K. and Germany but dicey in France.

Star Power

	1997	1998	1999
64			
62			
60			
58			
56			
54			
52			
50			
48			
46			

Box Office Bait

MOVIE	STUDIO	N.AMERICAN GROSS	RELEASE
A Time To Kill	WB	$108,766,007	7/24/96
Contact	WB	$100,769,177	7/11/97
Angels in the Outfield	BV	$50,236,831	7/15/94
Amistad	Dreamworks	$44,107,804	12/10/97
Boys on the Side	WB	$23,432,802	2/3/95

Career Trajectory

Ralph Fiennes Rank 98 Bankability 56

Real Name Ralph Nathaniel Fiennes
D.O.B. 12/22/62
Place of Birth Suffolk, England
Contact (A) Bryan Lourd, CAA

Willingness to Travel/Promote	Professionalism	Career Mgmt	Talent
61	81	70	76

INSIDE DIRT

He didn't get the bump off *The English Patient* he should have.

◆ *The English Patient* made him a leading man for the educated mass audience.

◆ He harkens back to those matinee idols of the 1930s and 1940s. His appeal has less to do with his acting than his looks.

◆ Careerwise, *Strange Days* was a huge mistake. He was trying to break out of that straitjacketed British image he has—and he didn't.

◆ If he wants to become an international star in Hollywood, he has to get a personality.

◆ He's a powerhouse talent with tremendous versatility.

◆ He hasn't played yet in what I call a broad commercial film. *The Avengers* flopped.

◆ He has to learn how to enjoy life.

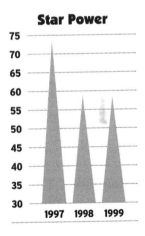

Star Power

| | 1997 | 1998 | 1999 |

Box Office Bait

MOVIE	STUDIO	N.AMERICAN GROSS	RELEASE
The Prince of Egypt	Dreamworks	$101,217,900	12/18/98
Schindler's List	Univ	$96,065,768	12/15/93
The English Patient	Miramax	$78,651,430	11/15/96
Quiz Show	BV	$24,814,770	9/14/94
The Avengers	WB	$23,322,832	8/14/98

Career Trajectory

Brendan Fraser

Rank 99   **Bankability 56**

Real Name	Brendan James Fraser
D.O.B.	12/3/68
Place of Birth	Indianapolis, Indiana, USA
Contact	(A) Peter Levine, CAA

Willingness to Travel/Promote **65**   **Professionalism 73**   **Career Mgmt 78**   **Talent 64**

INSIDE DIRT

If his looks start going, he could always slide back into art films.

♦ What a piece of brilliance, following up *George of the Jungle* with *Gods and Monsters*. It makes everyone out there happy for him and root for him because he's been in little movies as well as big ones.

♦ He should do one *George of the Jungle* for every three intelligent films.

♦ He's done some pretty big movies. But he hasn't really convinced the world that it wasn't the concept that carried the movie and not him.

♦ People shouldn't forget he started out his career as an incredible dramatic actor.

♦ As long as he keeps his looks, he'll always have big studio pictures to fall back on.

♦ He's an actor whom I instinctively respect very much.

Star Power

55
50
45
40
35
30
25
20
15
10

1997 1998 1999

Box Office Bait

MOVIE	STUDIO	N.AMERICAN GROSS	RELEASE
The Mummy	Univ	$153,783,825	5/7/99
George of the Jungle	BV	$105,263,257	7/16/97
Encino Man	BV	$40,028,108	5/23/92
Now and Then	NL	$27,109,131	10/20/95
Blast From the Past	NL	$26,415,951	2/12/99

Career Trajectory

Minnie Driver Rank 100 Bankability 56

Real Name Amelia Driver
D.O.B. 1/31/71
Place of Birth London, England
Contact (A) Brian Swardstrom, Endeavor

Willingness to Travel/Promote	Professionalism	Career Mgmt	Talent
65	**58**	**67**	**63**

INSIDE DIRT

She can't carry a movie, but she's a wonderful co-lead.

♦ It's brilliant how she's manipulated the press into believing she's this beauty! I mean, girl, how long can you keep up this $2,000 makeup job every time you go out?

♦ I find her to be an extraordinarily engaging screen presence.

♦ The jury's still out as to whether she can even act or not.

♦ She has basically picked artsy roles. She won't become a superstar.

♦ I'm personally charmed by her, but she's a pain in the ass on a movie set. She makes just one silly demand after another. She'll say she's not coming out of her trailer for an hour because she's doing—whatever.

♦ Minnie thought she was a star before she became one.

Star Power

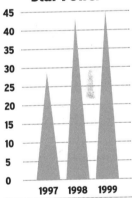

| | 1997 | 1998 | 1999 |

Box Office Bait

MOVIE	STUDIO	N.AMERICAN GROSS	RELEASE
Tarzan	BV	$161,851,795	6/15/99
Good Will Hunting	Miramax	$138,339,411	12/5/97
Golden Eye	MGM	$106,429,941	11/17/95
Sleepers	WB	$53,300,852	10/18/96
South Park: Bigger, Longer & Uncut (voice)	Para	$50,587,886	6/30/99

Career Trajectory

Ethan Hawke Rank **101** Bankability **56**

Real Name   Ethan Hawke
D.O.B.   11/6/70
Place of Birth   Austin, Texas, USA
Contact   (A) Bryan Lourd, CAA

Willingness to Travel/Promote	Professionalism	Career Mgmt	Talent
63	**60**	**47**	**60**

INSIDE DIRT

He could have been another Leonardo DiCaprio.

- Ethan Hawke had his moment, and he didn't take off. I'm not sure he can ever get it back. In that sense, he's a younger version of John Travolta.

- He had a rough patch where his public awareness went down. But he's coming out of it.

- He'll be a bigger star than he is today.

- His vanity picture, *Hamlet,* is set in present-day Manhattan. And it's so very bad. I think he'll forever be one of those brooding, self-involved people who destines your movie to less rather than more.

- He has crossover appeal to the foreign market. Japan especially likes Ethan Hawke.

- There's a rumor from reliable sources that Ethan Hawke has three nipples.

Star Power

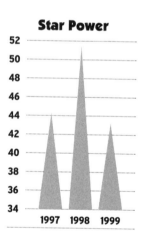

1997	1998	1999

(52, 50, 48, 46, 44, 42, 40, 38, 36, 34)

Box Office Bait

MOVIE	STUDIO	N.AMERICAN GROSS	RELEASE
Dead Poets Society	BV	$94,544,861	6/2/89
Alive	BV	$36,733,909	1/16/93
White Fang	BV	$34,576,736	1/18/91
Great Expectations	Fox	$26,333,044	1/30/98
Dad	Univ	$22,123,131	10/27/89

Career Trajectory

Susan Sarandon

Rank 102 **Bankability 56**

Real Name Susan Abigail Tomaling
D.O.B. 10/4/46
Place of Birth New York, USA
Contact (A) Sam Cohn/Martha Luttrell, ICM

Willingness to Travel/Promote	Professionalism	Career Mgmt	Talent
46	83	74	83

INSIDE DIRT

A goddess, yes, but not a fully bankable goddess.

♦ She's a great example of someone who knows how to be very selective with her projects and still maintain her star standing.

♦ The enduring question is, how and why does she put up with Tim Robbins? Everyone inevitably asks this after spending a half hour with her.

♦ She's a great mom to her kids; she protects them from all the showbiz stuff.

♦ She and Tim tend to dismiss those who have different politics than they do, as being unworthy and contemptible.

♦ In the past five years, Susan has really opened up and made herself more accessible to her fans and the press. She used to be incredibly guarded.

♦ She's still one of America's leading ladies of film.

Star Power

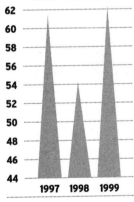

62
60
58
56
54
52
50
48
46
44
1997 1998 1999

Box Office Bait

MOVIE	STUDIO	N.AMERICAN GROSS	RELEASE
The Rocky Horror Picture Show	Fox	$112,892,319	9/26/75
The Client	WB	$92,112,663	7/20/94
Stepmom	Sony	$91,030,827	12/25/98
The Witches of Eastwick	WB	$63,749,955	6/12/87
Bull Durham	Orion	$50,346,467	6/15/88

Career Trajectory

Madonna   Rank **103**   Bankability **56**

Real Name   Madonna Louise Veronica Ciccone
D.O.B.   8/16/58
Place of Birth Bay City, Michigan, USA
Contact   (A) Bryan Lourd, CAA

Willingness to Travel/Promote   **Professionalism**   **Career Mgmt**   **Talent**
67   **56**   **28**   **58**

INSIDE DIRT

In her case, an especially strong script and director is paramount.

- She's had a dreadful run of movies for the most part, and she's been dreadful in them.

- Her problem in movies is the same as Demi's: a total lack of vulnerability.

- She points to the social trends and exploits them shamelessly.

- She's pure self-invention and my hat's off to her for that. But I can't respond to her in any other than a crass commercial way.

- Her film company is very approachable. There's no star trip about it. If you've got an idea that you feel passionate about and is worthy of her, there's an open door there.

- Her willingness to travel? It's high if you're willing to shell out for twelve people to stay with her in the Hotel du Cap.

Star Power

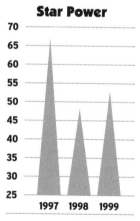

Box Office Bait			
MOVIE	STUDIO	N.AMERICAN GROSS	RELEASE
A League of Their Own	Columbia	$107,439,000	7/1/92
Dick Tracy	BV	$103,738,726	6/15/90
Evita	BV	$50,038,461	12/25/96
Desperately Seeking Susan	Orion	$27,398,584	3/29/85
Truth or Dare	Miramax	$15,012,935	5/10/91

Career Trajectory

Mark Wahlberg

Rank 104 **Bankability 56**

Real Name	Mark Robert Michael Wahlberg
D.O.B.	6/5/71
Place of Birth	Dorchester, Massachusetts, USA
Contact	(A) Ariel Emmanuel, Endeavor

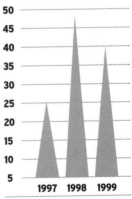

Willingness to Travel/Promote	Professionalism	Career Mgmt	Talent
59	56	61	59

INSIDE DIRT

His appeal is domestic, not foreign.

◆ He's the antiactor. He's the guy who came from another medium and was completely different—weird, edgy, and iconoclastic. But the age demographic that likes that iconoclasm is also fickle and will move on quickly.

◆ He's getting paid too much on a global basis for what he's really worth. His quote was $3 to $4 million a picture in mid-1999.

◆ It's his bad-boy attitude that's kept him from being a bigger star. He's hard to work with, he's demanding for no reason, and he walks out on interviews.

◆ He didn't take *Boogie Nights* and run with it in a way that would have made him a major star.

◆ *Three Kings* showed he's not just a bad-boy hunk—he has acting muscles, too.

Star Power

```
50
45
40
35
30
25
20
15
10
 5
    1997  1998  1999
```

Box Office Bait

MOVIE	STUDIO	N.AMERICAN GROSS	RELEASE
The Big Hit	Sony	$27,007,143	4/24/98
Boogie Nights	NL	$26,384,919	10/12/97
Renaissance Man	BV	$24,332,324	6/3/94
Fear	Univ	$20,829,193	4/12/96
The Corruptor	NL	$15,119,975	3/12/99

Career Trajectory

Renée Zellweger

Rank 105   **Bankability 56**

Real Name	Renee Kathleen Zellweger
D.O.B.	4/25/69
Place of Birth	Katy, Texas, USA
Contact	(A) Brandt Joel, CAA (M) Jim Morey

Willingness to Travel/Promote	Professionalism	Career Mgmt	Talent
65	**81**	**61**	**76**

INSIDE DIRT

She's got legs, because she knows how to pick material.

♦ She should be working more. She's truly talented. It's partly the curse of "the new one to watch." And it's weighted with so much baggage that usually it backfires, as it did with Julia Ormond.

♦ Renée Zelwegger means nothing overseas.

♦ I worked with her before she did *Jerry Maguire*. She came in to replace an actress and she gave it 300 percent. She was terrific.

♦ Renée whines about everything. She's not hard to deal with, no; she's just a whiner. She's a good Jewish girl.

♦ I think she'll have a long career because she's cute and really talented. But she'll never be the big star they envisioned her to be.

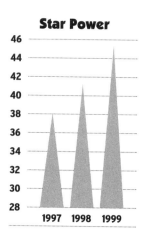

Star Power

46
44
42
40
38
36
34
32
30
28

1997 1998 1999

Box Office Bait

MOVIE	STUDIO	N.AMERICAN GROSS	RELEASE
Jerry Maguire	Sony/TS	$153,620,822	12/13/96
One True Thing	Univ	$23,337,196	9/18/98
Reality Bites	Univ	$20,982,557	2/18/94
8 Seconds	WB	$19,570,825	2/25/94
My Boyfriend's Back	BV	$3,335,984	8/6/93

Career Trajectory

7

Hollywood Vine

It all seemed a bit cloak and dagger.

My source, a former executive of a major star's production company and a repository of Big Dish, had tucked himself into a corner seat of a dusky Hollywood café. Street traffic poured in from a nearby exit—the better to discourage eavesdropping. I asked him to take off the shades, he asked me to turn off the tape recorder.

"Who's that person watching us over there?" he asks suspiciously. "Is *he* recording us?"

"That's a cell phone," I reply.

"Really? Well, maybe he's phoning us in to his lawyers."

It was going to be a long lunch.

The day before, he had promised he would "consider" talking to me about the star's "secret life" and the "bizarre workings" of the production office. How could I get him to spill the beans?

"Did you read my screenplay?" he asked warily.

I assured him that such a unique and compelling piece of writing should really be discussed in depth—another day—to do it justice.

He smiled and asked me for my business card. I obliged. Things were going to be just fine.

"James, I know where every bone in that company is buried because I personally buried it."

A half hour and several napkins full of scribbles later, I had gained enough trust from my source to switch on the microcassette. Two hours after that, my little Panasonic had collected enough gleaming bones to fill a Benedictine crypt.

And so it went, day after day, week after week, as I negotiated with my sources to gather, like a cautious terrier, dozens of buried tales from the dark and light side of Hollywood life. Unfortunately for the reader, some of these "bones" can never see the light of day in print, unless I want to be buried along with them and never eat lunch in this town again. But thankfully, most can.

Gossip—the word in Old English means a person who has contracted spiritual affinity with another—suffers a bad rap in Hollywood. As Glynda might say about the witches in Oz, there is good gossip, and there is bad gossip.

"Good" doesn't necessarily imply good behavior, as when sources enthuse that Jeff Bridges is a "dream" to work with and has "one of the best reputations in town." Nor does "bad" necessarily mean that a star does bad things, as in an executive's comment (and widely held view in Hollywood) that "Val Kilmer is an abusive man who has caused many, many delays on his films."

Simply put, "good" means credible gossip that comes from reliable sources. "Bad" doesn't.

Part of the reason for good gossip's potency in Hollywood is its usefulness. "The grapevine" is vital to the smooth functioning of many jobs in Hollywood. Whenever directors or producers consider a star for a part, they conduct an asking-around phase to other members of the community. How did that star behave on his last film and the film before that?

As I contemplated the possibility that CAA might be wiretapping our water glasses, I thought back to a conversation with Tekla Morgan, a noted film bonder in Hollywood. Bonding companies risk millions of dollars to guarantee a film's completion. So it's no surprise that to help assess that risk, they also take advantage of good gossip.

"We call around to production managers and UPMs [unit production managers] and ask them what they think about the stars," she said. "That helps us decide whether to say yes or no to bonding a film. Studios do it all the time, too."

Everyone does it. Gossip is simply shared tribal wisdom, and the Hollywood Tribe is sharing it all the time.

Useful gossip also may include leaking information to achieve a particular end. An ambitious agent may want to cheat the news of his client's potential $15-million–plus–back end movie deal onto the front pages of the

Hollywood trade papers in order to beef up the chances that the deal will be closed. Or a crewmember may whisper tales of treachery about a "difficult" co-worker into the ears of the film's producers, in order to hasten that co-worker's dismissal from the set.

But good or bad, corroborated or not, gossip is like a recreational drug with a high market value, much in demand for its quick, pleasurable rush. And the Thai stick of Hollywood gossip is "negative" dirt, especially concerning sex and drugs.

Breathe the name of Sharon Stone on almost any movie set and what do you get? An earful about betrayal, greed, vindictiveness, revenge—plenty of ammo for a Jackie Collins masterpiece. A tale involving an ersatz golden shower is especially popular.

Demi Moore, Marlon Brando, Russell Crowe, Johnny Depp, Mira Sorvino, Melanie Griffith, Sean Penn, Tommy Lee Jones, and Gwyneth Paltrow don't exactly come off as Hollywood darlings, either. As for Val Kilmer? Godzilla gets better reviews. It's no surprise Val ranks the lowest in professionalism (19 out of 100) of any actor in this book.

Why is this industry addicted to gossip? For the same reason so many in it are addicted to drugs. Hollywood is a town ruled by fear and desperation. Here job security is perilous, the fate of a megamillion-dollar movie can hang on the whim of a studio suit (and vice versa), and fear of failure is a common smell.

Stars fret that their window of opportunity for the top-dollar market is shrinking by the month; the big wave they're riding today could be a wipe-out tomorrow as more and more teen turks and TV pinups flood the feature market to replace them. (Not to mention their horror over those spreading crow's feet.)

Even success is something for people to fear: It might only be setting them up to fail next time.

With this kind of dull panic clutching their collective throats, is it any wonder that Hollywood professionals obsess over gossip? Only in a world where the status quo can change so drastically so fast—video clerk one day, millionaire the next; "in bed together" Wednesday, libel suit Thursday—is "the grapevine" so tended to and the soil so ripe for its often sour grapes.

Meanwhile, back at lunch, my source is waxing forth while eyeing a trendy, if unidentifiable, entree.

"This town is living proof that knowledge—including gossip—is power," he remarks, imperiously dismissing a hovering busboy. "And no one wants to give up that power easily."

He offers the following scenario: Assume you're a producer "about to break." You have a $40-million-dollar action flick, a house in the Hamptons, a six-digit producing fee, and an impressionable, buxom Baltic twinkie (and potential trophy wife) all riding on your ability to hook Star X for your lead role. Why reveal valuable information on that actor to other agents or producers—all of whom might be trying to snag the same Star X for their own tacky exploitation projects?

"Why risk ditching your dream package?" my source concludes.

These last words were hitched to a rather pained expression, as if he himself might have succumbed to this risk in the past.

I think back to a comment from a producer I once met, who stressed that gossip also can backfire if it's unreliable to begin with. "The danger is that telling tales about the stars becomes a self-fulfilling prophecy," said David Levy, a producer on several Robert Altman films. "If the kernel isn't valid in the first place, these things can spread around and become part of the lore and prejudice of the community. They're prophecies—but they're false prophecies."

He added a caveat: "But as a producer, I wouldn't let that stop me asking around about someone." Hooray for pragmatism.

Another reason Hollywood professionals are nervous about spreading gossip, particularly the reliable negative gossip, is the fear of being found out. "But don't tell anyone I told you so!" was a typical refrain sung by many of the songbirds I met. Like the pledge of silence taken by members of the Cosa Nostra (another dysfunctional extended family), Hollywood's jealously guarded tribal secrets speak to its fear of professional reprisals. You never know when the hand that feeds you may be the hand on the knife that stabs you in the back.

Some gossip is more taboo than others, of course. This is the gossip that is the most coveted and carefully guarded of all.

For years, no one spoke openly, or at least on the record, about Robert Downey Jr.'s drug problem—until it became a matter of law following his arrest and conviction for substance abuse. Now it's mentioned casually all over town. In such cases, the legal system itself sanctifies the gossip and makes it "credible" and true. Few in town, however, wish to wait until actors get arrested to know how they behave in and around their jobs.

(Paradoxically, while Downey Jr. scores low in professionalism due to his drug run-ins, his professional conduct on a set is highly praised.)

Bonding companies also cultivate a highly reliable grapevine identifying the substance abusers in Hollywood. Courtney Love is one of the handful of actors on such a "watch list." During the shooting of *The People vs. Larry Flynt,* Love's risk factor was considered so high that, to mitigate that risk, the film's insurance company required that someone be present "to baby-sit her twenty-four hours a day, seven days a week," as one executive put it. "But the production company really wanted Courtney to play the role, so they were willing to pay the very high premiums the insurance companies charge for 'watch list' stars."

There is also the taboo of Improper Sexual Orientation For A Major Star. No matter where I went to research this book—offices, cafés, movie sets, back alleys, emergency-stopped elevators—one of the first questions off people's tongues when trading gossip was: "So is Star X really gay?" So much innuendo and outuendo has spread up the Hollywood grapevine regarding this topic that pruning shears are in order. The answer is—maybe. Suffice it to say that the real dirt lies with the star's assistants booking the hotel rooms and the publicist squashing the stories. And the wife, of course.

Which brings us back to my Deep Throat at the café.

He is deep in the throes of unearthing more bones. There are tales of high-level marketing execs traveling thousands of miles to meet with the star, only to be turned away "for no reason" and without so much as a hello, after waiting three days on the set.

There are whispered mentions of the star's secret nocturnal liaisons with members of the same sex in fancy hotel rooms (all of which are scanned at the star's request by former CIA operatives hired to check for bugging devices). When one such nighttime visitor leaks a story to the local press, it is instantly killed by the efficient and ruthless hand of the star's publicist. The star's reputation remains unblemished.

My source acknowledges that he, like all employees of major stars, has signed confidentiality agreements assuring his silence about such personal and highly inflammable information. But his temptation to talk today betrays his frustration with the Hollywood game, and he is unrepentant about his apparent legal breach.

"Why do publicists and managers and agents want people to sign these confidentiality statements?" he offers. "It's not only so they can hide the stars' private lives; it's also because it's a status symbol. 'Brad Pitt has it done so I'm going to have it done, too.' It's part of the internalized glamour of this business."

In other words, keeping secrets in Hollywood is seductive because it maintains status, just as telling them is seductive because it can change that status. It all depends on your vested interests.

"Why do people sign these statements? People here would sign over their firstborn just to get a job as a PA [production assistant] or a chauffeur! People are so desperate in this town—pathetic and desperate and hungry."

And afraid, he adds. Secrets about the stars must be vigilantly guarded because, above all, the stars are investments. There is simply too much hard cash to be made by too many people to risk losing these powerful assets.

"Publicists and agents and managers will always protect their investments," he shrugs. "They'll die to protect their investments. They're too scared to do anything else."

In the end, it all seemed rather cynical and sad. Hollywood is a tribe that has become so industrious and self-destructive that it creates its own monsters to prove the power of its gods. Fear feeds the star system—fear of failure, fear of power, fear of secrets, and gossip about that power—because it is valuable and essential in creating those stars. It is a nearly perfect self-absorbed and self-perpetuating closed system, like the mythical serpent that eats its own tail.

We finish lunch, and as I pay the bill I feel as greasy and used up as the remains of our meal. Then I remember something encouraging said to me by another source—one of the more bearable and intelligent producers who boasts hot stars on her project rosters.

"Let's put this all in perspective," she cautioned. "Nobody will go to war over gossip. Nobody will kidnap somebody's daughter over gossip. It's simply the currency of the business."

I load up another microcassette and breathe a sigh of relief. This town isn't so bad after all.

8

Rx for Tired Stars

The perils of major stardom are plentiful. Oh, for the good old employment safety net of the studio contract system.

Driven by the ever-present bottom line, studios are more willing than ever to consider less powerful actors for their films if a major star proves too expensive or temporarily unavailable. Past bankability is no longer a guarantee for hiring these so-called box office guarantors. Hence, there's more risk with each new role choice a star makes. More stress. More manic phone calls to the agent. More skipped Kundalini Yoga classes.

All the symptoms are there for potential career coronary arrest if such a high-risk lifestyle is not treated properly. The early warning signs:

Intense feelings of insecurity: Stars' careers are less stable, assured, and long-lasting in studio films than ever before.

Overconsumption of fatty substances: Stars' agents are boosting star salaries up at the time when studios are looking to push costs down.

Increased evidence of aging: Many of the most bankable male stars are heading into their fifties, sixties, even seventies. Most movie audiences, on the other hand, are just heading out of their teens and early twenties. Is there still potential for any market romance between the two?

Fear of severe incapacitation: All those barely post-puberty TV heartthrobs are coming up from behind, ready to steal the older guys' thunder, their girls, and their box office.

So what's an aging, overpriced, panic-stricken, soon-to-be-marginalized Hollywood star to do? Such severe performance anxiety would drive any actor to send his manager out for a crate of Career-Strength Viagra.

A better cure is an intense regime of mid-career therapy. The following remedial options are recommended:

1. **Stop blaming the marketplace for your problems. Blame your agent and manager instead.** Rant at them to work harder. Nearly every industry professional we spoke to (except for most agents and managers) agreed that stars' reps are not working hard enough for their clients. About the only thing most agents do is negotiate deals. Whatever happened to finding them work?

   "Agents and managers have got to get infinitely more proactive in finding good material and in helping that material get produced," Miramax's Mark Gill suggests. Adds Peter Dekom, a business consultant, "The problem is that agents today don't want to bring a major star client a film which isn't already fully financed because they're afraid they'll look foolish to their client. Fear of looking foolish has made many agents no longer perform valuable services for actors."

   With looking foolish, of course, comes the agent's fear that a star will ditch him or her and be happily poached by another agent. (Managers aren't known for poaching much.) The end result is that stars don't get enough really good scripts because their agents are filing them where the sun don't shine.

2. **Take more character roles.** After a certain age, those sexy leading roles aren't as feasible as they once were. There's an almost inevitable transition from leading man or lady to a good solid character actor, but most stars don't want to make it.

   Take the case of Robert De Niro: "Bobby's problem is that he considers himself a leading man, so he shuns supporting roles," notes a director. "He could make a fortune playing number two to an A-list star."

   There are a few exceptions. Dustin Hoffman and Jack Nicholson are both sixty-three years old and still nab leading roles. So do Eastwood and Connery, both seventy. (That threshold is a lot earlier for women, usually around forty.) These superstars have managed to avoid the grandpa roles and still are perceived as driving the story lines. Lucky them.

But for most stars, the world changes when those paunches and wrinkles make their dreaded debut. Diversifying into smaller roles, ego humbling as that may be, is the correct remedy here.

3. **Play comedy.** This is one of the best ways to ensure a berth on future power lists like this one. The willingness and ability to take on comic roles is vital to extending career longevity, because comedy is age-resistent. Many female stars have done so successfully; Sharon Stone helped rescue her career by playing the title role in *The Muse.* Some male action stars haven't been so fortunate: Harrison Ford in *Sabrina* (though it hardly hurt his bankability) and Sylvester Stallone, painfully, in *Oscar.*

4. **Stop saying yes to mediocre films.** This means Gene Hackman, Dennis Hopper, and Michael Caine, especially. Those guys just can't say no to any bill-paying job, although Caine vindicated himself nobly with *Little Voice* and then got the big payoff with *The Ciderhouse Rules.* Vince Vaughn (*Psycho*) is doing a great job of following in their footsteps.

   Sure, stars still need to work even when the best offers don't flood their agents' offices. Most fear they've got only three to five years to make the big money before the offers start petering out. How do they know which roles are right for them?

   Take a cue from Sean Connery: At least he has had the sense to wait a couple of years before finding the right role to say "yes" to. Patience is a virtue, especially when the alternative is *Krippendorf's Tribe*—a truly lesser opus for Mr. Richard Dreyfuss.

5. **Read the script first, the role second.** Question: How did Meryl Streep and Jack Nicholson end up starring in a god-awful movie like *Ironweed*?

   Answer: They read the script for their own juicy parts, not for the movie itself.

   A star may love a meaty role, but it should be in a *movie* that people will love, too—or at least will find tolerable enough to squander nine dollars on. "Actors who are going to survive in this business are the ones who know how to read scripts," says business consultant Dekom. "If they don't have that skill set, they'll have to get it or leave it to their managers to pick their roles for them."

6. **Don't play against your bankable "type"—at least not too soon.** When Sharon Stone moved from bimbo to thought-provoking woman of sub-

stance (à la *Intersection, Last Dance, The Mighty*), many in Hollywood saw it as a recipe for box-office poison.

"She's not a thought-provoking or intellectual woman to begin with, so people don't want to see her that way," insists producer Howard Rosenman (*Father of the Bride*), formerly with Brillstein/Grey Prods. "Once actors undercut their own iconography, they're doomed."

That doesn't hold true, of course, for stars lucky enough to boast tremendous range—the Meryl Streeps and Robert DeNiros out there. But for those whom audiences have "branded" early on, it certainly applies. "For Jim Carrey to have become suddenly serious in his recent films was wrong," contends Rosenman. "He should have done it gradually, going from *Liar, Liar* to another calibration up in seriousness. Instead, he went into an unusually serious mode with *The Truman Show* and undercut his whole base. Audiences weren't ready for that, and it hurt him."

In contrast, box-office *wunderkind* Adam Sandler boasts one of the best-managed careers in Hollywood precisely because he has managed it with his core audience in mind. Continues Rosenman: "Look at how carefully he's chosen his roles. In his first movie he never touched a girl. Then, in his following movies, he kissed a girl, and then he was in bed with the girl, and then finally he goes on to fuck the girl. It's brilliant, and Adam himself planned it that way. And that's why he's going to become a major, major star."

Rounding his bases so carefully is one reason why Sandler, the day we spoke to Rosenman, was handed another check for his backend participation in the smash hit *The Waterboy*—this one for a mere $9 million. That's one fine iconography for you.

7. **Lower your price (occasionally) and expand your market to independent films.** A star may be fetching an absurdly astronomical paycheck for his walk-through in the next *Armageddon* rip-off or *Die Hard* clone, but can money really buy him love—of the actor's craft?

Everyone has a little Larry Olivier in him itching to worm its way out. The best way to express that itch is in independent films, where the most challenging and itching parts are.

Bruce Willis is a handy role model here. He has expanded his audience by doing quality "art house" films at a fraction of his asking price, *Pulp Fiction* and *Breakfast of Champions* being two examples. Any star who has ever appeared in a Robert Altman or Woody Allen film has done the same, banking on prestige rather than box office to build his career.

As one marketing executive put it: "It's the Clint Eastwood strategy of doing one for the studios to keep your brand awareness high and then one for yourself."

Clint, by the way, is another example of how stars can stretch those atrophying career muscles: by directing. Mel Gibson, Kevin Costner, Robert DeNiro, Sally Fields, Antonio Banderas, Al Pacino, Jodie Foster, and Warren Beatty have tried it. So, too, have Barbra Streisand, Johnny Depp, Roberto Benigni, Danny DeVito, Sean Penn, Tim Robbins, Kevin Spacey, Edward Norton, and Danny Glover, among many others.

Warning: This cure isn't foolproof. Case histories include infirmities like Sly Stallone's *Cop Land.* In any case, beware of possible infection from a current North American epidemic of overindulgent passion projects from actors-turned-directors.

8. **Hook up with younger stars.** Al Pacino did it with Chris O'Donnell and he won an Oscar. Paul Newman matched up with Tom Cruise for *The Color of Money* and won an Oscar nomination.

It's the old Mae West syndrome: Surround yourself with young bucks and they'll forget you're an aging diva or that you ever started taking those hormone pills in the first place. There's no better way to beef up your eighteen-to-twenty-five-year-old male demographic.

Like an overdose of Viagra, this cure is not recommended for use with very nubile romantic co-leads. Michael Douglas paired up with Gwyneth Paltrow in *A Perfect Murder* and "came off looking like a hoary old cradle robber," declared an executive. Ditto Warren Beatty with Halle Berry in *Bullworth.* Robert Redford tried it to equally delightful effect in those love scenes for *Up Close and Personal.* Sighed a female fan: "It was like watching Michelle Pfeiffer make out with Grandpa."

THE
B
LIST

Roberto Benigni

Rank 106   **Bankability 55**

Real Name	Roberto Benigni
D.O.B.	10/27/52
Place of Birth	Misericordia, Arezzo, Italy
Contact	(Atty) John Delaverson, Loeb & Loeb

Willingness to Travel/Promote	Professionalism	Career Mgmt	Talent
76	80	82	74

INSIDE DIRT

He's a good actor, but he really has got to calm down.

- Some people in the business are getting pissed off at his histrionics.

- We journalists were onto his schtick a long time ago. He pretends not to speak English but he speaks it fluently. Even his slapstick can get old fast if you've seen it a hundred times before—which obviously the Oscar audience hadn't.

- A friend caught him on the street flipping out of his staged accent and talking practically like an American.

- At the end of the day there's not a lot of room for him in the world of high-profile roles. He should stick to character comedy.

- He epitomizes over-the-top.

Star Power

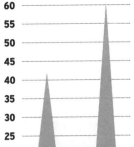

Values shown: 60, 55, 50, 45, 40, 35, 30, 25, 20, 15 — years 1997 1998 1999

Box Office Bait

MOVIE	STUDIO	N.AMERICAN GROSS	RELEASE
Life Is Beautiful	Miramax	$57,216,351	10/23/9
Son of the Pink Panther	MGM	$2,365,290	8/27/93
Night on Earth	FL	$2,011,294	5/1/92
Down by Law	Island	$1,288,149	9/20/86
Johnny Stecchino	NL	$616,854	10/9/92

Career Trajectory

Rupert Everett

Rank 107 **Bankability 55**

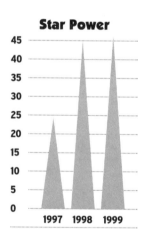

Real Name	Rupert Everett
D.O.B.	5/29/59
Place of Birth	Norfolk, England
Contact	(A) Nick Styne/Aleen Keshishian, ICM

Willingness to Travel/Promote	Professionalism	Career Mgmt	Talent
80	**82**	**80**	**79**

INSIDE DIRT

When he came out and played gay he really became a star.

- He's one of the only male stars in Hollywood who can come out of the closet and get away with a straight relationship on screen—look at *An Ideal Husband.* He almost shagged Julia Roberts in *My Best Friend's Wedding* and nobody said "yuck."

- He just shot *Pink Triangle,* a documentary about gays in the Holocaust. He was sweet, and he even thanked the crew. He's never a diva.

- Is he playing his career right by doing more gay-oriented projects? No.

- He owes his brilliant career a lot to friends like Madonna and Julia Roberts. They bond with him because he's a safe date and an amusing hunk, so they put him in their movies.

- What a comeback star.

- Ooooph. Sexy.

Star Power

A chart showing values 0 to 45 for years 1997, 1998, 1999.

Box Office Bait

MOVIE	STUDIO	N.AMERICAN GROSS	RELEASE
My Best Friend's Wedding	Sony/TS	$127,120,029	6/20/97
Shakespeare in Love	Miramax	$100,241,322	12/11/98
Inspector Gadget	BV	$64,779,601	7/23/99
An Ideal Husband	Miramax	$16,454,382	6/18/99
A Midsummer Night's Dream	Fox Search	$16,027,451	5/14/99

Career Trajectory

Daniel Day-Lewis

Rank 108   **Bankability 55**

Real Name	Daniel Michael Blake Day-Lewis
D.O.B.	4/29/57
Place of Birth	London, England
Contact	ICM (London)

Willingness to Travel/Promote	Professionalism	Career Mgmt	Talent
53	76	49	92

INSIDE DIRT

What career? He's off making shoes in Italy.

- He's now working as a cobbler for a famous shoemaker in Florence—and it's not for a movie role. He's tired of the pressures of being a star. He wants to learn a trade that won't upset his psyche.

- He's perceived as probably the highest-quality actor in the world. But his career hasn't been as fanciful as his talent.

- Doing all that heavy drama hurt him in Japan.

- You have to go to extreme lengths to create the right acting environment for Daniel's work. He's obsessively compulsive. Before shooting a prison scene, they had to find him a real prisoner's hood and put him in solitary confinement for a night.

- He's a nineteenth-century recluse stuck in a twentieth-century industry.

Star Power

	1997	1998	1999

(Chart axis values: 80, 75, 70, 65, 60, 55, 50, 45, 40, 35)

Box Office Bait

MOVIE	STUDIO	N.AMERICAN GROSS	RELEASE
Last of the Mohicans	Fox	$72,155,275	9/25/92
Gandhi	Columbia	$55,962,711	1982
The Age of Innocence	Columbia	$31,925,717	9/17/93
In The Name of the Father	Univ	$25,096,862	12/29/93
A Room with a View	CINECOM	$20,766,644	3/7/86

Career Trajectory

Gérard Depardieu

Rank 109　**Bankability 54**

Real Name	Gérard Depardieu
D.O.B.	12/27/48
Place of Birth	Chateauroux, Indre, France
Contact	(A) John Ptak CAA

Willingness to Travel/Promote 60　**Professionalism** 58　**Career Mgmt** 70　**Talent** 65

INSIDE DIRT

French. Esoteric. And past.

- It's a pretty sad time in Hollywood if he's considered the biggest French star. In reality, there are at least five other top male French actors that are much more bankable, more respected, and easier to work with than Gérard.

- He's clearly a character actor. He's not a leading man in American movies, and no one in Hollywood cares if he's a leading man in French movies.

- He's crossed over, but he's very typecast and is spending a lot of time doing French films. That's where he can utilize his tremendous energies better, as in *Cyrano*. He's still not very comfortable with English.

- The most powerful actor in France? Hardly. Try Daniel Auteuil. Ever heard of him?

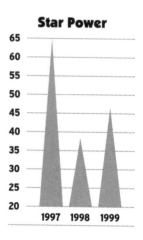

Star Power

65, 60, 55, 50, 45, 40, 35, 30, 25, 20

1997　1998　1999

Box Office Bait

MOVIE	STUDIO	N.AMERICAN GROSS	RELEASE
The Man in the Iron Mask	MGM	$56,968,169	3/13/98
Green Card	BV	$28,576,997	12/19/90
My Father the Hero	BV	$25,479,558	2/4/94
1492: Conquest of Paradise	Para	$7,148,891	10/8/92
Cyrano de Bergerac	Orion	$5,804,286	11/16/90

Career Trajectory

Robert Duvall Rank 110 Bankability 54

Real Name Robert Duvall
D.O.B. 1/5/31
Place of Birth San Diego, California, USA
Contact (A) Todd Harris, WMA

Willingness to Travel/Promote	Professionalism	Career Mgmt	Talent
62	80	64	78

INSIDE DIRT

He's an actor's actor.

♦ He picks really good roles, shows up on time, and is ready to go. He's a good guy.

♦ He's review-proof in a way that Dustin Hoffman and others from the New York method acting school are; they're almost never criticized even when they give a bad performance. That's because they've spent their whole careers working to be perceived as "actors."

♦ When he directed *The Apostle*, it was an extraordinary performance in an extraordinarily mediocre script.

♦ Even in a movie like *Deep Impact*, he brings a certain gravity to the role that distinguishes him.

♦ He's supposed to be unbelievably difficult, although my dealings with him on *The Apostle* were fantastic.

♦ Robert is great as a supporting cast member, not as a lead.

Star Power

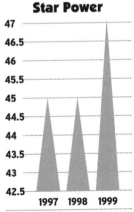

| | 1997 | 1998 | 1999 |

Box Office Bait

MOVIE	STUDIO	N.AMERICAN GROSS	RELEASE
Deep Impact	Para	$140,464,664	5/8/98
The Godfather (with re-issue)	Para	$136,228,625	3/15/72
Phenomenon	BV	$104,632,573	7/3/96
Apocalypse Now (with re-issue)	MGM	$84,456,197	8/15/79
Days of Thunder	Para	$82,663,996	6/27/90

Career Trajectory

Morgan Freeman

Rank 111 **Bankability 54**

Real Name	Morgan Freeman
D.O.B.	6/1/37
Place of Birth	Memphis, Tennessee, USA
Contact	(A) Jeff Hunter WMA (NY)

Willingness to Travel/Promote 70   **Professionalism** 84   **Career Mgmt** 75   **Talent** 80

INSIDE DIRT

A safe black actor.

- Even though he's older, he's one of the best actors working today, black or white. He's the black actor with the greatest career longevity.

- His career is protected by his high level of craft.

- When Morgan is in your movie, you're announcing you have a classy film.

- He's usually very cautious about what he commits to.

- A terrific actor and great guy. He's had a lot of success at a mature age and has a full life outside of his celebritydom. He's a real class act.

- Morgan Freeman won't do anything for love. It's always about money.

Star Power

Year	Value
1997	56
1998	58
1999	64

(Chart scale: 46, 48, 50, 52, 54, 56, 58, 60, 62, 64)

Box Office Bait

MOVIE	STUDIO	N.AMERICAN GROSS	RELEASE
Robin Hood: Prince of Thieves	WB	$165,493,908	6/14/91
Deep Impact	Para	$140,464,664	5/8/98
Driving Miss Daisy	WB	$106,593,296	12/13/89
Unforgiven	WB	$101,101,229	8/7/92
Seven	NL	$100,123,974	9/22/95

Career Trajectory

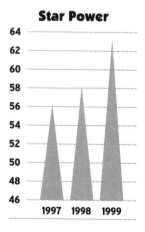

Kevin Kline Rank **112** Bankability **54**

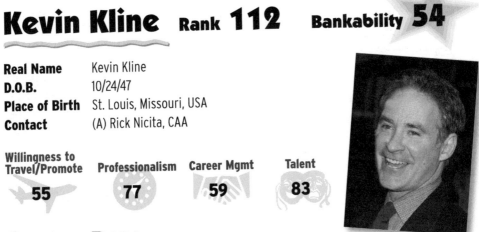

Real Name Kevin Kline
D.O.B. 10/24/47
Place of Birth St. Louis, Missouri, USA
Contact (A) Rick Nicita, CAA

Willingness to Travel/Promote	Professionalism	Career Mgmt	Talent
55	**77**	**59**	**83**

INSIDE DIRT

A terrific actor who has probably been hurt by *Wild Wild West*.

♦ He's a very deep and smart guy. The problem is, he's never going to be a megastar.

♦ *In and Out* proved he can be funny and commercial. But when he's in bad material like *Wild Wild West,* not even he can save it. Oh my god that was awful.

♦ A lot of leading men wouldn't have taken the gay role in *In and Out*. But Kevin isn't afraid to take parts like that.

♦ Talented, totally professional, and nice. He puts his personal life first. He'd like to be more of a leading man, but he knows he's really a character actor.

♦ I'd cut off my little finger to work with Kevin Kline because I think he's a true genius of an actor.

Star Power

60	
55	
50	
45	
40	
35	
30	
25	
20	
15	
	1997 1998 1999

Box Office Bait

MOVIE	STUDIO	N.AMERICAN GROSS	RELEASE
Wild Wild West	WB	$110,726,211	6/30/99
The Hunchback of Notre Dame (voice)	BV	$100,137,089	6/21/96
In and Out	Para	$63,855,317	9/19/97
Dave	WB	$63,193,194	5/7/93
A Fish Called Wanda	MGM	$59,991,944	7/15/88

Career Trajectory

Liv Tyler

Rank 113 **Bankability 54**

Real Name	Liv Tyler
D.O.B.	7/1/77
Place of Birth	Portland, Maine, USA
Contact	(A) Scott Landis, CAA

Willingness to Travel/Promote **64**

Professionalism **67**

Career Mgmt **48**

Talent **54**

INSIDE DIRT

She makes very old men feel autumnal.

♦ She's a teen fave. She's a Pantene shampoo goddess and a dirty-old-man goddess.

♦ Of all the ingenues, she's the most vulnerable to a career plunge. She's overexposed herself in too many films without a breakout role.

♦ She looks like someone out of a Gainsborough painting, this rosy-cheeked cow maiden from the heath. She seems to fit more into period films.

♦ I think she's a former flavor of the month.

♦ She needs to be in a class-act film where she's not the sex object and doesn't have to rely solely on her charm.

♦ She really has to grow up. Buyers don't care about her yet.

♦ She's incredibly talented. You can't take your eyes off her.

♦ Movie stardom will happen for her. She's got the look.

Star Power

Year	Value
1997	41
1998	38
1999	46

(chart values: 28–46 scale)

Box Office Bait

MOVIE	STUDIO	N.AMERICAN GROSS	RELEASE
Armageddon	BV	$201,578,182	7/1/98
That Thing You Do!	Fox	$25,731,918	10/4/96
Cookie's Fortune	October	$10,856,097	4/2/99
U-Turn	Sony/TS	$6,658,193	10/3/97
Inventing The Abbotts	Fox	$5,737,888	4/4/97

Career Trajectory

Jennifer Love Hewitt

Rank 114   **Bankability 54**

Real Name	Jennifer Love Hewitt
D.O.B.	2/21/79
Place of Birth	Waco, Texas, USA
Contact	(A) Ames Cushing, WMA

Willingness to Travel/Promote	Professionalism	Career Mgmt	Talent
64	68	73	54

INSIDE DIRT

She hasn't been in that breakout movie yet.

♦ She could become a star, but the chances are equal that she won't. She's been in enough roles where the audience knows her, but she's never been the force behind the film.

♦ She could break out of the pack more than, say, Sarah Michelle Gellar or Rachel Leigh Cook.

♦ If she plays her career correctly and develops it in a mature way, she could give Julia Roberts a run for her money. She still has time. She's young.

♦ I'm sorry, she's just not interesting. To think that *she* played Audrey Hepburn in that TV movie! Not since Faye Dunaway played Joan Crawford has there been such inadvertent comedy in casting.

Star Power

45
40
35
30
25
20
15
10
5
0

1997 1998 1999

Box Office Bait

MOVIE	STUDIO	N.AMERICAN GROSS	RELEASE
I Know What You Did Last Summer	Sony	$72,586,134	10/17/97
Sister Act 2	BV	$57,319,029	12/10/93
I Still Know What You Did Last Summer	Sony	$39,989,008	11/13/98
Can't Hardly Wait	Sony	$25,605,015	6/12/98
House Arrest	MGM	$7,031,471	8/14/96

Career Trajectory

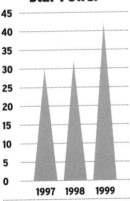

Kenneth Branagh

Rank 115　　**Bankability 53**

Real Name	Kenneth Branagh
D.O.B.	12/10/60
Place of Birth	Belfast, Northern Ireland
Contact	(A) Rick Nicita CAA

Willingness to Travel/Promote	Professionalism	Career Mgmt	Talent
70	85	62	81

INSIDE DIRT

He has an unerring sense of what is desired of him in a scene.

♦ Besides his artistic integrity, he's so terribly bright. He knows so much about so many of the jobs involved on the production that he's invaluable.

♦ He's superb in working with children. In *The Gingerbread Man,* when the director wasn't nearby, he became the parental figure, a kind of director on the spot for them. Ken had an instant understanding of this.

♦ He's eminently approachable and a great listener.

♦ He has no star syndrome whatsoever.

♦ Right after *Dead Again* he rushed back here to England to do projects locally, instead of Stateside. I think he could have had a big career if he had "gone Hollywood."

♦ His natural resources are only tapped to about 70 percent.

Star Power

A bar chart titled "Star Power" with a vertical axis from 25 to 70. Bars for 1997 (approx. 65), 1998 (approx. 47), and 1999 (approx. 44).

<table>
<tr><th colspan="4">Box Office Bait</th></tr>
<tr><th>MOVIE</th><th>STUDIO</th><th>N.AMERICAN GROSS</th><th>RELEASE</th></tr>
<tr><td>Wild Wild West</td><td>WB</td><td>$110,726,211</td><td>6/30/99</td></tr>
<tr><td>Dead Again</td><td>Para</td><td>$37,378,123</td><td>8/23/91</td></tr>
<tr><td>Much Ado About Nothing</td><td>Goldwyn</td><td>$22,548,086</td><td>5/7/93</td></tr>
<tr><td>Mary Shelley's Frankenstein</td><td>Tri-Star</td><td>$22,006,296</td><td>11/4/94</td></tr>
<tr><td>Henry V</td><td>S Goldwyn</td><td>$10,161,099</td><td>11/8/89</td></tr>
</table>

Career Trajectory

Juliette Binoche

Rank 116 **Bankability 53**

Real Name	Juliette Binoche
D.O.B.	3/9/64
Place of Birth	Paris, France
Contact	(A) Adam Isaacs UTA

Willingness to Travel/Promote
72

Professionalism
82

Career Mgmt
71

Talent
70

INSIDE DIRT

She hasn't crossed over to American audiences.

♦ She's a major international star. Her forte is France and Germany.

♦ The French did a great job of exporting her to the States. They're not so good at sending over male stars.

♦ She should do more intelligent, commercial English-language movies as a co-lead or a lead.

♦ Who is she? I haven't a clue. The *Oscar*?

♦ She's in control of managing her own career and isn't being dictated to by others.

♦ She still likes to do her little French art films, and good for her.

♦ She's very beautiful and very talented and God would I like her phone number.

Star Power

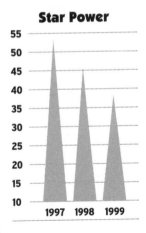

1997 1998 1999

Box Office Bait

MOVIE	STUDIO	N.AMERICAN GROSS	RELEASE
The English Patient	Miramax	$78,651,430	11/15/96
Damage	NL	$7,522,045	12/23/92
The Unbearable Lightness of Being	Orion	$9,821,042	1988
The Horseman on the Roof	Miramax	$1,334,174	5/17/96
White	Miramax	$1,235,434	6/10/94

Career Trajectory

Jeremy Irons Rank 117 Bankability 53

Real Name	Jeremy John Irons
D.O.B.	9/19/48
Place of Birth	Cowes, Isle of Wight, England
Contact	(A) Fred Specktor, CAA

Willingness to Travel/Promote	Professionalism	Career Mgmt	Talent
58	72	52	78

INSIDE DIRT

He's chosen his roles much better than his movies.

♦ He doesn't work much—what's he done after *Lolita*?

♦ He picks good directors and good casts. He's always in good surroundings.

♦ He's another one of these actors who presence in a film guarantees it won't work, like *Damaged*. Ever since he played Claus Von Bulow, he hasn't been really good in anything.

♦ He's so attracted to these roles which are ice cold, so who cares?

♦ He's one of our generation's great actors. He always shines whether the movie is good or bad.

♦ As a character type, he's the classy British gent who looks like he has never digested his food properly.

♦ He's got to stop playing those troubled, sex-repressed Brits. Enough already!

Star Power

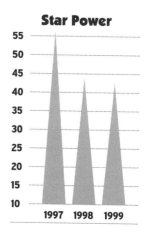

1997 1998 1999

Box Office Bait			
MOVIE	STUDIO	N.AMERICAN GROSS	RELEASE
The Lion King (voice)	BV	$312,855,561	6/15/94
Die Hard with a Vengeance	Fox	$100,003,359	5/19/95
The Man in the Iron Mask	MGM	$56,968,169	3/13/98
The Mission	WB	$17,218,023	10/31/86
Reversal of Fortune	WB	$15,353,573	10/17/90

Career Trajectory

Ewan McGregor

Rank 118   **Bankability 53**

Real Name	Ewan Gordon McGregor
D.O.B.	3/31/71
Place of Birth	Crieff, Pertshire, Scotland
Contact	(A) Brandt Joel, CAA

Willingness to Travel/Promote	Professionalism	Career Mgmt	Talent
70	**77**	**68**	**56**

INSIDE DIRT

He's taken the Michael Caine route: Never turn down a role.

♦ He's made too many films of a medicore nature, like *Rogue Trader*. That lessens his value.

♦ He comes off as a bit punk and has more of a problem with romantic roles.

♦ *Emma* proved his versatility as an actor.

♦ He should be in more romantic movies. He's sexy and interesting.

♦ He's especially strong in the UK and Germany. France is dicey.

♦ He supports his films and he's fantastic to work with.

♦ The jury's out on McGregor. He's not a traditional leading man—he doesn't have the looks.

♦ He's not much bigger after *Star Wars*. After all, that franchise didn't help Mark Hamil's career much, did it?

Star Power

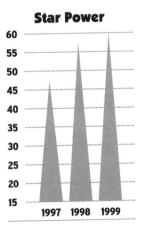

| 60 |
| 55 |
| 50 |
| 45 |
| 40 |
| 35 |
| 30 |
| 25 |
| 20 |
| 15 |
| 1997 1998 1999 |

Box Office Bait

MOVIE	STUDIO	N.AMERICAN GROSS	RELEASE
Star Wars Episode One: The Phantom Menace	Fox	$412,775,151	5/19/99
Emma	Miramax	$22,231,658	8/2/96
Trainspotting	Miramax	$16,525,842	7/19/96
Little Voice	Miramax	$4,595,000	12/4/98
The Life Less Ordinary	Fox	$4,266,243	10/24/97

Career Trajectory

Kristin Scott-Thomas

Rank 119 **Bankability 53**

Real Name	Kristin Scott Thomas
D.O.B.	5/24/60
Place of Birth	Redruth, Cornwall, England
Contact	(A) Kevin Huvane/Bryan Lourd CAA

Willingness to Travel/Promote	Professionalism	Career Mgmt	Talent
71	85	69	72

INSIDE DIRT

She's more bankable in Europe than America.

♦ A class act who lends immediate credibility to a film.

♦ She's not gregarious. That may inhibit her ability to work the town, although I doubt that's a high priority for her. But everybody likes her.

♦ On the set, she hits her marks over and over again. She's incredibly professional and sweet. She brings up the quality of other actors working with her.

♦ Like Binoche or Emma Thompson, she appears to be in control of managing her own career and isn't being dictated to by others.

♦ After *The English Patient,* she should try movies where she shines in a different capacity, like comedies or romantic comedies.

Star Power

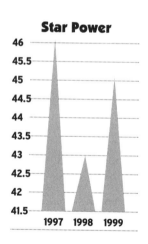

Chart values: 46, 45.5, 45, 44.5, 44, 43.5, 43, 42.5, 42, 41.5 — 1997 1998 1999

Box Office Bait

MOVIE	STUDIO	N.AMERICAN GROSS	RELEASE
Mission: Impossible	Para	$180,981,866	5/22/96
The English Patient	Miramax	$78,651,430	11/15/96
The Horse Whisperer	BV	$75,383,563	5/15/98
Four Weddings and a Funeral	GRAM	$52,636,671	3/9/94
Under the Cherry Moon	WB	$10,090,429	7/2/86

Career Trajectory

Heather Graham

Rank 120 **Bankability 53**

Real Name Heather Joan Graham
D.O.B. 1/29/70
Place of Birth Milwaukee, Wisconsin, USA
Contact (A) Mike Davis, CAA (M) Heather Reynolds, First Artist (BM) (Business Manager) Erica DeYoung–Gudvi, Chapnick & Oppenheim

Willingness to Travel/Promote	Professionalism	Career Mgmt	Talent
75	72	79	59

INSIDE DIRT

Is everyone going crackers over Graham?

- After playing Rollergirl and the nymphette in *Bowfinger*, she's going to skate far.
- She's no Goldie Hawn.
- At least real comediennes like Goldie and Carole Lombard could play ditzy with depth. But Graham has no depth. She just plays cookie-cutter roles.
- Yes, *Austin Powers* was huge. But what's better—to be a co-lead in something that's big and have Mike Myers get all the credit, or to be a lead in something smaller and get the credit yourself?
- Heather should look to the path of Cameron Diaz and walk there. Cameron has a great comedic sense—and comedy has been the entry for women to become superstars more than any other genre.
- She's being marketed as the perfect balance of naughty and nice.

Star Power

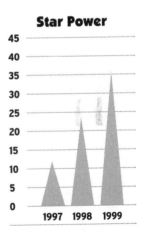

Chart showing values for 1997, 1998, 1999 with y-axis from 0 to 45.

Box Office Bait

MOVIE	STUDIO	N.AMERICAN GROSS	RELEASE
Austin Powers: The Spy who Shagged Me	New Line	$205,444,716	6/11/99
Lost In Space	New Line	$69,117,629	4/3/98
Bowfinger	Universal	$66,365,290	8/13/99
Boogie Nights	New Line	$26,400,640	10/12/97
License to Drive	Fox	$21,066,484	7/6/88

Career Trajectory

Chris Rock   Rank **121**   Bankability **53**

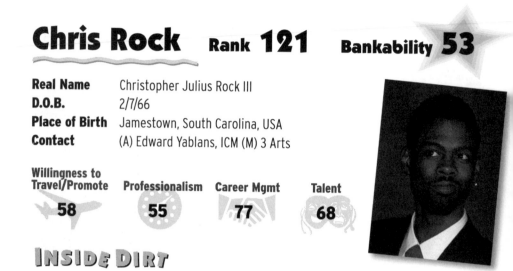

Real Name	Christopher Julius Rock III
D.O.B.	2/7/66
Place of Birth	Jamestown, South Carolina, USA
Contact	(A) Edward Yablans, ICM (M) 3 Arts

Willingness to Travel/Promote	Professionalism	Career Mgmt	Talent
58	**55**	**77**	**68**

INSIDE DIRT

Of all the black actors, he's the most likely to cross over.

♦ It's the Eddie Murphy syndrome: You make enough people laugh out there and you've got star potential.

♦ He and Chris Tucker are going to be gigantic in the foreign market.

♦ Chris is really clever with his book and TV and movie deals. But it's going to be very hard for him to sustain a film career, because the stuff he's best at is the political/social commentary kind of comedy. Those aren't the kind of roles that come easily in Hollywood.

♦ The marketplace is pretty racist. It doesn't tolerate too many black stars at the same time, and right now Eddie Murphy and Will Smith are running away with it.

Star Power

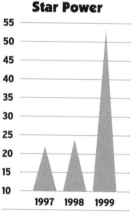

Box Office Bait

MOVIE	STUDIO	N.AMERICAN GROSS	RELEASE
The Rock	BV	$134,069,511	6/7/96
Face Off	Para	$112,273,211	6/27/97
Con Air	BV	$100,927,613	6/6/97
Moonstruck	MGM	$79,765,241	12/16/87
City of Angels	WB	$78,647,175	4/10/98

Career Trajectory

Cher

Rank 122   **Bankability 52**

Real Name Cherilyn Sarkisian LaPierre
D.O.B. 5/20/46
Place of Birth El Centro, California, USA
Contact (A) Toni Howard/Risa Shapiro, ICM

Willingness to Travel/Promote	Professionalism	Career Mgmt	Talent
50	53	43	66

INSIDE DIRT

I wouldn't have her headline the next summer blockbuster.

◆ Cher's screen presence is great, but the film's storyline and cast have to be greater before she's a bankable factor.

◆ She knows how to use the press. She's traded some intimacies—no boyfriend, not much sex, a gay daughter, and plastic surgery—to gain the admiration of her fans. Consequently, there's a new, younger generation that's embracing her.

◆ *Tea with Mussolini* was served very cold.

◆ Her hit song definitely put some casting heat back on her.

◆ She canceled my project five times before deciding to do it—and then she didn't show up on the set. She's horrible to work with, but I like her personally.

◆ At fifty-something, she's still got this timeless face—let's not talk about the nips and tucks needed to create it.

Star Power

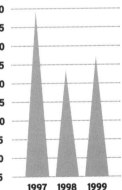

50
45
40
35
30
25
20
15
10
5
        1997 1998 1999

Box Office Bait

MOVIE	STUDIO	N.AMERICAN GROSS	RELEASE
Moonstruck	MGM	$79,765,241	12/16/87
The Witches of Eastwick	WB	$63,749,955	6/12/87
Mask	Univ	$48,245,400	3/8/85
Mermaids	Orion	$35,124,004	12/14/90
Silkwood	Fox	$39,611,111	12/14/83

Career Trajectory

Geena Davis Rank **123** Bankability **52**

Real Name	Virginia Elizabeth Davis
D.O.B.	1/21/57
Place of Birth	Wareham, Massachusetts, USA
Contact	(A) Kevin Huvane, CAA

Willingness to Travel/Promote	Professionalism	Career Mgmt	Talent
50	**64**	**32**	**57**

INSIDE DIRT

One more dud and it will be good night, sweetheart.

♦ A gifted comedienne who's too daffy and comic-book looking for leading roles.

♦ She ruined her career by taking off with Renny Harlin.

♦ We don't care about her at all in France.

♦ She's a complete pro. If necessary, she'll do another take till the cows come home.

♦ She'a always the same in everything. She doesn't have that chameleon quality.

♦ She needs to pull a rabbit out of her hat fast—and it won't be playing opposite a mouse in *Stuart Little*.

♦ When you're playing bow and arrows seven hours a day—for the Olympics, not a movie—your career is in trouble.

♦ If she hits the right role, she's golden.

♦ She has a no-breast clause in her contract, but she still gets Sharon Stone rejects.

Star Power

60		
55		
50		
45		
40		
35		
30		
25		
20		
15		
1997	1998	1999

Box Office Bait

MOVIE	STUDIO	N.AMERICAN GROSS	RELEASE
Tootsie	Columbia	$177,200,000	12/17/82
A League of Their Own	Columbia	$107,439,000	7/1/92
Beetlejuice	WB	$73,707,461	3/30/88
Fletch	Univ	$50,641,507	5/31/85
Thelma & Louise	MGM	$43,295,821	5/24/91

Career Trajectory

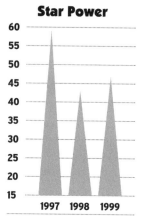

Joseph Fiennes

Rank 124 **Bankability 52**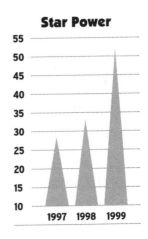

Real Name	Joseph Alberic Fiennes
D.O.B.	5/27/70
Place of Birth	Salisbury, Wiltshire, England
Contact	(A) Peter Levine, CAA

Willingness to Travel/Promote 51 **Professionalism** 61 **Career Mgmt** 65 **Talent** 73

INSIDE DIRT

He doesn't support his films.

♦ He's so much more fun to watch than his earnest brother. In *Shakespeare in Love* he has a boyish quality and lightness. If Ralph had done that part, it would have seemed like the soufflé had fallen.

♦ What a pain in the ass to work with! Thank god he has a warmer screen presence than his brother, which is to say he's above zero. He's astonishingly self-centered, even by actor standards.

♦ He'll have a longer career than Ralph.

♦ For *Shakespeare in Love,* he refused to do one lick of publicity. No wonder he didn't get an Oscar nomination, even though it was a great performance. I believe he'll have a short career.

♦ He's a decent actor and girls love watching him. Is that enough for stardom? No.

Star Power

	1997	1998	1999

(chart values on y-axis: 10, 15, 20, 25, 30, 35, 40, 45, 50, 55)

Box Office Bait

MOVIE	STUDIO	N.AMERICAN GROSS	RELEASE
Shakespeare in Love	Miramax	$100,241,322	12/11/98
Elizabeth	GRAM	$30,012,990	11/6/98
Stealing Beauty	Fox/S	$4,718,580	6/14/96

Career Trajectory

Salma Hayek

Rank 125 **Bankability 52**

Real Name	Salma Hayek Jimenez
D.O.B.	9/2/66
Place of Birth	Coatzacoalcos, Veracruz, Mexico
Contact	(A) John Fogelman/Theresa Peters, WMA (M)

Willingness to Travel/Promote	Professionalism	Career Mgmt	Talent
72	76	75	62

INSIDE DIRT

She's got two trump cards: exotic looks and comic talent.

♦ She's top loaded—with charisma.

♦ She was exploited more than she needed to be in *Wild Wild West*.

♦ With the increasing importance of the Latin market in this country, she's poised to take off.

♦ Salma has to take a couple of really good roles or she'll be stuck in the bombshell category. That's why we've cast her as Freda Kahlo in *Freda*.

♦ I'm not convinced she has the talent to go the distance.

♦ She's smart. She knows she won't be a bombshell forever, so she's producing TV for companies like Telemundo.

♦ Professionally, she's a 10. She returns calls, she follows through, and she's great on the set.

♦ What can I say? I'm in love with her.

Star Power

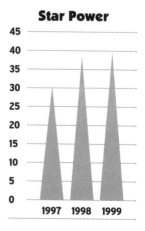

	1997	1998	1999

Box Office Bait

MOVIE	STUDIO	N.AMERICAN GROSS	RELEASE
Wild Wild West	WB	$110,726,211	6/30/99
The Faculty	Miramax/D	$40,064,955	12/25/98
Fools Rush In	Sony/C	$29,481,428	2/14/97
From Dusk Till Dawn	Miramax/D	$25,836,616	1/19/96
Desperado	Sony/C	$25,405,445	8/25/95

Career Trajectory

Christina Ricci Rank 126 Bankability 51

Real Name	Christina Ricci
D.O.B.	2/12/80
Place of Birth	Santa Monica, California, USA
Contact	(A) Toni Howard/Jason Barrett, ICM

Willingness to Travel/Promote	Professionalism	Career Mgmt	Talent
65	76	73	74

INSIDE DIRT

She's very much of a Sundance darling, like Parker Posey.

◆ If you put her in a good, small, and ambitious project, she's magic—witness *The Opposite of Sex*.

◆ I predicted *200 Cigarettes* would be a bomb. It's the idea of putting quirky indie actors into MTV-type movies where they all play crazies. Just throw enough of these films against the wall and hope one of them sticks.

◆ As a buyer, I definitely keep her on my radar.

◆ She has mild value overseas.

◆ She brought depth to her role in *The Ice Storm*. But she seems to play the same sarcastic, disenfranchised girl in every film.

◆ I'm concerned about her physique. She's pudgy at the moment.

◆ Very original taste in material. *Buffalo 66* showed she wasn't afraid of taking risks.

◆ Christina's a pretty radical hardcore chick.

Star Power

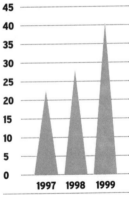

45
40
35
30
25
20
15
10
5
0

1997 1998 1999

Box Office Bait

MOVIE	STUDIO	N. AMERICAN GROSS	RELEASE
The Addams Family	Para	$113,379,166	11/22/91
Casper	Univ	$100,280,870	5/26/95
Small Soldiers (voice)	Dreamworks	$55,143,823	7/10/98
Addams Family Values	Para	$45,703,556	11/19/93
Mermaids	Orion	$35,124,004	12/14/90

Career Trajectory

Freddie Prinze, Jr.

Rank 127 **Bankability 51**

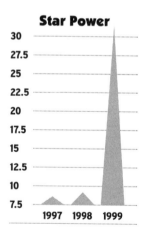

Real Name	Freddie Prinze, Jr.
D.O.B.	3/8/76
Place of Birth	Los Angeles, California, USA
Contact	(A) Jane Berliner, CAA

Willingness to Travel/Promote	Professionalism	Career Mgmt	Talent
68	**81**	**74**	**70**

INSIDE DIRT

He's on his way to something major.

- He's on the up and up. He's right behind Adam Sandler in his off-the-edge, off-kilter comic potential.

- I found him very, very bland in *Wing Commander*. And our company actually bought the film.

- I think he's a passing phenomenon.

- *Wing Commander* was the best-selling video game in Germany, which helps him there. But anyone could have played the lead, including my mother.

- He's the male equivalent of Sarah Michelle Geller—a "maybe" as a crossover star.

- Freddie is a charmer and a lovely guy. In *She's All That* he wasn't just the lead—he was the best-regarded person on the set, the one whom the other actors turned to as a confidant and a leader.

- Twelve-year-old girls swoon over him.

Star Power

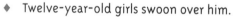

30
27.5
25
22.5
20
17.5
15
12.5
10
7.5

1997 1998 1999

Box Office Bait

MOVIE	STUDIO	N.AMERICAN GROSS	RELEASE
I Know What You Did Last Summer	Sony/C	$72,586,134	10/17/97
She's All That	Miramax	$63,319,509	1/29/99
I Still Know What You Did Last Summer	Sony	$39,989,008	11/13/98
Wing Commander	Fox	$11,576,087	3/12/99
To Gillian On Her 37th Birthday	Tri-Starumph	$4,185,584	10/18/96

Career Trajectory

Jessica Lange Rank 128 Bankability 51

Real Name Jesse Lange
D.O.B. 4/20/49
Place of Birth Cloquet, Minnesota, USA
Contact (A) Toni Howard, ICM

Willingness to Travel/Promote	Professionalism	Career Mgmt	Talent

| 45 | 70 | 50 | 79 |

INSIDE DIRT

She's no longer a leading lady, even though she wants to be.

♦ For such a powerful actress and great beauty, it's stunning that she isn't getting more parts. It's the same problem with Sally Field, Meryl Streep, and Glenn Close—all those aging leading ladies on the CAA client list.

♦ Jessica can't sustain a movie anymore—only a Movie of the Week.

♦ She refused to do my film because she didn't want to play a fifty-year-old mom. But I've got news for her: She doesn't look like she can play women in their forties anymore.

♦ When I see her I think, Can't I spend the weekend with her? She's so earth-motherish and sexy. For us Jewish guys, she's like this shiksa goddess.

Star Power

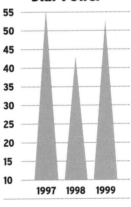

55
50
45
40
35
30
25
20
15
10
1997 1998 1999

Box Office Bait

MOVIE	STUDIO	N.AMERICAN GROSS	RELEASE
Tootsie	Columbia	$177,200,000	12/17/82
Cape Fear	Univ	$79,118,315	11/13/91
All That Jazz	Fox	$44,511,111	1979
Rob Roy	MGM	$31,369,938	4/7/95
Crimes of The Heart	DeG	$22,841,950	12/12/86

Career Trajectory

Michael Keaton

Rank 129 **Bankability 51**

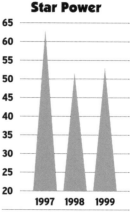

Real Name Michael John Douglas
D.O.B. 9/5/51
Place of Birth Coraopolis, Pennsylvania, USA
Contact (A) Chris Andrews, ICM

Willingness to Travel/Promote	Professionalism	Career Mgmt	Talent
49	80	50	74

INSIDE DIRT

He has great range, but he needs better vehicles to show it off.

♦ Keaton just doesn't have international appeal. He's like white bread. He fades into the wallpaper.

♦ Poor Michael Keaton. A while ago he got that hair transplant in the front of his head. Now his hair is receding in the back. He wears this baseball cap on the set, and when he takes it off he looks like a poodle.

♦ On *Pacific Heights* he was always trying to be very cool. As a crew member, you couldn't have much eye contact with him. We didn't warm up to him.

♦ He could still be another Robin Williams: someone who began as a wild comedian, then made movies that crossed over into other genres. But it sure hasn't happened yet.

Star Power

Chart showing values from 20 to 65 for years 1997, 1998, 1999.

Box Office Bait

MOVIE	STUDIO	N.AMERICAN GROSS	RELEASE
Batman	WB	$251,188,924	6/23/89
Batman Returns	WB	$162,831,698	6/19/92
Beetlejuice	WB	$73,707,461	3/30/88
Jackie Brown	Miramax/D	$39,647,595	12/25/97
The Paper	Univ	$36,819,152	3/18/94

Career Trajectory

Nick Nolte Rank **130**   Bankability **51**

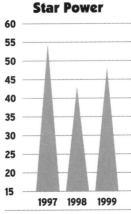

Real Name	Nick Nolte
D.O.B.	2/8/40
Place of Birth	Omaha, Nebraska, USA
Contact	(A) Steve Dontanville, WMA

Willingness to Travel/Promote	Professionalism	Career Mgmt	Talent
60	66	59	73

INSIDE DIRT

He belongs in those smaller, contained movies.

◆ He's done very well for himself with *Affliction* and his Oscar nomination. Despite his image as a drinker and a rabble-rouser, he's very professional when he's working. He's a very talented actor, and he does publicity.

◆ I love him because he's not afraid to do low-budget pictures.

◆ During the filming of *Breakfast of Champions* he wore his pajamas and silk robe everywhere. In Twin Falls, Idaho, he was walking around in those PJs in the middle of the day, looking for the car dealership where he'd meet the salesman he was going to play. He didn't even care. He's funny that way.

◆ Nick's a good guy. But this growth hormone thing he advocates—I don't know. He takes them religiously. He thinks it's the new fountain of youth.

Star Power

Bar chart showing values for 1997, 1998, 1999 with a y-axis from 15 to 60.

Box Office Bait

MOVIE	STUDIO	N.AMERICAN GROSS	RELEASE
Another 48 Hrs	Para	$80,692,414	6/8/90
Cape Fear	Univ	$79,118,315	11/13/91
Prince of Tides	Columbia	$74,632,400	12/25/91
The Deep	Columbia	$69,480,000	1977
Down and Out in Beverly Hills	BV	$62,134,225	1/31/86

Career Trajectory

Claire Danes Rank **131** Bankability **51**

Real Name	Claire Catherine Danes
D.O.B.	4/12/79
Place of Birth	New York, New York, USA
Contact	(A) Nick Stevens, UTA

Willingness to Travel/Promote	Professionalism	Career Mgmt	Talent
60	75	76	72

INSIDE DIRT

She's a teen idol in Japan.

♦ She's vulnerable, she's sexy, and she's a survivor—it's a great combination.

♦ She still hasn't made a false step. She's never lumped in with all the other teen and early twenty-something actresses. She's only taken projects with pedigree.

♦ I'm surprised her bankability scores are so high. The jury is still out on her.

♦ With the right role, she could break through like Julia Roberts did with *Pretty Woman*.

♦ She's beautiful but unusual looking. She has a unique star quality.

♦ She needs the ballast of a strong costar on screen. Left to her own devices, she can be a little moody and vague.

♦ She should get a man on her arm. Sex off-screen plays very well in Europe, and she could use the boost.

Star Power

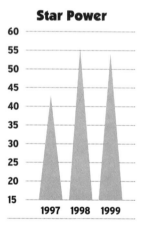

1997 1998 1999

Box Office Bait

MOVIE	STUDIO	N.AMERICAN GROSS	RELEASE
Little Women	Columbia	$50,003,303	12/21/94
Romeo and Juliet	Fox	$46,338,728	11/1/96
The Rainmaker	Para	$45,911,897	11/21/97
How to Make an American Quilt	Univ	$23,586,725	10/6/95
Home for the Holidays	Para	$17,514,057	11/3/95

Career Trajectory

Bill Paxton   Rank **132**   Bankability **51**

Real Name	William Paxton
D.O.B.	5/17/55
Place of Birth	Fort Worth, Texas, USA
Contact	(A) Brian Swardstrom, Endeavor

Willingness to Travel/Promote **71**   **Professionalism** **74**   **Career Mgmt** **50**   **Talent** **59**

INSIDE DIRT

He always plays the same role: the good ol' boy.

- He's the luckiest guy in Hollywood. He's been in two of the biggest grossing films, *Twister* and *Titanic.*

- He's a great second banana to the special effects.

- So he was in *Twister,* big deal. Sam Neill was in *Jurassic Park*—do you think anyone remembers him?

- He's not a lead actor, but he's a great complement to one in any film.

- He desperately craves to be taken seriously.

- He appeals more to men than women. He's kind of a tough cookie, although he has his soft side.

- He's still friends with friends whom he knew when he had no money. He has no trappings or ideas of himself as a movie star. A stand-up guy.

- Everybody likes good ol' Bill. He's a pro. And very flirtatious.

- Bor-r-ring.

Star Power

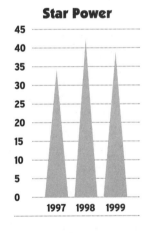

45		
40		
35		
30		
25		
20		
15		
10		
5		
0		
1997	1998	1999

Box Office Bait

MOVIE	STUDIO	N.AMERICAN GROSS	RELEASE
Titanic	Para	$600,788,188	12/19/97
Twister	WB	$241,721,524	5/10/96
Apollo 13	Univ	$172,036,360	6/30/95
True Lies	Fox	$146,273,950	7/15/94
Stripes	Columbia	$90,859,087 E	1981

Career Trajectory

Elizabeth Hurley

Rank 133   **Bankability 51**

Real Name   Elizabeth Hurley
D.O.B.   6/10/65
Place of Birth   Hampshire, England
Contact   (A) Tracey Jacobs, UTA

Willingness to Travel/Promote	Professionalism	Career Mgmt	Talent
67	71	76	52

INSIDE DIRT

She's too beautiful to be taken seriously as an actress.

- She's been underused. She has personality, but it hasn't shone through in her choices of projects.

- She's a very astute businessperson, but that astuteness can sometimes be interpreted as being bitchy.

- I think she's got some global appeal because of her TV ads for hair products.

- I just have one question for Liz Hurley: Why does she always wear exactly the same frock with the slit all the way up to her Suzie?

- She should say novenas every day to Gianna Versace for putting her in that safety pin dress. Overnight she was in every magazine around the world.

- Instead of just being the girl on Hugh Grant's arm, now she's become Ms. Elizabeth Hurley who happens to be his girlfriend.

Star Power

38	
37	
36	
35	
34	
33	
32	
31	
30	
29	
	1997 1998 1999

Box Office Bait

MOVIE	STUDIO	N.AMERICAN GROSS	RELEASE
Austin Powers: The Spy Who Shagged Me	NL	$199,647,588	6/11/99
Austin Powers: Int'l Man of Mystery	NL	$53,882,132	5/2/97
Passenger 57	WB	$44,041,843	11/6/92
My Favorite Martian	BV	$36,830,057	2/12/99
EDTV	Univ	$22,362,500	3/26/99

Career Trajectory

Alicia Silverstone

Rank 134 **Bankability 51**

Real Name	Alicia Silverstone
D.O.B.	10/4/76
Place of Birth	San Francisco, California, USA
Contact	(A) Michael Packenham, Premiere Artists

Willingness to Travel/Promote	Professionalism	Career Mgmt	Talent
61	68	60	69

INSIDE DIRT

She'll be an actress in need of a transition soon.

♦ I still think she was a flash in the pan.

♦ *Clueless* and *Batman* indicate that Alicia may have peaked too early.

♦ If she's smart, she'll niche herself into bratty comedy roles to keep her mainstream appeal.

♦ The Japanese like her because she's blonde, cute, and attractive.

♦ Her roles need to have more meat, less popcorn.

♦ Nabbing a studio producing deal at eighteen just set her up to fail. She tried to overcompensate in proving she wasn't an airhead.

♦ She's kind of fallen off the map.

♦ What are her chances of having a long-term career? A lot slimmer than she is.

Star Power

Star Power chart (values 10–55) for 1997, 1998, 1999.

Box Office Bait

MOVIE	STUDIO	N.AMERICAN GROSS	RELEASE
Batman and Robin	WB	$107,285,004	6/20/97
Clueless	Para	$56,628,979	7/19/95
Blast From The Past	NL	$26,415,951	2/12/99
Excess Baggage	Sony/C	$14,355,189	8/29/97
The Crush	WB	$13,589,383	4/2/93

Career Trajectory

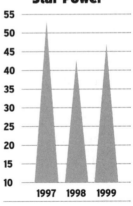

Billy Bob Thornton

Rank 135   **Bankability 50**

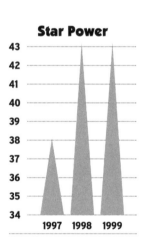

Real Name	Billy Bob Thornton
D.O.B.	8/4/55
Place of Birth	Hot Springs, Arkansas, USA
Contact	(A) Todd Harris, (M) WMA Keith Addis
	Industry Entertainment

Willingness to Travel/Promote	Professionalism	Career Mgmt	Talent
40	**64**	**72**	**75**

INSIDE DIRT

A great actor. He's just not great looking.

- He isn't going to become the leading man that he thinks he's going to become. Look at *Pushing Tin*—he's a character actor.

- Like Whoopi, his contract stipulates that he won't fly. So when he needed to get from New York to L.A. for *Sling Blade,* Harvey [Weinstein] had him ponied across the country in a white Town Car.

- He seems to enjoy using his current power in the business to snub his nose at the studios. He refuses to fly—but he'll do it if they charter him a private 707.

- As a director, will his career take off? The movie that answers that is *All the Pretty Horses.* Which is wonderful.

Star Power

A bar chart with values on the y-axis from 34 to 43, and years 1997, 1998, 1999 on the x-axis. 1997 bar reaches about 38, 1998 bar reaches 43, 1999 bar reaches 43.

Box Office Bait

MOVIE	STUDIO	N.AMERICAN GROSS	RELEASE
Armageddon	BV	$201,578,182	7/1/98
Indecent Proposal	Para	$105,544,089	4/9/93
Tombstone	BV	$56,505,065	12/25/93
Primary Colors	Univ	$39,017,984	3/20/98
On Deadly Ground	WB	$38,572,114	2/18/94

Career Trajectory

184

David Duchovny

Rank 136 **Bankability 50**

Real Name David Duchovny
D.O.B. 8/7/60
Place of Birth New York, New York, USA
Contact (A) Risa Shapiro, ICM

Willingness to Travel/Promote	Professionalism	Career Mgmt	Talent
50	57	40	45

INSIDE DIRT

He's a would-be Richard Gere.

♦ He's boxed himself into a Fox Mulder mold. People just don't see him outside his TV persona. It's the same syndrome the *Star Trek* actors fell into, only Duchovny doesn't have pointed ears.

♦ He's got a blandness about his acting that women really like.

♦ When he's in an *X Files* movie I give him an eight out of ten for bankability. For anything else, he gets a four.

♦ He's a one-trick pony. He has no range as an actor.

♦ I've heard he can be pretty difficult to work with.

♦ He's a nice guy but he takes himself too seriously. He thinks he's a great actor. Come off it.

♦ He became a little too famous a little too fast.

Star Power

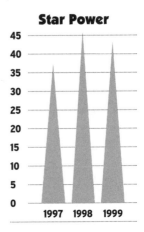

1997 1998 1999

Box Office Bait

MOVIE	STUDIO	N.AMERICAN GROSS	RELEASE
The X-Files	Fox	$83,892,374	6/19/98
Working Girl	Fox	$62,152,437	12/21/88
Don't Tell Mom the Babysitter's Dead	WB	$25,186,641	6/7/91
Bad Influence	Tri-StarUMPH	$12,364,045	3/9/90
Chaplin	Tri-Star	$9,329,605	12/25/92

Career Trajectory

Judi Dench   Rank **137**   Bankability **50**

Real Name	Judith Olivia Dench
D.O.B.	12/9/34
Place of Birth	York, England, UK
Contact	(A) Gene Parseghian, WMA

Willingness to Travel/Promote	Professionalism	Career Mgmt	Talent
65	**89**	**71**	**84**

INSIDE DIRT

She's pigeonholed into literate, period costume pieces.

♦ She's the first port of call for sixty-year-old woman roles, historical or otherwise.

♦ She's not a voracious Hollywood competitor. She'll retain her base by doing legitimate theater.

♦ She does theater regularly, TV in the U.K., and major features. She's had an extraordinary career.

♦ They were about to tear down the stage set from *Shakespeare in Love* after the shoot, but Judi bought it so it could be used for students of theater. That's class.

♦ She not only brings up the standard for a film; she brings the other actors up along with her.

♦ We should all be so lucky to have Dame Judi Dench in our film.

♦ How many more queens are there left for her to play?

Star Power

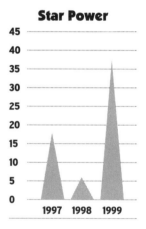

45
40
35
30
25
20
15
10
5
0

1997 1998 1999

Box Office Bait

MOVIE	STUDIO	N.AMERICAN GROSS	RELEASE
Tomorrow Never Dies	MGM	$125,210,295	12/19/97
Goldeneye	MGM	$106,429,941	11/17/95
Shakespeare in Love	Miramax	$100,241,322	12/11/98
A Room With a View	CINECOM	$20,766,644	3/7/86
Tea With Mussolini	MGM/UA	$13,301,729	5/14/99

Career Trajectory

Matt Dillon   Rank **138**   Bankability **50**

Real Name	Matt Dillon
D.O.B.	2/18/64
Place of Birth	New Rochelle, New York, USA
Contact	(A) Chris Andrews, ICM (M) AMG

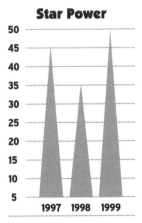

Willingness to Travel/Promote	Professionalism	Career Mgmt	Talent
58	**69**	**49**	**68**

INSIDE DIRT

He has star quality—why not exploit that more?

♦ He's grown up enough now to realize that being the baddest boy on the block isn't the persona he wants for his entire career. So now he's playing comic villains, as in *There's Something About Mary*. Smart.

♦ He should do more movies like *Drugstore Cowboy*.

♦ He's getting into directing and producing. He's very strategic about his career. And his name has very high recognition value.

♦ I think Matt's value has a real threshold—they're trying to overprice him. They want between $1 and $3 million for him.

♦ He's a very serious actor who puts his craft before compensation.

♦ Matt Dillon will act in anything. Meet his price and watch him say yes.

Star Power

| 50 |
| 45 |
| 40 |
| 35 |
| 30 |
| 25 |
| 20 |
| 15 |
| 10 |
| 5 |

1997 1998 1999

Box Office Bait

MOVIE	STUDIO	N.AMERICAN GROSS	RELEASE
There's Something About Mary	Fox	$176,472,910	7/15/98
In and Out	Para	$63,855,317	9/19/97
Malcolm X	WB	$48,140,491	11/18/92
Wild Things	Sony/C	$30,147,739	3/20/98
The Outsiders	WB	$27,555,556	1983

Career Trajectory

Holly Hunter Rank **139** Bankability **50**

Real Name	Holly Hunter
D.O.B.	3/20/58
Place of Birth	Conyers, Georgia, USA
Contact	(A) Steven Dontanville, WMA

Willingness to Travel/Promote   **Professionalism**   **Career Mgmt**   **Talent**

 64   **77**   **60**   **79**

INSIDE DIRT

She's shrinking.

- She a really gracious, giving, intelligent, and charming individual.

- She was a treat to work with on *Raising Arizona*. She, her boyfriend, and Joel and Ethan Cohen were a group of smart, not-very-Hollywood guys.

- She's too attracted to the Beth Henleyesque roles. There are too many *Home for the Holidays* and *Living Out Louds* in her life—really eccentric movies that don't have any commercial viability.

- She needs to be a third lead in something big. She needs to be in another *Broadcast News* again.

- She's chosen very good roles—except for *Once Around,* where she was supposed to be Boston Italian, and definitely wasn't.

- For someone with a Southern accent you could cut with an ax, she's done very well.

Star Power

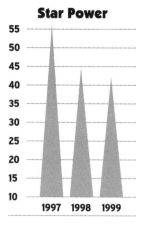

	1997	1998	1999

(y-axis: 10, 15, 20, 25, 30, 35, 40, 45, 50, 55)

Box Office Bait

MOVIE	STUDIO	N.AMERICAN GROSS	RELEASE
The Firm	Para	$158,308,178	6/30/93
Broadcast News	Fox	$49,154,886	12/16/87
Always	Univ	$41,847,970	12/22/89
The Piano	Miramax	$40,156,190	11/12/93
Copycat	WB	$32,018,307	10/27/95

Career Trajectory

Marlon Brando

Rank 140 **Bankability 49**

Real Name	Marlon Brando Jr.
D.O.B.	4/3/24
Place of Birth	Omaha, Nebraska, USA
Contact	(A) Rick Nicita, CAA

Willingness to Travel/Promote	Professionalism	Career Mgmt	Talent
9	25	27	84

INSIDE DIRT

He loathes acting. He only does it for the money.

- He never shows up for rehearsals.

- He stormed off the set of *Don Juan DeMarco* in Hawaii. They finally found him on another island, still in costume and holed up in some bar. When they begged him to return to the set, he just picked up a bottle of ketchup and poured it over his costume. When he did come back, they had to cover the stain with a boa.

- I have known him to wear an earphone so his assistant off-camera can read him his lines, which he just repeats on camera. And to think he was one of our country's greatest actors.

- I turned down an aisle of Gelson's Market and there, walking like a giant walrus, was Marlon Brando in a muu-muu with a gallon tub of Breyer's under his arm. He was eating it with a plastic spoon.

Star Power

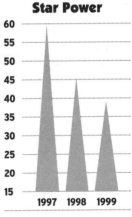

60, 55, 50, 45, 40, 35, 30, 25, 20, 15

1997 1998 1999

Box Office Bait

MOVIE	STUDIO	N.AMERICAN GROSS	RELEASE
The Godfather (with re-issue)	Para	$136,228,625	3/15/72
Superman	WB	$134,218,018	12/15/78
Apocalypse Now (with reissue)	MGM	$84,456,197	8/15/79
The Island of Dr. Moreau	NL	$27,682,712	8/23/96
Sayonara	WB	$23,333,333	1957

Career Trajectory

Jennifer Aniston

Rank 141   **Bankability 49**

Real Name	Jennifer Anistonapoulas
D.O.B.	2/11/69
Place of Birth	Sherman Oaks, California, USA
Contact	(A) Patrick Whitesell, CAA (M) 3 Arts

Willingness to Travel/Promote   **Professionalism**   **Career Mgmt**   **Talent**

 65   **78**   **82**   **48**

INSIDE DIRT

I've never seen her do anything outside of her TV persona.

- She's personable and unchallenging, and that isn't the kind of appeal that lasts—at least not in movies.

- Aniston has overperformed. There's no way she should have been the lead in as many movies as she has. She's riding the popularity of her show. Her career management has been spectacular.

- She'll be okay as long as her price isn't too high. But she's never going to be a Meg Ryan.

- She's taking this Brad Pitt thing too seriously. She'd better lighten up.

- Overseas, Jennifer Aniston means zip. Zero. Nothing. *Friends* worked in some territories, but they just don't care about her feature films.

- She *wishes* she were Sandra Bullock!

- The depth of her range can be measured in millimeters.

Star Power

	1997	1998	1999
41			
40			
39			
38			
37			
36			
35			
34			
33			
32			

Box Office Bait

MOVIE	STUDIO	N.AMERICAN GROSS	RELEASE
Picture Perfect	Fox	$30,828,720	8/1/97
The Object of My Affection	Fox	$29,106,737	4/17/98
Office Space	Fox	$10,824,921	2/19/99
She's The One	Fox/S	$9,538,948	8/23/96
Leprechaun	Trimark	$8,530,048	1/6/93

Career Trajectory

Christian Slater

Rank 142   **Bankability 49**

Real Name	Christian Michael Leonard Hawkins
D.O.B.	8/18/69
Place of Birth	New York, New York, USA
Contact	(A) David Unger, ICM

Willingness to Travel/Promote 60
Professionalism 59
Career Mgmt 50
Talent 64

INSIDE DIRT

He's phenomenal to work with, no matter what people say about him.

- His career has suffered from people's assumptions that actors are dumb, that he's just part of the drug culture.

- His run-ins with drugs and the cops haven't negatively affected our assessment of his bankability. I've never heard any bad stuff about him being problematic on a film.

- As a director he's very smart and very clear on what he wants. Christian's problem is that he became a star very young. He's never been given the inducements to be an adult, to be confident in his decisions.

- A very charming and positive fellow to have around.

- My opinion on his career? What do you call the tail end of a lit bottle rocket fading into the moonlight?

Star Power

Year	
1997	
1998	
1999	

(chart values range 15–60)

Box Office Bait

MOVIE	STUDIO	N.AMERICAN GROSS	RELEASE
Robin Hood: Prince of Thieves	WB	$165,493,908	6/14/91
Interview With the Vampire	WB	$105,248,316	11/11/94
Star Trek VI	Para	$74,739,913	12/6/91
Broken Arrow	Fox	$70,770,147	2/9/96
Young Guns II	Fox	$40,445,599	8/3/90

Career Trajectory

Harvey Keitel Rank 143 Bankability 49

Real Name	Harvey Keitel
D.O.B.	5/13/39
Place of Birth	Brooklyn, New York, USA
Contact	(A) David Schiff, UTA

Willingness to Travel/Promote	Professionalism	Career Mgmt	Talent
50	**71**	**63**	**82**

INSIDE DIRT

Too many dark and brooding roles.

- He's an actor's actor who can't carry a movie on his own.

- He was considered a champion of indie films until he made too many movies. Now he's just considered a bottom feeder.

- He's a survivor.

- Actors love to work with him. He brought in William Hurt for *Smoke,* and Bruce Willis and Demi and Cameron Diaz for other films, too.

- He could do comedy, but he doesn't because then he wouldn't be a "serious" actor.

- He's very big overseas. His name can get you foreign financing.

- His association with De Niro, Scorsese, and Pesci plays very well in Italy.

- He's very sexy.

- Ask someone to tell you how he left *Eyes Wide Shut.* It's an eye opener.

Star Power

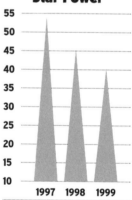

	1997	1998	1999

Box Office Bait			
MOVIE	STUDIO	N.AMERICAN GROSS	RELEASE
Sister Act	BV	$139,605,150	5/29/92
Pulp Fiction	Miramax	$107,921,755	10/14/94
Rising Sun	Fox	$61,202,789	7/30/93
Bugsy	Tri-Star	$49,091,562	12/13/91
Cop Land	Miramax	$44,810,734	8/15/97

Career Trajectory

Diane Keaton

Rank 144   **Bankability 49**

Real Name	Diane Hall
D.O.B.	1/5/46
Place of Birth	Los Angeles, California, USA
Contact	(A) John Burnham, WMA

Willingness to Travel/Promote	Professionalism	Career Mgmt	Talent
69	84	58	82

INSIDE DIRT

A grande dame of acting.

♦ With a Diane Keaton movie, you definitely appeal to an upscale, specifically female audience.

♦ I'd put her on the same level as Meryl Streep in terms of the quality of the projects she's involved in.

♦ She's becoming a very fine director.

♦ No, her directing hasn't helped her bankability as an actress.

♦ I fought to have her in *Father of the Bride*. I finally convinced Disney to cast her, because at the time she was box-office poison.

♦ She's nice. I like her. She's very, very professional. She's on time, she's not a prima donna. She does her lines and helps other actors. She's really great that way.

♦ She's toast. She's a TV actress.

Star Power

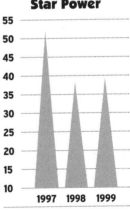

55
50
45
40
35
30
25
20
15
10

1997 1998 1999

Box Office Bait

MOVIE	STUDIO	N.AMERICAN GROSS	RELEASE
The Godfather (with re-issue)	Para	$136,228,625	3/15/72
First Wives Club	Para	$105,475,862	9/20/96
Father of the Bride	BV	$89,325,780	12/20/91
Father of the Bride Part II	BV	$76,592,999	12/8/95
The Godfather III	Para	$66,520,529	12/25/90

Career Trajectory

Cuba Gooding, Jr.

Rank 145   **Bankability 49**

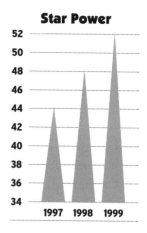

Real Name	Cuba Gooding, Jr.
D.O.B.	1/2/68
Place of Birth	The Bronx, New York, USA
Contact	(A) Kevin Huvane, CAA

Willingness to Travel/Promote
65

Professionalism
75

Career Mgmt
69

Talent
63

INSIDE DIRT

He should stay away from really heavy parts.

♦ Cuba is known for taking parts that were originally conceived as white parts and convincing the director that he could play them. He's done that on at least two films and gotten the parts.

♦ I'd certainly have no hesitation in bonding a film of his.

♦ He's talented but not that talented. Yet his natural charm has served him very well. You want to see him on-screen.

♦ People love his energy level. He's fun to watch. They love the fact that he'll let himself go and even go over the top. And that energy isn't intimidating to white audiences, which can only help his career.

♦ He's a charismatic character actor.

Star Power

52
50
48
46
44
42
40
38
36
34

1997 1998 1999

Box Office Bait

MOVIE	STUDIO	N.AMERICAN GROSS	RELEASE
Jerry Maguire	Sony/TS	$153,620,822	12/13/96
As Good As It Gets	Sony/TS	$148,478,011	12/24/97
A Few Good Men	Columbia	$141,340,178	12/11/92
Coming To American	Para	$128,152,301	6/29/88
Outbreak	WB	$67,598,303	3/10/95

Career Trajectory

Gary Oldman Rank **146** Bankability **49**

Real Name	Leonard Gary Oldman
D.O.B.	3/21/58
Place of Birth	New Cross, London, England
Contact	N/A

Willingness to Travel/Promote	Professionalism	Career Mgmt	Talent
59	**56**	**50**	**76**

INSIDE DIRT

He can be a very dark and negative presence on a set.

◆ With filmmakers he respects, he's great. With people he doesn't, he's uncooperative and nonresponsive.

◆ My understanding is that he'd rather direct than act. And when he acts, he wants to be paid more than his value.

◆ It seemed that while the other people on the set were doing one movie, Gary's mind was off doing another movie of his own. It's his world and we're all just living in it.

◆ He takes these cliché Russian villain roles because they pay a lot. But he also produces, so I give him credit for that.

◆ He's out of his alcohol, drugs, and bad-marriage (to Uma Thurman stage), so that's good news.

◆ One of our great unsung actors.

Star Power

51
50
49
48
47
46
45
44
43
42

1997 1998 1999

Box Office Bait

MOVIE	STUDIO	N.AMERICAN GROSS	RELEASE
Air Force One	Sony/C	$172,956,409	7/25/97
Bram Stoker's Dracula	Columbia	$82,416,928	11/13/92
JFK	WB	$70,354,327	12/20/91
Lost in Space	NL	$69,102,910	4/3/98
The Fifth Element	Sony/C	$63,820,180	5/9/97

Career Trajectory

Alec Baldwin Rank **147** Bankability **48**

Real Name	Alexander Rae Baldwin III
D.O.B.	4/3/58
Place of Birth	Massapequa, New York, USA
Contact	(A) Jim Wiatt, WMA

Willingness to Travel/Promote	Professionalism	Career Mgmt	Talent
48	47	42	65

INSIDE DIRT

He's made some abysmal choices.

♦ A good actor who can't get his price these days.

♦ After doing *The Hunt for Red October* he turned down the next two Jack Ryan franchises, which were blockbusters. Why? To do a minor stage production of *A Streetcar Named Desire*. This guy could have been the biggest star in the business. What an incredibly stupid decision.

♦ He's tried to take over some movies as artistic director. Now he wants to be a director, and people are very reluctant to go along with him.

♦ I think that he's much more intelligent and less self-involved than most actors.

♦ He missed his chance as a leading man. *Outside Providence* shows his chops as a character actor.

♦ He's so mean to everybody. He's one of the greatest self-destructive personalities I've witnessed in this business.

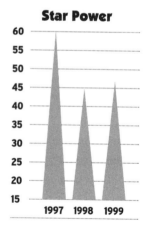

Star Power

(Bar chart with y-axis from 15 to 60, years 1997, 1998, 1999)

Box Office Bait			
MOVIE	STUDIO	N.AMERICAN GROSS	RELEASE
Hunt for Red October	Para	$120,702,326	3/2/90
Beetlejuice	WB	$73,707,461	3/30/88
Working Girl	Fox	$62,152,437	12/21/88
Malice	Columbia	$46,038,636	10/1/93
Mercury Rising	Univ	$32,983,332	4/3/98

Career Trajectory

Catherine Deneuve

Rank 148 **Bankability 48**

Real Name	Catherine Dorléac
D.O.B.	10/22/43
Place of Birth	Paris, France
Contact	(A) Adam Isaacs, UTA

Willingness to Travel/Promote	Professionalism	Career Mgmt	Talent
55	81	78	73

INSIDE DIRT

I wish she were still as bankable as she is sensual.

- She's still regarded as gorgeous, classy, and sexy.

- Except for Sophia Loren, she's the only woman who could ever get away with doing a sex scene in a Hollywood movie with a young hunk half her age. Men like Clint Eastwood can do it but not women. Not yet.

- The last film we really knew her for in Spain was *Indochine,* and that really did poorly, even with its Oscar.

- As a headliner, she doesn't cut it anymore. In a European art film with an ensemble cast, maybe. But people don't go to the movies just to see her.

- She's the goddess. She's the female equivalent of Ian McKellan. But there are only so many roles for that niche.

- French women remain sexual all their lives.

Star Power

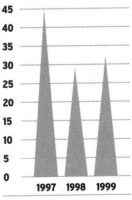

45
40
35
30
25
20
15
10
5
0
1997 1998 1999

Box Office Bait

MOVIE	STUDIO	N.AMERICAN GROSS	RELEASE
The April Fools	WB	$11,111,111	1969
Indochine	SPC	$5,590,893	12/23/92
Belle De Jour (re-release)	Miramax	$3,997,109	6/28/95
The Convent	Strand	$41,100	12/8/95

Career Trajectory

Sally Field Rank **149** Bankability **48**

Real Name	Sally Mahoney
D.O.B.	11/6/46
Place of Birth	Pasadena, California, USA
Contact	(A) Jennifer Gabler-Rawlings, CAA

Willingness to Travel/Promote	Professionalism	Career Mgmt	Talent
49	**80**	**55**	**72**

INSIDE DIRT

I think she'll succeed as a director.

♦ She'll survive as a character actress instead of a leading actress.

♦ It's unfair, but that Oscar speech she made—"You *really, really* like me!"—was almost as damaging to her movie career as playing *The Flying Nun* on TV. God knows an honest emotion in Hollywood pegs you as someone to avoid.

♦ She's as tough as nails. She's self-determined. She understands show business better than almost any woman I know, in that she knows the finite length of a female movie star's career. She's decided she's not going to get eaten up by that. So she's producing, and she's directing.

♦ She knows how to mobilize the forces. She knows how to get the gatekeepers to support her.

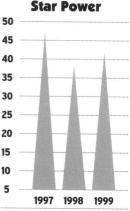

Star Power

1997 1998 1999

Box Office Bait

MOVIE	STUDIO	N.AMERICAN GROSS	RELEASE
Forrest Gump	Para	$329,690,974	7/6/94
Mrs. Doubtfire	Fox	$219,194,773	11/24/93
Smokey and the Bandit	Univ	$126,737,428	5/27/77
Smokey and the Bandit II	Universal	$86,469,940	1980
Steel Magnolias	Tri-Star	$81,920,597	11/15/89

Career Trajectory

Melanie Griffith

Rank 150   **Bankability 48**

Real Name Melanie Griffith
D.O.B. 8/9/57
Place of Birth New York, New York, USA
Contact (A) Nicole David, WMA

Willingness to Travel/Promote	Professionalism	Career Mgmt	Talent
50	49	54	43

INSIDE DIRT

Her age has taken her out of leading roles.

- She's not a movie star anymore. I think she may find some solace in TV.

- She's obsessive about how she's photographed in a shot. Certain casting agents won't consider her for parts that have to be played haggard or bedraggled, anything with reality.

- She's a bag of collagen.

- On *Nobody's Fool,* she checked into the presidential suite at the Plaza without getting approval from the producers. They were furious at her, and then Melanie tried to get them fired. She expects very much to be treated like a movie star.

- I like that Melanie is very loyal to her makeup artists.

- She's very jealous of Antonio.

- Her career has definitely been helped by sleeping with a hot tamale like Banderas.

Star Power

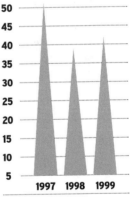

	1997	1998	1999

Box Office Bait

MOVIE	STUDIO	N.AMERICAN GROSS	RELEASE
Working Girl	Fox	$62,152,437	12/21/88
Nobody's Fool	Para	$39,485,639	12/25/94
Pacific Heights	Fox	$27,892,883	9/28/90
Now and Then	NL	$27,109,131	10/20/95
Shining Through	Fox	$21,353,158	1/31/92

Career Trajectory

199

Danny Glover Rank **151** Bankability **48**

Real Name	Danny Glover
D.O.B.	7/22/47
Place of Birth	San Francisco, California, USA
Contact	(A) Lee Stollman, WMA

Willingness to Travel/Promote	Professionalism	Career Mgmt	Talent
65	**79**	**67**	**64**

INSIDE DIRT

He's very hardworking and prepared.

♦ He's smart. He's always done both art films and big movies like *Lethal Weapon*. Now his agents are forbidding him to do the little movies until he gets another action movie. That's probably a good career decision, because *Beloved* tanked.

♦ He's one of the very few stars who instinctively responds to material.

♦ He's been known to bring a lot of family members to his shoots—up to twenty.

♦ He directed a short film for us. Even TV repairmen followed him down the street. He's created a persona of a man of the people. They love him for being Danny Glover, not because he's a star.

♦ When he's working, you'd better give him his Wheat Chex for breakfast or you're in trouble.

Star Power

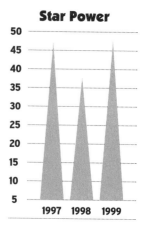

50		
45		
40		
35		
30		
25		
20		
15		
10		
5		
1997	1998	1999

Box Office Bait

MOVIE	STUDIO	N.AMERICAN GROSS	RELEASE
Lethal Weapon 2	WB	$147,253,986	7/7/89
Lethal Weapon 3	WB	$144,731,527	5/15/92
Lethal Weapon 4	WB	$129,734,803	7/10/98
The Prince of Egypt (voice)	Dreamworks	$101,217,900	12/18/98
The Color Purple (with re-issue)	WB	$95,767,388	12/18/85

Career Trajectory

Chris O'Donnell

Rank 152 **Bankability 48**

Real Name	Christopher Eugene O'Donnell
D.O.B.	6/26/70
Place of Birth	Winnetka, Illinois, USA
Contact	(A) Kevin Huvane, CAA (M) Susan Bymel

Willingness to Travel/Promote	Professionalism	Career Mgmt	Talent
65	76	49	60

INSIDE DIRT

He's in danger of becoming a former flavor of the month.

♦ He had his heyday. He needs to get back to basics—strong movies.

♦ In 1999 I thought the shrewdest thing Chris ever did was to commit to *The Bachelor.* He was on his way out the door as the kid who's just a little too square and a little too bland. Well, unfortunately, he still is—the movie tanked.

♦ He's very charismatic and professional.

♦ Nobody cares about the boy next door. The girl next door, yes. But the boy? Bo-r-ring. Put him on TV.

Star Power

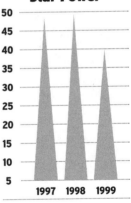

50
45
40
35
30
25
20
15
10
5

1997 1998 1999

Box Office Bait

MOVIE	STUDIO	N.AMERICAN GROSS	RELEASE
Batman Forever	WB	$183,997,904	6/16/95
Batman and Robin	WB	$107,285,004	6/20/97
Fried Green Tomatoes	Univ	$81,192,860	12/27/91
Scent of a Woman	Univ	$62,724,644	12/23/92
The Three Musketeers	BV	$53,661,805	11/12/93

Career Trajectory

Anne Heche Rank **153** Bankability **48**

Real Name	Anne Heche
D.O.B.	5/25/69
Place of Birth	Aurora, Ohio, USA
Contact	(A) Steve Dontanville, WMA

Willingness to Travel/Promote ✈ **62** **Professionalism** **56** **Career Mgmt** **54** **Talent** **50**

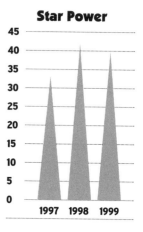

INSIDE DIRT

She's using this Ellen thing to her advantage.

♦ In Germany she's not a factor. Her whole publicized relationship with Ellen Degeneres is a total non-issue there.

♦ I can't see her as a love interest for a man in a movie. It's an overwhelming reality that she has changed totally the nature of her acting career.

♦ Anne will say hello to you depending on whether she thinks you can help her. And she's very arbitrary in her decisions.

♦ Anne's a very passionate and committed girl.

♦ She dumped Steve Martin when she found out he wasn't much of a career booster for her.

♦ She's starting to direct now.

♦ She wasn't fussy or a problem on *Volcano*. I could say she was sweet but that just meant she said hello.

Star Power

(Chart showing values peaking near 30 in 1997, ~40 in 1998, ~27 in 1999, with y-axis from 0 to 45 and x-axis labeled 1997 1998 1999)

Box Office Bait

MOVIE	STUDIO	N.AMERICAN GROSS	RELEASE
Six Days, Seven Nights	BV	$74,339,294	6/12/98
I Know What You Did Last Summer	Sony/C	$72,586,134	10/17/97
Volcano	Fox	$47,067,010	4/25/97
Wag The Dog	NL	$43,022,524	12/25/97
Donnie Brasco	Sony/TS	$41,909,762	2/28/97

Career Trajectory

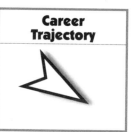

Jamie Lee Curtis

Rank 154   **Bankability 48**

Real Name	Jamie Lee Curtis
D.O.B.	11/22/58
Place of Birth	Los Angeles, California, USA
Contact	(A) Rick Kurtzman, CAA

Willingness to Travel/Promote **53**   **Professionalism** **67**   **Career Mgmt** **55**   **Talent** **58**

INSIDE DIRT

Her choices of roles have hurt her career.

♦ You can't sell Jamie Lee unless it's an ensemble piece and the director is right.

♦ She's never opened a movie. She's a supporting actress.

♦ Her action career was over after *True Lies*. Arnold was the reason for its success, not her.

♦ Jamie Lee is history.

♦ Since she wants to be near her kids, she chooses short-term work where she doesn't leave town. That's limited her film roles.

♦ I find her incredibly masculine. She joined a motorcycle group as a biker, too.

♦ Why did such a nice, friendly gal marry that icky Christopher Guest?

♦ She's a down-home girl with the crew. She'll stop in the street to talk to people. Everyone loves her.

Star Power

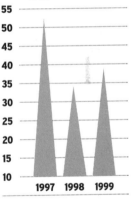

	Box Office Bait		
MOVIE	**STUDIO**	**N.AMERICAN GROSS**	**RELEASE**
True Lies	Fox	$146,273,950	7/15/94
Trading Places	Para	$90,404,800	1983
A Fish Called Wanda	MGM	$59,991,944	7/15/88
My Girl	Columbia	$57,896,291	11/22/91
Forever Young	WB	$55,942,630	12/16/92

Career Trajectory

Woody Allen Rank **155** Bankability **47**

Real Name Allan Stewart Konigsberg
D.O.B. 12/1/35
Place of Birth Brooklyn, New York, USA
Contact (A) John Burnham, WMA

Willingness to Travel/Promote **17**
Professionalism **80**
Career Mgmt **75**
Talent **87**

INSIDE DIRT

His willingness to travel and promote is zilch.

♦ *Celebrity* was a dog. A lot of people here in England are saying Woody is past his sell-by date.

♦ He has an incredibly obsessive level of detail in his work.

♦ He's beloved in France, where they worship auteurs.

♦ Even during the Soon Yi and Mia disaster, he still managed to make movies like *Bullets Over Broadway*. He has an almost supernatural ability to compartmentalize. That kept him going when lesser mortals would have given up.

♦ He hates doing publicity. He told me when he made *Manhattan* that the publicity for the movie was up on the screen and that word-of-mouth would be enough.

♦ That young New York angst has now become senior citizen angst. And senior citizen angst is seriously unattractive.

Star Power

	1997	1998	1999
70			
65			
60			
55			
50			
45			
40			
35			
30			
25			

Box Office Bait

MOVIE	STUDIO	N.AMERICAN GROSS	RELEASE
Antz (voice)	Dreamworks	$90,646,554	10/2/98
Hannah and Her Sisters	Orion	$40,084,041	2/7/86
Manhattan	UA	$39,072,576	1979
Annie Hall	MGM	$27,324,847	1977
Casino Royale	Columbia	$22,666,667	1967

Career Trajectory

Ed Harris   Rank **156**   Bankability **47**

Real Name   Edward Allen Harris
D.O.B.   11/28/50
Place of Birth   Englewood, New Jersey, USA
Contact   (A) Rick Kurtzman, CAA

Willingness to Travel/Promote	Professionalism	Career Mgmt	Talent
52	77	55	70

INSIDE DIRT

He made a smart career move by directing the Jackson Pollock film.

- He's one of the best character actors around, and he consistently gives the highest-quality performances. And he's pretty easy to work with. People like him.

- He's very professional. He's extremely intense and private, and keeps to himself on movies.

- I think he regrets that he's not perceived as a leading man.

- He's a middle-aged balding guy with great blue eyes whose reps tell him he shouldn't play second and third leads because he's a movie star. As a result, they're keeping a brilliant actor from truly acting.

- Even though he doesn't like doing publicity, he does it when he needs to. Because of that he got nominated for *The Truman Show*. You gotta give the boy credit.

Star Power

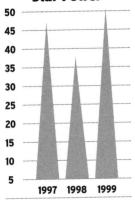

50
45
40
35
30
25
20
15
10
5

1997 1998 1999

Box Office Bait

MOVIE	STUDIO	N. AMERICAN GROSS	RELEASE
Apollo 13	Univ	$172,036,360	6/30/95
The Firm	Para	$158,308,178	6/30/93
The Rock	BV	$134,069,511	6/7/96
The Truman Show	Para	$125,618,201	6/5/98
Stepmom	Sony	$91,030,827	12/25/98

Career Trajectory

Mira Sorvino Rank 157 Bankability 47

Real Name Mira Sorvino
D.O.B. 7/28/67
Place of Birth Tenafly, New Jersey, USA
Contact (A) Michelle Stern, WMA (M) Jean Fox

Willingness to Travel/Promote	Professionalism	Career Mgmt	Talent
63	43	61	70

INSIDE DIRT

She desperately needs reinvention.

- She had Gwyneth Paltrow's career before Gwyneth Paltrow. She was Hollywood's darling and Oscar queen. Talk about a career reversal.

- She brings an attitude and is difficult and unpleasant to work with. That's the career killer in Mira Sorvino's life. Any woman from Harvard with her theatrical pedigree should be one of our leading dramatic actresses.

- French people like Mira.

- She's still a starlet, not a star.

- As bonders, we're often told by people that they celebrate her last day on the job.

- Mira is young and insecure. She just needs a little extra care and approval. This is a girl who brings her mom and dog onto the set. She's got a side to her that's really sweet.

- She's a Sharon Stone in training.

- I would absolutely work with Mira again.

Star Power

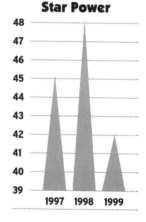

MOVIE	STUDIO	N.AMERICAN GROSS	RELEASE
Box Office Bait			
Romy and Michelle's High School Reunion	BV	$29,235,353	4/25/97
Mimic	Miramax	$25,454,187	8/22/97
Quiz Show	BV	$24,814,770	9/14/94
At First Sight	MGM/UA	$22,326,247	1/15/99
The Replacement Killers	Sony/C	$19,204,929	2/6/98

Career Trajectory

John Cleese Rank **158** Bankability **46**

Real Name John Marwood Cleese
D.O.B. 10/27/39
Place of Birth Weston-Super-Mare, Somerset, England
Contact (A) Rick Nicita, CAA

Willingness to Travel/Promote	Professionalism	Career Mgmt	Talent
52	77	48	79

INSIDE DIRT

There's no longer a market for him as a lead in farcical comedy.

- I'd be careful buying a film starring him. *Out of Towners* tanked.

- *Monty Python* was a smash in Germany, but now they've become tired of that genre.

- His principal value is a character actor, or a writer-producer-director behind the camera. You don't build a movie around him.

- Yes, his time is past. But his type of comedy is incredibly in vogue—look at what Adam Sandler does. It's just that John's old. If he were young, he'd be enormous.

- Cleese wrote intelligent, falling-down fart comedies where people got organs caught in doors. What's the difference between that and *South Park*?

- The more John insists he doesn't want to work, the more producers pay him to do it. And he does.

Star Power

	1997	1998	1999

(Chart showing values: 50, 45, 40, 35, 30, 25, 20, 15, 10, 5 on the y-axis with declining peaks for 1997, 1998, 1999)

Box Office Bait

MOVIE	STUDIO	N.AMERICAN GROSS	RELEASE
George of the Jungle	BV	$105,263,257	7/16/97
A Fish Called Wanda	MGM	$59,991,944	7/15/88
Silverado	Columbia	$32,192,570	7/10/85
The Great Muppet Caper	Univ	$31,206,251	1981
The Out-of-Towners	Para	$28,535,768	4/2/99

Career Trajectory

Laurence Fishburne

Rank 159   **Bankability 46**

Real Name	Lawrence Fishburne III
D.O.B.	7/30/61
Place of Birth	Augusta, Georgia, USA
Contact	(A) Sam Gores, Paradigm (M) Helen Sugland

Willingness to Travel/Promote	Professionalism	Career Mgmt	Talent
62	80	64	79

INSIDE DIRT

He needs to lighten up with a good comedy.

- He's an incredible actor, but nine times out of ten he's playing people who are slightly psychotic. This, along with his demeanor, frightens the international marketplace.

- "The Fish" is a great guy to have on the set. He's a mature influence and really steps up the quality level of any movie. His presence makes actors act better.

- He needs to show more range in his work. And when he's interviewed, he needs to show a more playful side.

- Please, *Laurence* Fishburne? All of a sudden he changes his name from Larry and makes this big announcement about it. That's his first problem— he's a snob. He's trying too hard to present himself as a serious actor. It's as bad as Charlie Sheen insisting he's Charles.

Star Power

Chart showing values for 1997, 1998, 1999 on a scale from 37 to 46.

Box Office Bait

MOVIE	STUDIO	N.AMERICAN GROSS	RELEASE
The Matrix	WB	$168,220,229	3/31/99
The Color Purple (with reissue)	WB	$95,767,388	12/18/85
Apocalypse Now (with reissue)	MGM	$84,456,197	8/15/79
Boyz n' the Hood	Columbia	$56,128,253	7/12/91
A Nightmare on Elm Street 3	NL	$44,068,358	2/27/87

Career Trajectory

Richard Dreyfuss

Rank 160   **Bankability 46**

Real Name Richard Dreyfuss
D.O.B. 10/29/47
Place of Birth Brooklyn, New York, USA
Contact (A) Risa Shapiro/Ed Yablans, ICM
Industry Entertainment

Willingness to Travel/Promote	Professionalism	Career Mgmt	Talent
60	66	38	73

INSIDE DIRT

He could have been Dustin Hoffman.

◆ Richard in *Mr. Holland's Opus* was a stroke of casting genius. But following that up with a stupid comedy like *Krippendorf's Tribe* was a big mistake. He needed to pay the bills.

◆ He doesn't pick the right films.

◆ I've heard he's slightly difficult to work with. He has a very "method" approach to acting. He's not as bad as Bill Hurt, though.

◆ His value is strictly domestic—and within a very moderate budget.

◆ He can give off a very acerbic air.

◆ He's dependable, professional, smart. His biggest career problem? He's not sexy anymore.

◆ He's a short, Jewish-looking, middle-age man—*of course* he's not sexy.

Star Power

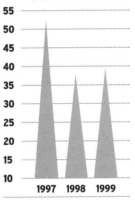

55
50
45
40
35
30
25
20
15
10
1997 1998 1999

Box Office Bait

MOVIE	STUDIO	N.AMERICAN GROSS	RELEASE
Jaws	Univ	$260,000,000	1975
Close Encounters of the Third Kind	Columbia	$166,000,000	1977
American Graffiti	Univ	$115,000,000	1973
Goodbye Girl	Columbia	$92,975,933	1977
Mr. Holland's Opus	BV	$82,564,043	12/29/95

Career Trajectory

Hillary Swank

Rank 161   **Bankability 46**

Real Name	Hillary Swank
D.O.B.	7/30/74
Place of Birth	Bellingham, Washington, USA
Contact	(A) Hylda Queally, WMA

Willingness to Travel/Promote	Professionalism	Career Mgmt	Talent
70	73	75	82

INSIDE DIRT

Just because she got an Oscar for a film most people didn't see doesn't make her bankable.

◆ Her problem is that it will never get better than winning an Oscar after your first major role.

◆ She's put herself on the map as a serious character actress.

◆ *Boys Don't Cry* did pretty poorly in Germany. It's the *Slingblade* syndrome: a very specific movie about weird problems blue collar people suffer in middle America. Nobody watches those movies overseas.

◆ Just because she got an Oscar for a film most people didn't see doesn't make her bankable.

◆ Great as she was in *Boys Don't Cry,* the film didn't give you any idea of what she can do as a female romantic lead—or as a male romantic lead, for that matter.

Star Power

50
45
40
35
30   Not Available
25
20
15
10
5

1997 1998 1999

Box Office Bait

MOVIE	STUDIO	N.AMERICAN GROSS	RELEASE
Buffy the Vampire Slayer	Fox	$15,227,253	7/31/92
Boys Don't Cry	Fox Search	$11,533,945	10/8/99
The Next Karate Kid	Columbia	$8,961,368	9/9/94

Career Trajectory

Willem Dafoe

Rank 162   **Bankability 46**

Real Name   William Dafoe
D.O.B.   7/22/55
Place of Birth   Appleton, Wisconsin, USA
Contact   (A) Scott Henderson, WMA

Willingness to Travel/Promote   **66**
Professionalism   **85**
Career Mgmt   **43**
Talent   **77**

INSIDE DIRT

If Willem has star attitude, then pigs have wings.

- Willem is a true artist and a complete pro.

- He's theater trained, he's worked all over the world and does two hours of yoga a day. Both his body and mind are super-flexible.

- He just shot *Pavillion of Women* in China, and I was amazed at his professionalism. Never any special requests, never a complaint. He read lines for his fellow actors and didn't want a stunt double. He insisted on waiting in line to eat with the Chinese crew. You'd think he was a day laborer.

- He can't get high-end work, but he's a phenomenal actor.

- Like Nicholson and Fishburne, when Dafoe arrives on the set people are suddenly more serious and focused in their work.

Star Power

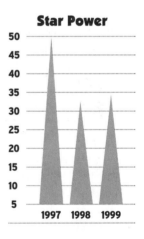

| | 1997 | 1998 | 1999 |

Box Office Bait

MOVIE	STUDIO	N.AMERICAN GROSS	RELEASE
Platoon	Orion	$137,963,328	12/19/86
Clear and Present Danger	Para	$122,010,252	8/3/94
The English Patient	Miramax	$78,651,430	11/15/96
Born on the 4th of July	Univ	$69,898,473	12/20/89
Speed 2: Cruise Control	Fox	$47,755,016	6/13/97

Career Trajectory

Chow Yun-Fat

Rank 163 **Bankability 46**

Real Name	Chow Yun-Fat
D.O.B.	5/18/55
Place of Birth	Lamma Island, Hong Kong
Contact	(A) Lee Stollman, WMA

Willingness to Travel/Promote **Professionalism** **Career Mgmt** **Talent**

 70   72   68   40

INSIDE DIRT

He's huge in Asia, but no one cares in America.

- Everyone thought the Asian invasion and buddy picture had peaked. Then Chow Yun-Fat proved them wrong.

- *Anna and the King* is a big film that increased his profile but probably not his bankability. How many Asian regal types can you play?

- Talent didn't get him *Anna and the King*; the producers were just betting on the Asian market.

- He's proven he can succeed in an American film.

- He's over before he began. He's just not proficient in English, and he's not a very good actor.

- In *Replacement Killers* he seemed to be reading off cue cards.

- He's very willing to promote.

- He was wonderful with the crew. He said thank you after each shot and even brought them cakes for their birthdays.

Star Power

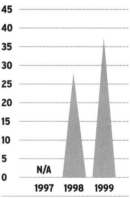

45
40
35
30
25
20
15
10
5
N/A
0
1997 1998 1999

Box Office Bait

MOVIE	STUDIO	N.AMERICAN GROSS	RELEASE
The Replacement Killers	Sony/C	$19,204,929	2/6/98
The Corruptor	NL	$15,119,975	3/12/99
Once a Thief	RIM	$6,810	1/14/94

Career Trajectory

Robert Downey, Jr.

Rank 164 **Bankability 46**

Real Name   Robert John Downey, Jr.
D.O.B.   4/4/65
Place of Birth New York, New York, USA
Contact   (A) Nick Styne, ICM

Willingness to Travel/Promote 65
Professionalism 68
Career Mgmt 37
Talent 77

INSIDE DIRT

His drug run-ins haven't adversely affected his bondability.

- Drugs doomed him. But today he's a complete professional. He's never cost anyone time or extra money.

- When he was shooting, there were restraints put on him by his parole board. He had to be in a halfway house every night. When he traveled he needed to have a counselor with him. But we had no problems.

- A brilliant, talented kid.

- The studios have delayed hiring him because insurance companies won't put up enough money for him.

- He definitely elevates the creative environment of any movie he's on.

- Now he's been sentenced to a few years of prison for breaking parole. But once he's back on the street, his career will be very hot again.

Star Power

(Bar chart with y-axis from 0 to 45, showing bars for 1997, 1998, 1999)

Box Office Bait

MOVIE	STUDIO	N.AMERICAN GROSS	RELEASE
Back to School	Orion	$91,300,000	6/13/86
U.S. Marshals	WB	$57,254,590	3/6/98
Natural Born Killers	WB	$50,271,653	8/26/94
Soapdish	Para	$36,416,994	5/31/91
Air America	Tri-Star	$30,506,847	8/10/90

Career Trajectory

Rowan Atkinson

Rank 165   **Bankability 46**

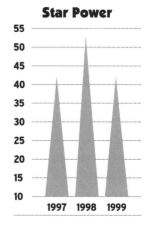

Photo: Shooting Star

Real Name   Rowan Sebastian Atkinson
D.O.B.   1/6/55
Place of Birth   Newcastle-upon-Tyne, England
Contact   (A) Ames Cushing, WMA

Willingness to Travel/Promote	Professionalism	Career Mgmt	Talent
35	63	60	68

INSIDE DIRT

He's Mr. Bean. What else can he do?

♦ He's huge overseas, but who cares over here? Benigni was in that category until this year, so maybe there's still hope for Rowan.

♦ He's a global star, not just a territorial star.

♦ If he's doing his "Bean" role or a comic cameo, he's valuable. But only within that limited range.

♦ He's his own island of success. He's completely eccentric. He has a huge following in England, with his hit comedy series and films. He hasn't bought into anything to do with Hollywood because he doesn't need to.

♦ I think he's been supplanted by Eddie Izzard as the U.K.'s leading comic force.

♦ I don't know who he is, and I'm a top entertainment attorney.

Star Power

1997	1998	1999

(bar chart with vertical axis marked 10, 15, 20, 25, 30, 35, 40, 45, 50, 55)

Box Office Bait

MOVIE	STUDIO	N.AMERICAN GROSS	RELEASE
The Lion King (voice)	BV	$312,855,561	6/15/94
Four Weddings and a Funeral	GRAM	$52,636,671	3/9/94
Bean (US Opening Date)	GRAM	$45,316,440	11/7/97
Hot Shots! Part Deux	Fox	$38,584,328	5/21/93
The Witches	WB	$10,295,199	8/22/90

Career Trajectory

9

The Bloom of Youth

It's the movies' millennial makeover: Studios are applying teenage actors to their comedy and horror flicks as heavily as a desperate old diva dipping into her Nivea Cream. It's a new wrinkle on an old story—beauty and youth sell, liver spots don't.

A lot of barely pubescent and early twentysomething mall rats are forking over nine bucks these days to go out to the movies—again and again—while baby boomers hole up in their homes watching Tom Hanks and Meryl Streep on video.

What's the impact of this ever-youthful shade on the face of moviegoing? The new "youth boom" isn't necessarily a permanent makeover. In fact, as America grays, seniors are expected to assert themselves increasingly as an economic and cultural force, and the much-hyped youth boom may fade as fast as a thirty-day rinse.

But for now, teens to twenty-five-year-olds are the hot market for the studios, creating new opportunities for young, fresh-faced talent. It's the mirror image of an indie phenomenon a generation ago.

Today's *Scream* and *I Know What You Did Last Summer* movie series are the spawn of the '80s low-budget *Nightmare on Elm Street* and *Friday the 13th* franchises, just as *American Pie* and *There's Something About Mary* are *Porky's* déjà-vu. In the black demographic, films like *A Thin Line Between Love and Hate* and *Hoodlum* owe a debt to that '70s trailblazer, *Shaft*.

Young TV actors crossing over into these genre movies hardly sport the star power of their feature film peers, but they're dressed to kill at the box office and constitute one of the fastest-growing sectors of Hollywood talent, especially among women. This tailored group includes such starlets as Sarah

Michelle Gellar, Rachel Leigh Cook, and Jennifer Love Hewitt—ladies whom critic Rex Reed has collectively dubbed "those thumb-sucking Lolitas with three names." They and their male counterparts may wow the media in the States, but most foreign-based film buyers don't even know their names.

As any David Caruso or David Schwimmer can tell you, there's a high fizzle rate in the saleability of these hot new faces. What does it matter if a Ryan Philippe or some other *Vanity Fair* cover kid suffers a short shelf life, after all? There's always another fresh-faced lollipop waiting to replace him on the candy stand.

A few years ago Alicia Silverstone fed the feeding frenzy. After one lucky movie, *Clueless*, she was promptly gussied up with a huge studio deal and offers for bigger films. "There's no such thing as being nurtured anymore the way Liz Taylor was, for example," says Rob Aft of Kuschner-Locke Entertainment. "Instead, we swoop down on these actors like ants at a picnic."

Interestingly, this continuing fashion parade of low-budget youth films has played more into the hands of female talent. As international marketing executive Bonnie Voland puts it: "Women are not only victims in these teen flicks, they're the stars. As actresses, their generation didn't have to fight for equality—they expected it. They're heroines, so they're able to drive the box office more than before because they appeal to girls as much as they appeal to boys."

Or as Fran Kazui, executive producer of TV's *Buffy the Vampire Slayer*, opines: "Buffy opened the door further for women and showed that proactive heroines command a new respect because of a new audience who accepts them."

Will this be the generation to strip the blush of male domination off the A list?

Keep dreaming.

10

Tribal Hollywood

In Hollywood, power has many incarnations. Power lunches. Power trips. Power to make movies. Power to sue over making movies. Power to sue those who sue you over making movies.

But to appreciate the true nature of power in Hollywood—even power that eludes the trial lawyers—you should consider two facts: First, Hollywood functions as a tribe. Second, real power in Hollywood is *tribal* power.

This realization hit me some years ago in a most exotic and tribal locale. It was a blazing hot August afternoon halfway into an eight-day environmental junket through the vanishing Amazon rain forests. We were on one of those consciousness-raising, spread-the-word-to-the-global-media shindigs that Hollywood gets so eager-beaver about.

Our riverboat was steaming down the Rio Negro, and on its deck was a chummy clan of Hollywood A-listers: Tom Cruise, Mimi Rogers, John Ritter, Paula Wagner, Rick Nicita, David Zucker, Debra Hill, Michael Fuchs, and Lewis Chesler. (I was the odd duck on the B list, invited as camp journalist and videographer.) At the moment we were shedding our Banana Republic khakis, undies, and any social shame to plunge into those muddy infested waters for a swim.

"Give a kiss to the piranhas," someone quipped to Cruise.

Splash.

Once in the water, I was nibbled like fish teeth by a question: How did we all end up *here,* skinny-dipping in the Amazon?

How could anyone have persuaded these insanely busy Hollywood powerbrokers—each making a salary the size of the GNP of a small African nation—to ditch their Beemers and corner suites and head for the jungle?

What was it that drove them all to strip down past their skivvies, and risk becoming fish bait?

The answer: pure, naked tribal power.

Besides money and the desire to see your best friend fail, nothing binds people together in Hollywood as securely as the knowledge of membership in a tribe. It may be a tribe that is opportunistic, cannibalistic, manic-depressive, and absurdly obsessive, but it is a tribe nonetheless.

This industry lives, works, dreams, plays, performs, and even sleeps as a tribe. (Concubine swapping isn't uncommon.) Like any tribe, it has its myths and symbols, its rituals and sacred rites, its totems and taboos. Some are temporary, some permanent. A ritual that is in vogue one year—stumping for the rain forests—may be overshadowed or replaced by another the next: stumping for AIDS awareness or Tibetan home rule.

Tribal Hollywood also has a social pecking order. This is not rigidly defined except at the top, where the tribal gods reside and where access to them is jealously guarded and controlled.

Herewith, a partial primer on that pecking order, from its deities to its bottom feeders. Consider it a tribal relic inspired by the jungle—the one in Hollywood, of course.

The Star Gods (and Star Monsters)

As with most tribes, Hollywood worships certain quasi-divine creatures. Here they are known as movie stars. There is no higher power in the tribe, attorneys notwithstanding.

The Star Gods' presumed talent and charisma enable the industry to construct its grand totems—feature-length motion pictures—and potentially reap millions in rewards. Hence, the tribe caters slavishly to the star gods' whims and needs. It offers them Manna like Valhalla-size palaces, jumbo Winnebagos, and use of the corporate jet. Tribal elders and others may make soul-selling sacrifices in their eagerness to appease their Star-God pantheon: honesty, sanity, and self-respect being three of the most popular.

Unlike the invisible gods of the Polynesian tribes that Margaret Mead rubbed up against, Hollywood's divinities demand to be seen. Their very human forms parade across movie screens the size of ancient ceremonial grounds, and the Hollywood media display their graven images in tabloids, TV shows, and magazines like so many gleaming, golden calves.

Like Zeus and the Olympian gods, the Star Gods often take on all-too-human characteristics. They may prove to be a bit fragile and ornery, or impossibly demanding and childish. No matter. The Hollywood Tribe continues to construct its Grand Totems in their image as all-powerful Deities.

The reason for such indulgence lies in the nature of the Star Gods' power. These creatures of flickering light and shadow exist as personifications of the Tribal Dream or Myth. It is a Dream that reveals that mere mortals can ultimately achieve eternal life, whether by "making it" on the silver screen (or a digital version thereof), or through the power of belief in an afterlife of their choosing.

Hence, the Dream must never be denied, for the Tribe's very existence depends upon it. This is, in fact, the Tribe's most enduring and transformational Myth: that human beings have the possibility not merely to Be, but to Become.

The Shamans

For those readers who skipped Cultural Anthropology 101 in college, shamans are tribal priests who wield their magic to divine the gods and, hence, control events. In Hollywood, you can find most of them tucked away on Wilshire Boulevard, between Robertson and Santa Monica Boulevard, or in the mystically named "Century City." They don Prada suits and ply their white witchcraft wearing Rolexes and wielding powerful Rolodexes in their Palm Pilots. Often they parade their magic by brandishing Hollywood's most currently fashionable personal totem, the cigar.

These are the "gatekeepers," the industry's top agents, managers, attorneys, and sometimes studio executives. They share privileged intimacies with, and control access to, Hollywood's pantheon of Star Gods. They are the rainmakers who, with a little dance, can command the deities to rain down their talent and bestow Hollywood with a bumper-crop harvest (at least a $10-million opening weekend at the box office, amen).

Usually no tribal members—be they producers, directors, screenwriters or junior studio execs—can so much as whisper to these Star Gods, much less slip them their next Oscar-winning screenplay—without first supplicating to these priestly powers.

"All producers want to do in this town is get past the gatekeepers to the talent so they can make their movies, and it's the hardest thing to do." This is a common complaint from Tribesmen. But with only a few persuasive phone calls, the Priests can easily summon the Star Gods to make another Tribal Totem. Hence they wield inordinate power and are feared and resented by all the Tribe.

Of course, leading "creatives" like top directors, producers, and screenwriters may also boast some shamanism of their own. They may have "connections" and "professional relationships" with the movie stars. Occasionally, Tribesmen favored with such powers can bypass the Shamans and place a direct phone call to the god Leonardo or the goddess Julia. But they can never afford to alienate the Shamans, for one day they, too, will surely need their power to locate other Magic.

The most legendary Über-Shaman of recent years was superagent Michael Ovitz, who has since shape-shifted like the immortal shamans of old to become a supermanager. But almost any head of a leading talent agency can achieve Über-Shaman status. Also in this charmed circle are ICM chief Jeff Berg; The William Morris Agency's Jim Wiatt; and top studio executives and creatives like Dreamwork's team of Steven Spielberg, Jeffrey Katzenberg, and David Geffen.

Anthropologists inform us that Tribal Shamans are traditionally known for creating mystical auras around themselves. And lo, Ovitz proclaims to read and follow Sun Tzu's *Art of War,* and once aligned his former Hollywood temple—the CAA headquarters—according to the ancient principles of Feng Shui. And lo, David Geffen practices Buddhism and "spirituality." It seems every agent and gatekeeper in town wants to get in on the spiritual act. Every few weeks, they can be found dumping their kids with the nannies and running off to another charity dinner for the Dalai Lama.

Chiefs and Warriors

These Tribesmen are found in two camps: that of the castle (the executive suites) and the trenches (the movie sets). The Castle Chiefs are absurdly rich studio moguls with eight-digit bonus packages and a host of stock options that would put Henry VIII's stashes to shame. They may as well be the heads of Boeing or AT&T or any other conglomerate balancing the bottom line. Also in this select group of elders are the Tribal Providers, a.k.a. bankers and financiers. They frequently have no contact with the Star Gods, and are most revered for their art of fine penmanship executed on the Tribes' most hallowed geometric configuration, the dotted line.

The Castle Warriors are the vastly less paid (but still overpaid by nontribal standards) midlevel production, distribution, and marketing executives, as well as studio publicists, development staffers (D-boys and D-girls), and other lackeys of the Chiefs. They may as well be welders and widget makers on Boeing's assembly line.

All Chiefs and Warriors are dedicated to ensuring that huge mountains of Manna are spent trying to erect the perfect Grand Totem for the ancestral Star Gods to inhabit. They must also keep the Star Gods amused and happy by ensuring that the Gulfstream IV jet winging them to Cannes for a world Totem unveiling has a private suite, a chef who cooks lactose-free, and a massage table with Evian access.

In the culture of the trenches, the Chiefs are the directors and producers. They are in charge of fighting the castle's war—that is, shooting a film. Often they are nagged and tortured by the Castle Chiefs who often presume to know more about the art of war than those in the trenches fighting it.

The Warriors are the lowly, vastly underpaid (compared to the Star Gods and Castle Chiefs they cater to), and overexploited crew members living the gypsy life of setting up and breaking camp month after month, Totem after Totem. Like most Warriors, they rightfully bemoan their lot. This is especially true when they are up sixteen hours a day servicing every whim of the Star Gods.

The latter, meanwhile, already enjoy twelve-hour turnaround times, private Winnebagos, entourages boasting gym trainers and occasional concubines, and salaries that bequeath them in one hour what the Warriors rustle up in a month. Who should be servicing whom here?

"The gods must be pampered," groaned a Trench Warrior after one fevered all-night shoot. "The gods really suck."

The Wisdom Keepers

These are the men and women with a vision of the Tribe's future, who view the world through a wide-angle lens. They may be journalists or database managers who analyze economic and social developments within the Tribe. Or they may be "industry veterans" such as Shaman/manager Bernie Brillstein, who boast a shrewd and seasoned worldview.

"Today is irrelevant," says Tribesman and producer Jana Sue Memel of Chanticleer Films. "The only thing that matters is where we'll be five years from now and what are the scenarios that will bring us there."

The Wisdom Keepers answer these and other questions, such as:

- What does the Internet portend for Tribal Hollywood?

- How will digital distribution impact the future design and marketing of its Grand Totems?

- Will future civilians who can see movies beamed down into their homes (and eventually into their optic nerves) ever again be inspired to go out and see the Grand Totems in public halls of Tribal Magic?

- Will the cathartic and communal experience of viewing this Magic even survive?

Only the Wisdom Keepers can tell.

The Tribal Concubines

Not only the Star Gods, but also the Shamans, Chiefs, and Warriors desire to be serviced once in a while. Tales abound of Tribesmen who have achieved their rites of passage up through the Tribe's pecking order via this time-honored, bed-bouncing sport. (One of the most revealing T-shirts ever to make its appearance on a Totemic set read: "Who do I have to fuck to get *out* of this film?")

The modus operandi of the Concubines are fairly obvious, as any Heidi Fleiss aficionado can tell you.

• • •

This is the basic lay of the Tribal land, as seen through its highly reactive and somewhat insecure social pecking order.

But what would Hollywood be without its Tribal ceremonies and tribal dress?

The Spring Festival of the Tribal Grand Totem

Around the time of Earth's vernal equinox, Hollywood Tribesfolk indulge in their annual rites of spring, celebrating the birth of the previous year's Grand Totems. One full moon before the rites' Grand Ceremonial Dance, various Wisdom Keepers consult the oracles of Tribal opinion as they prepare to honor a few select worthies within the Tribe. Any Tribesman from a Star God to a Warrior may be honored for his or her sacred devotion to the Tribal Dream.

Such is the importance of these spring rites that the Grand Ceremonial Dance, held in one of two stone temples in the heart of the City of Angels, may be witnessed by nearly all Earth's tribes, thanks to the ethereal spirits summoned and harnessed by select Warriors.

Inside the temple, the Star Gods, Shamans, and Chiefs sit closest to the raised ceremonial ground, while lesser Tribesmen serve as soothing background decor. Central to the Grand Ceremonial Dance is the bestowal of the golden craven images upon the Worthies. This is accompanied by frequent Tribal drumbeats, mystical music, and bizarre pagan dancing by Debbie Allen's tromping acolytes.

Special attention and devotion before, during, and after the Grand Ceremonial Dance is given to the Star Gods. Their exotic Tribal dress of fine cloths, rare gems, and occasionally plastic credit cards is an exalted display of the Deities' spring plumage, celebrating not only Totemic rebirth but the magnificent possibilities inherent in divine self-worship.

Dionysian revels proceed throughout the dark hours. In the morning, the Star Gods, Shamans, Chiefs, and Warriors commence a day of rest—satisfied that they have renewed their Tribal Dream, that they have Become what most of us can never Be.

11

The Internet and Beyond

Like Greek gods, classic film stars lived in a remote world. Garbo, Dietrich, Gable, and other grand old screen icons occasionally stepped down off their thrones to wander among the masses, viewable in glossy fanzine photo spreads or, at best, touchable at gala premieres and charity balls.

Today's stars are more accessible than ever. No longer remote and sanctified by distance, their names and faces are relentlessly mass-marketed and become consumer brands. Countless magazines and media outlets generate millions of miles of newsprint and videotape on these contemporary screen "legends." Many of the newest faces hail from TV, the most intimate and least remote of all star heavens.

The future will only find more ways to brings these luminous commodities closer to us, and Hollywood is terrified.

The Blair Witch Project sounded the alarm. "It scared the hell out of us—and not because of its storyline," says a studio denizen. "This is one episode where the Internet claimed a clear victory."

Blair Witch was marketed globally on the Internet as a "true story" and quickly spawned hundreds of fan sites and hundreds of millions of hits. The result: a film with no name actors had conjured up a box-office bonanza.

The Internet revolution continues. Today's computer world is run by techno-geeks—its version of those ancient tribal shamans. Where once these high priests served gods, now they serve databases. Wherever you look, more and more people are succumbing to the digital spell. A once-underground curiosity called "Microcinema" is now a full-fledged movement firmly entrenched on the Worldwide Web, featuring low-budget films shot on inexpensive formats such as DV and Hi-8 video. Numerous on-line channels offer short digital series and even produce feature films. Others screen feature trailers and shorts.

Meanwhile, Adam Sandler, ever the shrewd purveyor of new career options, made an animated short called "The Peeper" which premiered on the Net in late 1999.

All these media take advantage of the Internet's unique power to create a direct bridge between the filmmaker and the audience, eliminating the distributor and, hence, any middleman to call the shots.

Not to be drowned by a rising tide of web surfers, studios and their parent corporations are buying or creating their own Internet companies. Will Hollywood swallow the Internet?

The digital era has ushered in "consumerization" of the feature film production marketplace, too, threatening yet another sacred Hollywood cow. Digital movies are far easier and cheaper to produce than filmed movies—Thomas Vinterberg's 1998 Cannes festival entry, "Celebration," was the first commercially successful example. Upon completion, these "films" can be speedily downloaded to millions of computers, just as consumers download their favorite hit songs in MP3 and other formats today.

Sooner than Hollywood hopes, little Billy and Susie will be able to produce full-fledged motion pictures in their own bedrooms that once required entire soundstages and post-production departments to create. The "dream factory" has morphed into the Dream Digital Chip.

Just ask Gabrielle Kelly, a writer-producer in Hollywood and a self-proclaimed "clerk working in the Dream Factory." DVD technology and the Internet, she says, are giving new meaning to the term "niche marketing" in her own family.

"My thirteen-year-old daughter, Fiona, is turning into this mini-Spielberg," Kelly says incredulously. "She's writing, directing, art directing, costuming, and now editing her own featurette for her friends on her Web site. The credits are longer than the movie! But hey, she's ahead of me and I've been in the business a lot longer."

Will stars be needed to assure the appeal or success of these homegrown Internet masterpieces? Probably not—at least we hope not for Fiona's sake. But that doesn't mean movie stars won't be in demand, and won't be exploitable or marketable in other vehicles.

Hollywood has always been adept at increasing its options, even as it resists new technologies kicking and screaming. Once the industry tried to trample television and vanquish video. Today those formats are cash cows that sustain the entire business.

The studios may godfather hundreds of new cyberfilms in the coming years and adapt some of them into feature films. But they will never abandon their core market of action, adventure, and fantasy spectaculars, because they brook no competition on this level. Certainly they are betting that these "event" movies will never look as good on your home movie screen as they do in the sumptuous surroundings of a cineplex.

The coming years will continue to deliver newer and more impressive movie venues—perhaps harking back to those grand old movie palaces, where the early screen gods played.

12

The Dream Factory

Whatever their rankings—As, Bs, or Cs—actors share an enviable power: the power to transport us, the power to make us dream.

Like Charon's boat that carried Hades' lost souls to their destinations, the best actors lead us through the alphabet of our passions and fears to take us—where? To "the other side." It might be to a feeling or a realization, or to part of a new and common language that helps us wrestle with our darker selves. In any case, it's to a new emotional address.

Dreams have this power, too. Dreams happen when we close our eyes and open our souls, diving into a dark, measureless world.

It's that magic darkness that a movie theater re-creates. The lights go down, the music rises, and we hold our breath—not knowing where within ourselves this spirit troop of actors will carry us. For like spirits, actors are our mediums to other worlds. Maybe to fantasy and adventure. Maybe to laughter or to silence. Maybe, if we're lucky, to "the other side" of the screen, waiting just around the corner from over the rainbow.

Millennia since the first humans congregated to share their collective dreams, we are still tribal animals. No matter where technology carries us, we will always need the public cinema because we are by nature social and communicative. We need to share our experiences in public places. The blazing light of the movie screen is that same shared fire around which our ancestors sat telling stories, carrying their world on the shoulders of a tale.

Today those shoulders are the Hollywood studios and soundstages that create and tell our tribal stories.

It may be more than a half-century old, but the term "Dream Factory" still packs a powerful paradoxical punch. Dreams are abstract and insubstantial, while factories are about machinery, substance, and mass-produced products. Yet Hollywood's products are flickering dreams; they turn money into light. That contradiction is as powerful a "transporter" for our modern world as anything future space travel can dream up.

"Man created religion because he needed a structure for his gods," a friend once observed, "and he created Hollywood because he needed a structure for his dreams." Hollywood was built on our attraction to those dreams. Yet at some fundamental level we don't believe them, because we know they are only images—evanescent and insubstantial.

The market for celebrity lore and gossip taps into this mistrust. We praise our movie stars even as we vilify and trivialize them. Indeed, we exalt them by granting them such attention. We build a god on a pedestal, but it is human nature to tear down that idol eventually and raise up another in its place. It's a cycle of creation, destruction, and regeneration.

When we finish admiring the sultry powers of Sharon Stone, we mock her and move on to the newer powers of Gwyneth Paltrow or Salma Hayek. And on and on.

In short, we demystify these human gods to bring them nearer ourselves. In our world of cyber-connected but very separate spaces, maybe it's a way to span the emotional distance between us. Maybe it's one of the common languages to which these actor-spirits, leading us through the alphabet soup of our souls, have inadvertently carried us. Another side of "the other side," if you will.

The information in this book is a small attempt to demystify the gods. While its numbers measure the output of the Factory, my impulse to research it, write it, and tell its stories came straight from the Dream—the love of movies and the lure of their stars. The light of that fire never wanes, no matter how much of an "insider" you become.

Which, of course, is the paradox of this book: A power like that can never be measured at all.

THE **C** LIST

Chris Tucker Rank **166** Bankability **45**

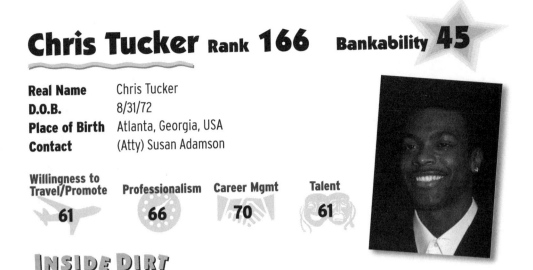

Real Name   Chris Tucker
D.O.B.   8/31/72
Place of Birth   Atlanta, Georgia, USA
Contact   (Atty) Susan Adamson

Willingness to Travel/Promote	Professionalism	Career Mgmt	Talent
61	66	70	61

INSIDE DIRT

He's going to be huge.

♦ He's too frenetic and too specific in his comedy to have the wide appeal of an Eddie Murphy. But he's got more chances to break big than Chris Rock because Rock is just too political.

♦ He's fun and dynamic and nonthreatening because he hasn't just been in black-oriented films.

♦ He's able to defy the "black factor" abroad and appeal to foreign audiences, too.

♦ His value is almost nil overseas.

♦ His kind of over-the-top comedy seems to be what the public clamors for. So he's given a wide berth.

♦ He doesn't mean anything to me or my company, although probably to New Line he does.

♦ I think he's so overrated. In *The Fifth Element,* I just wanted him to shut up.

Star Power

45
40
35
30
25
20
15
10
5
0

1997 1998 1999

Box Office Bait

MOVIE	STUDIO	N.AMERICAN GROSS	RELEASE
Rush Hour	NL	$141,153,686	9/18/98
The Fifth Element	Sony/C	$63,820,180	5/9/97
Money Talks	NL	$40,922,619	8/22/97
Jackie Brown	Miramax/Dimension	$39,647,595	12/25/97
Friday	NL	$27,909,510	4/26/95

Career Trajectory

Kevin Bacon Rank **167** Bankability **45**

Real Name	Kevin Bacon
D.O.B.	7/8/58
Place of Birth	Philadelphia, Pennsylvania, USA
Contact	(A) Lee Stollman, WMA

Willingness to Travel/Promote **61** **Professionalism** **70** **Career Mgmt** **46** **Talent** **64**

INSIDE DIRT

Like Matt Dillon, he'll act in almost any B movie if you meet his price.

- Definitely not a headliner.
- He's done some really small movies that never saw the light of day.
- During *Digging to China,* this redneck guy comes up to K.B. in a bar and for no reason says, "I'm gonna kick your ass." In a very Zen-composed moment, Kevin replies, "Just don't hit me in the face." He can really keep his cool.
- He's a wonderful actor.
- That trivia game *Six Degrees of Kevin Bacon* was the best thing that happened to his career recently.
- Everybody at the party wanted him to do the scene from *Footloose.* He did it, though he's sick of it. He's a great sport.
- *Footloose?* His career is more like *Footstiff.*

Star Power

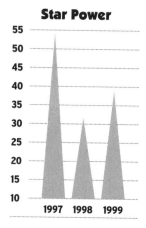

1997	1998	1999

Box Office Bait

MOVIE	STUDIO	N.AMERICAN GROSS	RELEASE
Apollo 13	Univ	$172,036,360	6/30/95
National Lampoon's Animal House	Univ	$141,600,000	7/28/78
A Few Good Men	Columbia	$141,340,178	12/11/92
Footloose	Para	$79,974,841	2/18/84
JFK	WB	$70,354,327	12/20/91

Career Trajectory

Neve Campbell

Rank 168   **Bankability 45**

Real Name	Neve Campbell
D.O.B.	10/3/73
Place of Birth	Guelph, Ontario, Canada
Contact	(A) Brandt Joel, CAA (M) Arlene Foster

Willingness to Travel/Promote   **Professionalism**   **Career Mgmt**   **Talent**

60   **71**   **72**   **50**

INSIDE DIRT

She's a regenerated TV actress.

- Her advantage is her disadvantage: another cute and sexy starlet.
- She's feeding off that old horror formula: nubile teens being terrorized with sexual glee.
- She's the flavor of the month for Generation Y.
- Ben Affleck does this hilarious imitation of her, in a really spacey voice: "Hi, yeah, yeah, I think I'm gonna do it, yeah."
- She doesn't have any heat on the foreign end—you can't build a budget around her. But she's okay in ensemble pieces.
- She doesn't yet have "openability," where people go to see a film just because she's in it. But she's on her way.
- I think *Movieline* was so right: "Actress Most Likely to Have Already Peaked."
- Ooof. Enough already.

Star Power

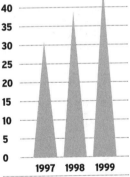

45
40
35
30
25
20
15
10
5
0
1997 1998 1999

Box Office Bait

MOVIE	STUDIO	N.AMERICAN GROSS	RELEASE
Scream	Miramax/Dimen	$103,001,286	12/20/96
Scream 2 (with re-issue)	Miramax	$101,363,301	12/12/97
Wild Things	Sony	$30,147,739	3/20/98
The Craft	Sony	$24,881,502	5/3/96
54	Miramax	$16,757,163	8/28/98

Career Trajectory

Angela Bassett

Rank 169   **Bankability 45**

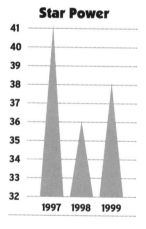

Real Name	Angela Bassett
D.O.B.	10/16/58
Place of Birth	New York, New York, USA
Contact	(A) Kevin Huvane, CAA

Willingness to Travel/Promote 57   **Professionalism** 78   **Career Mgmt** 64   **Talent** 66

INSIDE DIRT

She's filled with trepidation about her career as a black woman over forty.

♦ She never got the bump she should have from *What's Love Got to Do With It.*

♦ Despite those fierce-looking eyebrows, she's a genuine sweetheart. She's the kind of person who knows everyone's name. She even remembers to bring patches for the holes in their sweaters.

♦ She's made the right role choices for far.

♦ On *Waiting to Exhale* she drove herself to the set and was extremely deferential and professional. No attitude. Nothing phased her.

♦ She has a sense of humor and she can poke fun at herself. But deep down she's a serious gal.

♦ Stop lifting weights! Every time she wears a sleeveless dress in a film you're staring at her muscles and you forget how talented she is.

Star Power

41	
40	
39	
38	
37	
36	
35	
34	
33	
32	

1997 1998 1999

Box Office Bait

MOVIE	STUDIO	N.AMERICAN GROSS	RELEASE
Contact	WB	$100,769,177	7/11/97
Kindergarten Cop	Univ	$90,845,286	12/21/90
Waiting To Exhale	Fox	$67,001,595	12/22/95
Boyz n' The Hood	Columbia	$56,128,253	7/12/91
Malcolm X	WB	$48,140,491	11/18/92

Career Trajectory

Patrick Swayze

Rank 170   **Bankability 45**

Real Name	Patrick Swayze
D.O.B.	8/18/52
Place of Birth	Houston, Texas, USA
Contact	(A) Nicole David, WMA

Willingness to Travel/Promote	Professionalism	Career Mgmt	Talent
62	65	36	68

INSIDE DIRT

Maybe he could score a comeback like Travolta. But the clock's ticking.

◆ He's desperate to be in another hit movie, so he'll drive directors crazy with his obsessiveness. He'll ask them over and over, "Have you gotten *exactly* what you want? Shall we do it again?"

◆ Love his heart. He reached the pinnacle of his career after his first film. His charisma is tied to his virility and danceability.

◆ Get the ramrod out of your ass, Patrick! And nix the hair—it's not the '70s anymore.

◆ He should do a soap as a sexy older man. Otherwise, who's hiring him?

◆ If he ever found a role as the older mentor opposite a younger actor, he could really recapture his audience.

◆ He still gets solid TV numbers in Germany, but theatrically he's a dead issue.

◆ He's definitely over. And overpriced.

Star Power

60
55
50
45
40
35
30
25
20
15

1997 1998 1999

Box Office Bait

MOVIE	STUDIO	N.AMERICAN GROSS	RELEASE
Ghost	Para	$217,534,330	7/13/90
Dirty Dancing	VestRon	$63,422,230	8/21/87
Point Break	Fox	$40,706,215	7/12/91
Red Dawn	MGM	$38,890,177	8/10/84
To Wong Foo, Thanks For Everything – Julie Newmar	Univ	$36,422,690	9/8/95

Career Trajectory

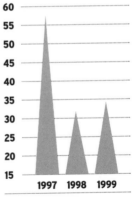

Real Name   Lisa Kudrow
D.O.B.   7/30/63
Place of Birth   Encino, California, USA
Contact   (A) Adam Venit, Endeavor (M) Scott Howard

Willingness to Travel/Promote	Professionalism	Career Mgmt	Talent
66	72	75	72

INSIDE DIRT

She's one of the smartest actresses in terms of picking her roles.

♦ She was wonderful in *The Opposite of Sex* because it was a parody of all those ditzy blondes she made her name playing. But now she's getting a bit long in the tooth.

♦ *Romy and Michelle's High School Reunion* put her on the up elevator from TV to feature-film stardom.

♦ The jury's still out on her. Her career could go the way of Shelley Long.

♦ Internationally, she's just not an issue at all. *Friends* doesn't travel.

♦ She has terrific charisma.

♦ I'd put faith in her if you had really strong material and a good director.

♦ Her career in comedy and romance will only blossom. If she does a *Pretty Woman,* it will be launched forever.

Star Power

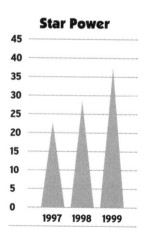

45
40
35
30
25
20
15
10
5
0
　　1997　1998　1999

Box Office Bait

MOVIE	STUDIO	N.AMERICAN GROSS	RELEASE
Analyze This	WB	$106,694,016	3/5/99
Romy and Michelle's High School Reunion	BV	$29,235,353	4/25/97
Mother	Para	$19,119,165	12/25/96
The Opposite of Sex	SPC	$6,367,164	5/22/98
The Unborn	Calfilm	$1,123,219	3/29/91

Career Trajectory

Dennis Hopper

Rank 172   **Bankability 45**

Real Name	Dennis Hopper
D.O.B.	5/17/36
Place of Birth	Dodge City, Kansas, USA
Contact	(M) Mike Menchel, AMG

Willingness to Travel/Promote	Professionalism	Career Mgmt	Talent
74	60	52	68

INSIDE DIRT

He's still the bad boy. He's always good press.

◆ He sees himself as a James Dean rebel, but he looks like a used car salesman.

◆ He's out of touch with where the world is now and what people want to see in terms of stories and acting.

◆ He can play a villain pretty good.

◆ One of the most pleasant guys you'll ever meet. I knew him when he was heavily into drinking and drugs. Now he's a card-carrying, right-wing Republican golfer.

◆ The German film he did, *Straight Shooter,* was an expensive dud. But he worked his ass off doing publicity for it.

◆ He's another guy whose career is living on fumes. Only in his case, he's breathing them in.

Star Power

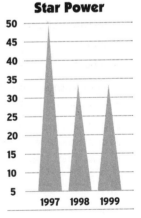

Values shown: 50, 45, 40, 35, 30, 25, 20, 15, 10, 5 — years 1997, 1998, 1999

Box Office Bait

MOVIE	STUDIO	N.AMERICAN GROSS	RELEASE
Speed	Fox	$121,221,490	6/10/94
Waterworld	Univ	$88,214,660	7/28/95
Apocalypse Now (with re-issue)	MGM	$84,456,197	8/15/79
Hoosiers	Orion	$28,607,524	11/14/86
Black Widow	Fox	$22,736,749	2/6/87

Career Trajectory

Gary Sinise   Rank **173**   Bankability **45**

Real Name	Gary Sinise
D.O.B.	3/17/55
Place of Birth	Blue Island, Illinois, USA
Contact	(A) Patrick Whitesell, CAA (M) Brillstein/Grey

Willingness to Travel/Promote	Professionalism	Career Mgmt	Talent
69	**70**	**55**	**76**

INSIDE DIRT

They really respect him overseas.

♦ He's a character actor. Period.

♦ He's too serious. He should lighten up a bit, laugh a little, and get a perspective on his work.

♦ He's going to be a very talented director. Very.

♦ He's more associated with cable movies or MOWs [movies of the week], which is a shame. He should have a broader base as a character actor who is truly pivotal to the storyline.

♦ He would have no impact on my financing decisions.

♦ Gary's gotten more comfortable doing publicity, which should extend his career.

♦ As an actor, he's like Marcel Marceau—he can make flowers appear from thin air and hand them to you. But he's not fall-down gorgeous. He's just plain Everyman—and who wants to pay $9.00 to relate to that?

Star Power

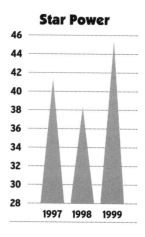

46
44
42
40
38
36
34
32
30
28

1997 1998 1999

Box Office Bait

MOVIE	STUDIO	N.AMERICAN GROSS	RELEASE
Forrest Gump	Para	$329,690,974	7/6/94
Apollo 13	Univ	$172,036,360	6/30/95
Ransom	BV	$136,485,602	11/8/96
Snake Eyes	Para	$55,585,389	8/7/98
The Quick and the Dead	Sony/TS	$18,543,150	2/10/95

Career Trajectory

Whoopi Goldberg

Rank 174   **Bankability 44**

Real Name	Caryn Johnson
D.O.B.	11/13/55
Place of Birth	New York City, New York, USA
Contact	(A) Arnold Rifkin, Cheyenne Enterprises

Willingness to Travel/Promote	Professionalism	Career Mgmt	Talent
53	64	40	67

INSIDE DIRT

She's had more flops than a cow pasture.

- She's a personality more than an actress.
- Some of her best stuff is dramatic, like *The Long Walk Home*.
- It's too bad Whoopi doesn't travel overseas much—she's dynamite with the press.
- Now she's on *Hollywood Squares*, confirming she has one of the worst-managed careers in Hollywood. Instead of "action!" and "cut!" it's all about "I'll take Whoopi to block."
- She needs to choose character-driven roles in better comedy scripts.
- Her anger can make for a very unpleasant set. She seems to always think the director is an idiot and the producer is a sleaze bag, which may not be far from the truth.
- When she tried to be romantic on screen, I almost barfed. *No one* wants to see Whoopi go there.
- At least in France, Whoopi will have a long career. But I don't know in what.

Star Power

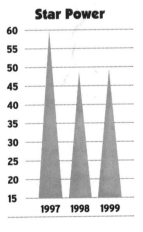

Box Office Bait			
MOVIE	STUDIO	N.AMERICAN GROSS	RELEASE
The Lion King (voice)	BV	$312,855,561	6/15/94
Ghost	Para	$217,534,330	7/13/90
Sister Act	BV	$139,605,150	5/29/92
The Rugrats Movie (voice)	Para	$100,494,675	11/20/98
The Color Purple (with re-issue)	WB	$95,767,388	12/18/85

Career Trajectory

Leslie Nielsen Rank 175 Bankability 44

Real Name Leslie Nielsen
D.O.B. 2/11/26
Place of Birth Regina, Saskatchewan, Canada
Contact (A) Bresler, Kelly & Assoc.

Willingness to Travel/Promote	Professionalism	Career Mgmt	Talent
83	81	75	59

INSIDE DIRT

He puts bums on seats in Britain.

- He's his own franchise. You know what a Leslie Nielsen movie is. You buy that ticket and you know you're going to be laughing at banana-peel comedy.

- He's professional, funny, and great to work with. He's written his own movie and stars in every scene.

- Hard to believe that one time he was a very serious actor. He's very grateful to be perceived as a comedian, and I think he'll stay there. It's going to be very hard for him ever to go back to serious parts.

- On the first day of his new movie he tripped over a cable and broke his nose. He handled it with such panache you'd think it was part of the film.

Star Power

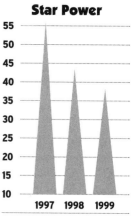

| | 1997 | 1998 | 1999 |

Box Office Bait

MOVIE	STUDIO	N.AMERICAN GROSS	RELEASE
Naked Gun 2 $1/_2$: The Smell of Fear	Para	$86,930,411	6/28/91
Airplane!	Para	$83,400,000	1980
Naked Gun: From the Files of Police Squad	Para	$78,041,829	12/2/88
The Naked Gun 33 $1/_3$: The Final Insult	Para	$50,996,948	3/18/94
Nuts	WB	$30,455,028	11/20/87

Career Trajectory

Anjelica Huston

Rank 176 **Bankability 44**

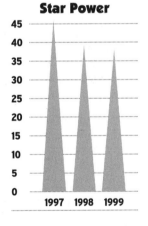

Real Name Anjelica Houston
D.O.B. 7/8/51
Place of Birth Santa Monica, California, USA
Contact (A) Toni Howard, ICM

Willingness to Travel/Promote **74** **Professionalism** **73** **Career Mgmt** **55** **Talent** **81**

INSIDE DIRT

She's had a quixotic career.

◆ Like Bette Midler, when they start casting you as the wicked witch, it's all over. Where do you go from there?

◆ She was smart to direct herself as the lead in "Agnes Browne," because no one else would have given her the role. She's lost momentum.

◆ She travels a lot and is good at supporting her films.

◆ She neither helps nor hurts a film package overseas. We're neutral about her.

◆ She's hurt by her own strength. She comes across as a very formidable screen presence. And in mainstream films, roles aren't there for that kind of persona—except as bitchy bosses and action heroines.

◆ Unlike Meryl Streep, she's too imposing to play maternal.

◆ Now she's producing and directing—the last refuge of the undervalued middle-aged actress in Hollywood.

◆ Great genes. Great talent.

Star Power

	1997	1998	1999

(chart showing values 45, 40, 35, 30, 25, 20, 15, 10, 5, 0)

Box Office Bait

MOVIE	STUDIO	N.AMERICAN GROSS	RELEASE
The Addams Family	Para	$113,379,166	11/22/91
Ever After	Fox	$65,703,412	7/31/98
Addams Family Values	Para	$45,703,556	11/19/93
Prizzi's Honor	Fox	$26,657,534	6/14/85
The Player	FL	$21,706,101	4/10/92

Career Trajectory

Bette Midler Rank 177 Bankability 44

Real Name	Bette Midler
D.O.B.	12/1/45
Place of Birth	Honolulu, Hawaii, USA
Contact	(A) Adam Venit, Endeavor

Willingness to Travel/Promote	Professionalism	Career Mgmt	Talent
72	66	 51	82

INSIDE DIRT

She's best when she's lewd.

- A marvelous comedienne and a full-scale dramatic talent.

- She's the greatest performer I've ever seen.

- She needs the right role. Everyone still wants her to sing.

- Up until *First Wives Club,* Bette was box-office poison overseas.

- Research screenings for *First Wives Club* showed that Japanese audiences preferred Bette over everyone.

- Her willingness to travel goes up depending on the amount of international magazine covers she sees other actresses on.

- Bette's negative is that she's had lots of flops and appeals to a much older record-buying and moviegoing public.

- I like her because she doesn't have the perfect Hollywood body.

- I don't see any long-term star allure. She's going to become a middle-age Jewish grandmother, a character comedienne. Her time has passed.

- Bette's a survivor.

Star Power

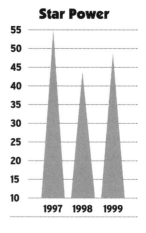

	Box Office Bait			
MOVIE	**STUDIO**	**N.AMERICAN GROSS**	**RELEASE**
First Wives Club	Para	$105,475,862	9/20/96
Oliver and Company (voice)	BV	$74,013,760	11/18/88
Ruthless People	BV	$71,624,879	6/27/86
Down and Out in Beverly Hills	BV	$62,134,225	1/31/86
Beaches	BV	$56,444,103	12/28/88

Career Trajectory

Dennis Quaid Rank **178** Bankability **44**

Real Name	Dennis Quaid
D.O.B.	4/9/54
Place of Birth	Houston, Texas, USA
Contact	(A) Jim Wiatt, WMA

Willingness to Travel/Promote — **72**

Professionalism — **73**

Career Mgmt — **37**

Talent — **69**

INSIDE DIRT

His acting abilities are very undervalued.

- Dennis has fortunately picked his mate well. Meg Ryan can still carry a movie; he can't.

- His best roles have been the crazy guys or bad seeds. In his case, that doesn't make for a leading man.

- I liked working with Dennis. He has other interests besides movies. During *Dragonheart* he was reading the Koran.

- His screen presence is a little surly and offputting.

- Wow, there's a career that's over. As Meg rises, he tanks. It probably doesn't hurt their marriage—he's like Mr. Mom.

- I think it's hard for Dennis to stand in the shadow of his wife. Their marriage is so strong because of their son Jack. They say playing baseball with Jack is the best thing about their lives.

Star Power

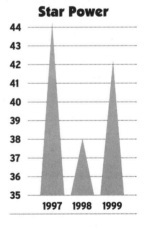

44, 43, 42, 41, 40, 39, 38, 37, 36, 35

1997 1998 1999

Box Office Bait

MOVIE	STUDIO	N.AMERICAN GROSS	RELEASE
The Parent Trap	BV	$66,308,518	7/29/98
Dragonheart	Univ	$51,385,101	5/31/96
Something to Talk About	WB	$50,835,801	8/4/95
Jaws 3-D	Univ	$42,245,180	1983
Postcards From the Edge	Columbia	$39,071,604	1990

Career Trajectory

Jet Li

Real Name	Li Lian Jie
D.O.B.	4/26/63
Place of Birth	Bejing, China
Contact	(A) Steve Chasman, Immortal Entertainment

Willingness to Travel/Promote	Professionalism	Career Mgmt	Talent
62	**70**	**65**	**54**

INSIDE DIRT

Unless he diversifies, he'll remain the millennial incarnation of Fu Man Chu.

◆ His type is the sidekick or best friend of the evil Asian.

◆ This whole preoccupation with East meets West in Hollywood has another five years left, so he'll be marketable at least until then.

◆ His value is so high in action territories like Latin America and Asia that it makes up for his lower profile elsewhere.

◆ In Hollywood, being Asian limits you even more than if you're black.

◆ I think he has a shot. He's a better actor and has a stronger persona than Chow Yun-Fat. And he had the good luck to be in *Lethal Weapon 4* and get noticed. Otherwise, who would have seen him in those chop-socky movies?

Star Power

34
32
30
28
26
24
22
20
18
16

1997 1998 1999

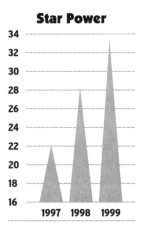

Career Trajectory

Box Office Bait

MOVIE	STUDIO	N.AMERICAN GROSS	RELEASE
Lethal Weapon 4	WB	$129,734,803	7/10/98
Black Mask	Artisan	$12,504,289	5/14/99

Andie MacDowell

Rank 180 **Bankability 44**

Real Name   Rosalie Anderson MacDowell
D.O.B.   4/21/58
Place of Birth   Gaffney, South Carolina, USA
Contact   (A) Risa Shapiro, ICM

Willingness to Travel/Promote 68 **Professionalism** 71 **Career Mgmt** 71 **Talent** 54

INSIDE DIRT

Four Weddings and a Funeral—how lucky can you get?

♦ She's not the girl next door so much as the wife next door.

♦ Andie is tougher to hire because she lives out of state and has a lot of motherly responsibilities.

♦ She's a weak actress who's been used correctly in nearly all her films. That's great career management.

♦ Typical model turned actress. It's all about attitude and persona with her as opposed to inhabiting a character. Except that in *Unstrung Heroes* she died—that always helps.

♦ Her acting is very intuitive. She needs an intuitive director to play off that, which is why Diane Keaton and Robert Altman work well with her.

♦ Andie's mistakes were *Multiplicity* and *Hudson Hawke*—any part where she plays second cheese to an underwritten male part in a studio tanker.

Star Power

Values on y-axis: 55, 50, 45, 40, 35, 30, 25, 20, 15, 10 across years 1997, 1998, 1999

Box Office Bait

MOVIE	STUDIO	N.AMERICAN GROSS	RELEASE
Michael	NL	$95,229,601	12/25/96
Groundhog Day	Columbia	$70,794,127	2/12/93
Four Weddings and a Funeral	GRAM	$52,636,671	3/9/94
Greystoke: The Legend of Tarzan...	WB	$45,858,563	3/30/84
St. Elmo's Fire	Columbia	$37,803,872	6/28/85

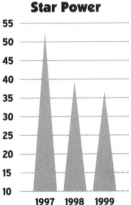

Career Trajectory

Michael J. Fox Rank 181 Bankability 44

Real Name Michael Andrew Fox
D.O.B. 6/9/61
Place of Birth Edmonton, Alberta, Canada
Contact (A) Kevin Huvane, CAA

Willingness to Travel/Promote	Professionalism	Career Mgmt	Talent
70	77	62	57

INSIDE DIRT

He's so strong in TV he really doesn't need a film career.

♦ I have a tremendous amount of respect for him. He was such a huge film star, and when he realized that that moment was over, he chose the right project to go back to TV with.

♦ He'll be a character actor. He's unlikely to be a leading actor in the future, despite TV's *Spin City*.

♦ Let's face it—he's only five foot four. Not exactly leading-man material.

♦ He's a sweetheart. He's always very polite to the stewardesses and signs everything for his fans. Nothing controversial there.

♦ He should do a second or third lead in a film, especially in an ensemble piece.

♦ The best character he's played is in real life: acknowledging his Parkinson's disease.

Star Power

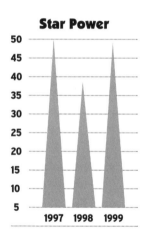

| | | 1997 | 1998 | 1999 |

Box Office Bait			
MOVIE	**STUDIO**	**N.AMERICAN GROSS**	**RELEASE**
Back to the Future	Univ	$210,609,762	7/3/85
Back to the Future II	Univ	$118,450,002	11/24/89
Back to the Future III	Univ	$87,630,852	5/25/90
The Secret of My Success	Univ	$66,987,694	4/10/87
The American President	Sony/C	$60,009,496	11/17/95

Career Trajectory

Bill Pullman Rank 182   Bankability 43

Real Name	Bill Pullman
D.O.B.	12/17/53
Place of Birth	Hornell, New York, USA
Contact	(A) J.J. Harris, UTA

Willingness to Travel/Promote	Professionalism	Career Mgmt	Talent
60	**66**	**55**	**65**

INSIDE DIRT

He's survived through the sheer diversity of his films.

◆ Bill's very nice, very easy to work with. I don't think he's going to be a star, though, despite *Independence Day*.

◆ Doing *The Last Seduction* in the middle of big-budget films like *Independence Day* gave weight to his more commercial performances.

◆ I've heard it over and over—Bill Pullman, Bill Paxton—they're both the same. But *The Last Seduction* distinguished him.

◆ He doesn't carry the baggage of trying to be too serious or heavy about being a great actor. He has more openness than that.

◆ He had a great sense of humor about himself. He jokes with the crew, too. He's just a cool guy.

Star Power

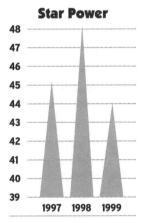

48		
47		
46		
45		
44		
43		
42		
41		
40		
39		
1997	1998	1999

Box Office Bait

MOVIE	STUDIO	N.AMERICAN GROSS	RELEASE
Independence Day	Fox	$306,169,255	7/3/96
Sleepless in Seattle	Tri-Star	$126,007,337	6/25/93
A League of Their Own	Columbia	$107,439,000	7/1/92
Casper	Univ	$100,280,870	5/26/95
While You Were Sleeping	BV	$81,052,361	4/21/95

Career Trajectory

Bridget Fonda

Rank 183   **Bankability 43**

Real Name	Bridget Fonda
D.O.B.	1/27/64
Place of Birth	Los Angeles, California, USA
Contact	(A) IFA

Willingness to Travel/Promote   **Professionalism**   **Career Mgmt**   **Talent**

69   **67**   **41**   **60**

INSIDE DIRT

For financing, she's neither a negative nor a positive.

♦ Bridget Fonda is the most boring actress that ever walked the face of the earth. How do you like that?

♦ I heard she split up with Eric Stoltz. That's all I've heard about her.

♦ Her name makes no difference when we bring her up in negotiating sessions.

♦ She's an extraordinary actress and a very, very bright woman.

♦ Unfortunately, she's chosen to do non-commercial projects, maybe because of how her parents raised her. Now she's an art-house actress. Sayonara, movie star.

♦ She's lucky her last name is Fonda. But the genes are getting weaker as they're passed down, not stronger.

Star Power

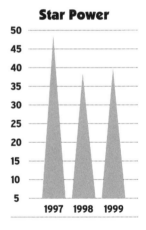

50
45
40
35
30
25
20
15
10
5

1997 1998 1999

Box Office Bait

MOVIE	STUDIO	N.AMERICAN GROSS	RELEASE
The Godfather III	Para	$66,520,529	12/25/90
Doc Hollywood	WB	$54,830,779	8/2/91
Single White Female	Columbia	$48,058,000	8/14/92
Jackie Brown	Miramax/Dimen	$39,647,595	12/25/97
It Could Happen to You	Tri-Star	$37,939,757	7/29/94

Career Trajectory

Jeff Goldblum Rank 184 Bankability 43

Real Name	Jeff Lynn Goldblum
D.O.B.	10/22/52
Place of Birth	Pittsburgh, Pennsylvania, USA
Contact	(A) Adam Venit, Endeavor (M) Keith Addis, Industry Entertainment

Willingness to Travel/Promote	Professionalism	Career Mgmt	Talent
65	**74**	**52**	**68**

INSIDE DIRT

He's a leading actor, but only in indie projects.

♦ He's been in some of the biggest movies ever, like *Independence Day*. But they're special-effects movies where the directors are the stars; their success didn't depend on him. So they haven't helped his bankability.

♦ Those bug eyes give him that edgy look.

♦ I don't think Jeff trusts himself enough. But he's intuitively a brilliant actor. He often plays the goon but he's extremely smart.

♦ It appears there's been a management decision to have him stay out of indie films. That's unwise.

♦ He's priced himself out of the marketplace. Jeff wants $3 million a movie now, and when people tell him that's ridiculous, he keeps reminding them he was in *Jurassic Park*. But on that basis the fucking dinosaurs should be getting $5 million.

Star Power

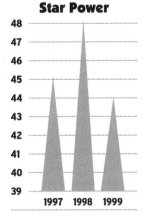

	1997	1998	1999

Box Office Bait

MOVIE	STUDIO	N.AMERICAN GROSS	RELEASE
Jurassic Park	Univ	$357,067,947	6/11/93
Independence Day	Fox	$306,169,255	7/3/96
The Lost World: Jurassic Park	Univ	$229,074,525	5/23/97
The Prince of Egypt	Dreamworks	$101,217,900	12/18/98
Nine Months	Fox	$69,689,009	7/12/95

Career Trajectory

Michael Jordan

Rank 185   **Bankability 43**

Real Name	Michael Jeffrey Jordan
D.O.B.	2/17/63
Place of Birth	Brooklyn, New York, USA
Contact	(M) David Falk

Willingness to Travel/Promote **84**   **Professionalism** **75**   **Career Mgmt** **58**   **Talent** **30**

INSIDE DIRT

He's no Laurence Olivier, that's for sure.

- He'll be stuck in those animated tentpole-type movies, like *Space Jam*.

- He's a guaranteed draw for thirteen-to-seventeen-year-old males.

- I often ask people who is the most famous person on the planet. More people tell me it's Michael Jordan than Clinton or the Pope.

- He's a sports figure, and that just doesn't have crossover potential in Europe.

- He's huge in China. *Space Jam* was a hit there.

- Nice guy. A bit detached. Prefers to have his Michael mafia around him to play poker with and hang as one of the boys. No false machismo on his part.

- He's very professional. Like Schwarzenegger, he always shows up, and he understands marketing very well.

- He's a perfect straight man to Tweety Bird.

Star Power

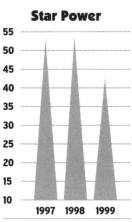

Chart values: 55, 50, 45, 40, 35, 30, 25, 20, 15, 10 — years 1997, 1998, 1999

Career Trajectory

Box Office Bait

MOVIE	STUDIO	N.AMERICAN GROSS	RELEASE
Space Jam	WB	$90,384,232	11/15/96
He Got Game	BV	$21,567,853	5/1/98

Robin Wright Penn

Rank 186   **Bankability 43**

Real Name	Robin Virginia Wright
D.O.B.	4/8/66
Place of Birth	Dallas, Texas, USA
Contact	(A) Hylda Queally, WMA

Willingness to Travel/Promote 52   **Professionalism** 58   **Career Mgmt** 45   **Talent** 65

INSIDE DIRT

Sean may have a lot of control over her career but not over her.

◆ She's a nice girl but a boring actress.

◆ She's an extraordinary actress who can do a lot of different things.

◆ She and Sean Penn have a very close but very turbulent relationship.

◆ Sean didn't want her to leave to go down to Australia to shoot *Paradise Road,* and there were reliable rumors he threw a restraining order on her. In the end, she went and made the movie anyway.

◆ Because Sean is so guarded with the press, she is, too. That antipathy has rubbed off on her.

◆ She married Sean Penn. That should explain the wrinkled face.

◆ Give her credit: She's chosen to have a career *and* a family.

Star Power

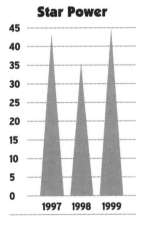

Bar chart showing values near 45 for 1997, approximately 37 for 1998, and near 45 for 1999.

Box Office Bait

MOVIE	STUDIO	N.AMERICAN GROSS	RELEASE
Forrest Gump	Para	$329,690,974	7/6/94
Message in a Bottle	WB	$52,799,004	2/12/99
The Princess Bride	Fox	$26,906,897	9/25/87
Toys	Fox	$21,326,485	12/18/92
She's So Lovely	Miramax	$7,260,472	8/29/97

Career Trajectory

Martin Lawrence

Rank 187　　**Bankability 43**

Real Name	Martin Lawrence
D.O.B.	4/16/65
Place of Birth	Frankfurt, Germany
Contact	(A) Jim Berkus, UTA (M) Michael Green

Willingness to Travel/Promote	Professionalism	Career Mgmt	Talent
49	**48**	**60**	**63**

INSIDE DIRT

He appeals to black audiences more than white ones.

- He recovered remarkably well from his nervous breakdown, when they found him wandering around in the streets of L.A. in his underwear.

- I think he's the new Eddie Murphy, but his niche is the sidekick or the best friend.

- Outside of *Bad Boys,* the international market doesn't remember him. And *Bad Boys* was basically Will Smith's film.

- He's nuts. He's wild.

- *Life* was too ethnic, too black American, to appeal to most of Europe. For me as a French buyer, a movie with Martin Lawrence would be a deterrent.

- As a black actor, he'll never cross over to global appeal. He's too "street," too urban.

Star Power

A bar chart titled "Star Power" with a vertical axis ranging from 31 to 40 and years 1997, 1998, 1999 on the horizontal axis.

Box Office Bait

MOVIE	STUDIO	N.AMERICAN GROSS	RELEASE
Boomerang	Para	$70,052,444	7/1/92
Bad Boys	Sony/C	$66,491,850	4/7/95
Life	Univ	$63,844,974	4/16/99
Nothing to Lose	BV	$44,477,235	7/18/97
Thin Line Between Love and Hate	NL	$34,767,836	4/3/96

Career Trajectory

Oprah Winfrey

Rank 188 **Bankability 43**

Real Name	Oprah Winfrey
D.O.B.	1/29/54
Place of Birth	Kosciusko, Mississippi, USA
Contact	(A) Kevin Huvane CAA

Willingness to Travel/Promote	Professionalism	Career Mgmt	Talent
84	75	60	62

INSIDE DIRT

She's a lean, mean promotion machine.

- She's very popular, very nonthreatening—and very definitely *not* a movie star.

- Here in Britain and everywhere, *Beloved* just died despite all the free hype she gave it on her show. Why? Because she pitched it as an issue film about slavery.

- *Beloved* was so unrelentingly dark and difficult to follow that even Oprah couldn't save it.

- Oprah will still keep working because she promotes whatever she does on her show.

- Yes, she's a promotion machine. But as an actress her success is extremely role-dependent. Otherwise she doesn't much matter.

- Oprah has such a mass following that I think she could star in the phone book and her fans would watch it and say: Wow, did you see page 23?

Star Power

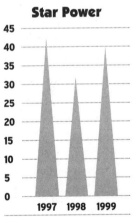

Values on chart: 45, 40, 35, 30, 25, 20, 15, 10, 5, 0 — 1997 1998 1999

Box Office Bait

MOVIE	STUDIO	N.AMERICAN GROSS	RELEASE
The Color Purple (with re-issue)	WB	$95,767,388	12/18/85
Throw Momma From The Train	Orion	$57,695,259	12/11/87
Beloved	BV	$22,843,047	10/16/98
Native Son	IND	$1,301,121	12/25/86
Listen Up	WB	$735,092	10/5/90

Career Trajectory

James Woods

Rank 189 **Bankability 43**

Real Name James Howard Woods
D.O.B. 4/18/47
Place of Birth Vernal, Utah, USA
Contact (A) Toni Howard, ICM

Willingness to Travel/Promote	Professionalism	Career Mgmt	Talent
65	46	62	78

INSIDE DIRT

Off the set he's Mr. Jovial. On the set he gets the Heinrich Himmler Award.

♦ Eventually you'll look at your casting list and come around to him for your paranoid schizophrenic.

♦ We would debate hard whether to bond him. He brings a lot of mental baggage. If the director is weak, Woods will eat him up and try to take control of the scene. And not just the scene but the entire film.

♦ He's a terrific ensemble player and a good video name.

♦ In Germany, his kind of sick characters don't repel us very much, maybe because we've had to live with the image of a bad guy in our past.

♦ As for selling Jimmy Woods overseas? You'd get a yawn.

♦ They say that insecurity is the greatest asset an actor can have. So Woods must have enormous talent.

Star Power

A bar chart titled "Star Power" with y-axis from 0 to 45 and x-axis years 1997, 1998, 1999.

Box Office Bait

MOVIE	STUDIO	N.AMERICAN GROSS	RELEASE
Contact	WB	$100,769,177	7/11/97
Hercules (voice)	BV	$99,111,505	6/13/97
The Specialist	WB	$57,344,996	10/7/94
The Way We Were	Columbia	$49,904,444	1973
Casino	Univ	$42,388,160	11/22/95

Career Trajectory

Emily Watson Rank 190 Bankability 43

Real Name	Emily Watson
D.O.B.	1/14/67
Place of Birth	London, England
Contact	(A) George Freeman ICM

Willingness to Travel/Promote	Professionalism	Career Mgmt	Talent
63	75	73	85

INSIDE DIRT

She needs a big studio picture to go on to the next level.

- Her acting is so penetrating. With each new role she cuts a fresh wound, and you can smell the blood.

- A luminous talent. But she's not yet perceived as an international star. My guess is that she wants that really badly.

- At the Golden Globes she was doing the Minnie Driver imitation. She had the long red gown, the coiffed hair, and the Harry Winston diamonds. She looked like she was trying too hard.

- She's picking more arty roles. That may limit her career, but it may also prolong it. In the art-film world, if you consistently do high-quality product, you work longer.

- She's been nominated for an Oscar twice in three years, and that ain't bad.

Star Power

41
40
39
38
37
36
35
34
33
32

1997 1998 1999

Box Office Bait

MOVIE	STUDIO	N.AMERICAN GROSS	RELEASE
The Boxer	Univ	$5,799,672	12/31/97
Hilary and Jackie	OCT	$4,874,838	12/30/98
Breaking the Waves	OCT	$4,012,819	11/15/96
Metroland	Lion	$299,463	4/9/99

Career Trajectory

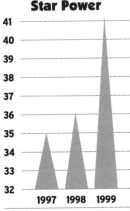

Helena Bonham Carter

Rank 191 **Bankability 43**

Real Name	Helena Bonham Carter
D.O.B.	5/26/66
Place of Birth	Golders Green, London, England
Contact	(A) Adam Isaacs, UTA

Willingness to Travel/Promote	Professionalism	Career Mgmt	Talent
52	68	63	63

INSIDE DIRT

Her name has sales value, especially in the U.K., Italy, and France.

◆ She's cooled off lately—*Theory of Flight* crash-landed, so that hurt her a bit. She was a little self-indulgent in it.

◆ Instead of going for the crass commercial hit, she's chosen roles that make her an art-film actress.

◆ She gives a project instant pedigree.

◆ She wanted to play a Jewish woman who marries a Nazi in our film. I asked her, "Why do you relate to this?" and she said, "Because I'm Jewish." I was stunned. She looks like an English beauty rose.

◆ No, she's not difficult to work with.

◆ In the beginning she was wildly applauded in public just for staring at her shoes—everyone thought she had a neck problem. Now she's poised and self-confident. She's finally come into her own.

Star Power

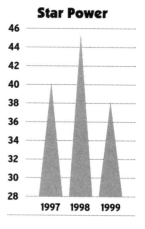

1997 1998 1999

Box Office Bait

MOVIE	STUDIO	N.AMERICAN GROSS	RELEASE
Howards End	SPC	$25,960,280	3/13/92
Mary Shelley's Frankenstein	Tri-Star	$22,006,296	11/4/94
Room with a View	Cinecom	$20,766,644	3/7/86
Hamlet	WB	$20,684,776	12/19/90
The Wings of the Dove	Miramax	$13,661,362	11/7/97

Career Trajectory

Halle Berry Rank **192** Bankability **42**

Real Name	Halle Berry
D.O.B.	8/14/68
Place of Birth	Cleveland, Ohio, USA
Contact	(A) Josh Lieberman, CAA

Willingness to Travel/Promote	Professionalism	Career Mgmt	Talent
59	**80**	**67**	**72**

INSIDE DIRT

She's a terrific team player.

- She goes after what she wants and manages her career shrewdly.

- She's gorgeous, but she doesn't have any clout to headline a film.

- She's adorable and sweet and lovely to work with. The biggest drama on the set was that her dog had puppies. Everyone cared so much about her they felt this was her extended family.

- She was totally prepared for all her scenes. A day before she wrapped, she gave a speech to the crew and did a top-10 list, roasting the director in a very loving way.

- She's a fun, vivacious lady. She's one of those women who's totally beautiful but isn't conscious of it.

- Forget makeup. Here's a girl who looks good rolling out of bed.

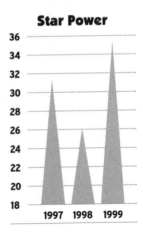

Star Power

36
34
32
30
28
26
24
22
20
18

1997 1998 1999

Box Office Bait

MOVIE	STUDIO	N.AMERICAN GROSS	RELEASE
The Flintstones	Univ	$130,512,915	5/27/94
Boomerang	Para	$70,052,444	7/1/92
The Last Boy Scout	WB	$58,926,549	12/13/91
Executive Decision	WB	$56,679,192	3/15/96
Jungle Fever	Univ	$32,550,172	6/7/91

Career Trajectory

Jean Reno Rank **193** Bankability **42**

Real Name	Juan Moreno
D.O.B.	7/30/48
Place of Birth	Casablanca, Morocco
Contact	(A) Matt Del Tiano, CAA

Willingness to Travel/Promote	Professionalism	Career Mgmt	Talent
72	**75**	**67**	**76**

INSIDE DIRT

His value in Europe is extraordinary.

♦ He and Depardieu are the only two male French stars who have truly crossed over.

♦ He's very smart. He'll always work in France. Being an American movie star is icing on the cake for him.

♦ He promotes his films. His English is good, and he's charming.

♦ He came to the London screening to promote one of his films and meet all the distributors. He knew the film needed help.

♦ His bankable value is minimal. But in the films we've done with him, he's been nothing but professional.

♦ Jean Reno is dynamite. I'd put him in anything. He's vulnerable yet he's a protector. Women like him a lot and so do men.

♦ He's a low-maintenance guy.

Star Power

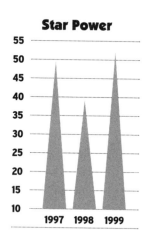

55
50
45
40
35
30
25
20
15
10

1997 1998 1999

Box Office Bait

MOVIE	STUDIO	N.AMERICAN GROSS	RELEASE
Mission: Impossible	Para	$180,981,866	5/22/96
Godzilla	Sony/TS	$136,314,294	5/20/98
Ronin	MGM	$41,609,593	9/25/98
French Kiss	Fox	$38,894,036	5/5/95
The Professional	Columbia	$19,284,974	11/18/94

Career Trajectory

Vince Vaughn Rank **194** Bankability **42**

Real Name Vincent Anthony Vaughn
D.O.B. 3/28/70
Place of Birth Minneapolis, Minnesota, USA
Contact (A) Nick Stevens, UTA

Willingness to Travel/Promote	Professionalism	Career Mgmt	Talent
58	60	50	49

INSIDE DIRT

He's already a B action star.

♦ I never understood why people thought he was ever going to be a megastar. I still don't.

♦ He's charming; he's good-looking. He throws around some attitude and it's kind of fun.

♦ I think he's said yes to too many scripts that he should have said no to.

♦ He seems like he's all surface. Is there anything underneath?

♦ He's good in ensemble roles, as a second lead. But I think he thought his looks would make him a leading man and his talent ain't backing that up.

♦ He's overrated. I don't think he's got enough heft to him to carry a film.

♦ Vince had all that hype and now where is he? Another flavor of the month.

Star Power

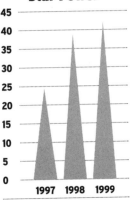

| | 1997 | 1998 | 1999 |

Box Office Bait

MOVIE	STUDIO	N.AMERICAN GROSS	RELEASE
The Lost World: Jurassic Park	Univ	$229,074,525	5/23/97
Rudy	Tri-Star	$22,620,994	10/13/93
Psycho	Univ	$21,380,220	12/4/98
Return To Paradise	Polygram	$8,288,513	8/14/98
Swingers	Miramax	$4,547,038	10/18/96

Career Trajectory

Andy Garcia Rank **195**   Bankability **42**

Real Name	Andrés Arturo García Menéndez
D.O.B.	4/12/56
Place of Birth	Havana, Cuba
Contact	(A) Clifford Stevens, Paradigm (NY)
	(M) Rick Yorn, AMG

Willingness to Travel/Promote	Professionalism	Career Mgmt	Talent
58	**76**	**38**	**66**

INSIDE DIRT

I gave him low points for his career management.

- He was pushed to become a big star once, when he did *Godfather III* and *Internal Affairs*. But in his case, he's not as smart as he thinks he is.

- He's very professional. He's always on time and very committed to his craft.

- When he shoots, he likes to stay where his family is. So if you do a movie with him, you have to figure out how to shoot his part in Los Angeles, irrespective of where the movie is set. *Things to Do in Denver . . .* was shot in L.A. for that reason.

- He's a nice guy. But he's cold as ice in everything he does. He's the box-office kiss of death.

- He really should be doing TNT movies.

Star Power

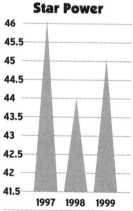

1997 1998 1999

Box Office Bait

MOVIE	STUDIO	N.AMERICAN GROSS	RELEASE
The Untouchables	Para	$76,254,308	6/3/87
The Godfather III	Para	$66,520,529	12/25/90
When a Man Loves a Woman	BV	$50,021,959	4/29/94
Black Rain	Para	$46,184,970	9/22/89
Dead Again	Para	$37,378,123	8/23/91

Career Trajectory

Elisabeth Shue

Rank 196 **Bankability 42**

Real Name	Elisabeth Shue
D.O.B.	10/6/63
Place of Birth	Wilmington, Delaware, USA
Contact	(A) Josh Lieberman, CAA

Willingness to Travel/Promote	Professionalism	Career Mgmt	Talent
51	65	69	70

INSIDE DIRT

She hasn't sold her soul to the studio devils.

- She's making very interesting choices.

- She's an extraordinary actress who has not pushed herself into the mainstream enough to generate commercial strength.

- Her management didn't take advantage of the career upcurve she got from *Leaving Las Vegas*. I thought her performance in that film vastly outshone Nic Cage's.

- First of all, she's gorgeous. Second, she can act. And third, she's bright. You get real value from Elisabeth.

- If she can work on a set with Nicolas Cage, she's got to be reasonably able to tolerate a lot of stuff.

- I don't think she can figure out what she wants to be. And therefore Hollywood can't figure out how to use her.

Star Power

Chart values: 55, 50, 45, 40, 35, 30, 25, 20, 15, 10 — years 1997, 1998, 1999

Box Office Bait

MOVIE	STUDIO	N.AMERICAN GROSS	RELEASE
Back to The Future II	Univ	$118,450,002	11/24/89
The Karate Kid	Columbia	$90,815,558	6/22/84
Back to The Future III	Univ	$87,630,852	5/25/90
Cocktail	BV	$78,059,216	7/29/88
The Saint	Para	$61,355,436	4/4/97

Career Trajectory

Greg Kinnear

Rank 197 **Bankability 42**

Real Name	Greg Kinnear
D.O.B.	6/17/63
Place of Birth	Logansport, Indiana, USA
Contact	(A) Bryan Lourd, CAA

Willingness to Travel/Promote	Professionalism	Career Mgmt	Talent
72	70	62	60

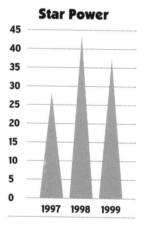

INSIDE DIRT

He's supporting actor material.

♦ He did such a terrific job in *As Good As It Gets*. But now they're actually casting gay men to play gay men, like Rupert Everett, so the whole character type he inhabited so effectively isn't really available to him anymore.

♦ The romantic leading man isn't his forte—he's too old and hasn't the looks.

♦ He'd better watch out, because John Henson, his replacement on E!'s *Talk Soup,* now has a movie development deal himself.

♦ He's quite good, but at $1 to 2 million he's overpriced.

♦ He's made great choices like *As Good As It Gets* and insufferable choices like *Dear God.*

♦ Greg, I have one word for you: cute. That's pretty much it.

♦ I just don't get his appeal. Vanilla, vanilla, vanilla. I'm sleeping already.

Star Power

	1997	1998	1999

(bar chart: 1997 ≈ 27, 1998 ≈ 41, 1999 ≈ 36; scale 0–45)

Box Office Bait

MOVIE	STUDIO	N.AMERICAN GROSS	RELEASE
As Good As It Gets	Sony/TS	$148,478,011	12/24/97
You've Got Mail	WB	$115,731,542	12/18/98
Beavis and Butt-Head Do America (voice)	Para	$62,813,703	12/20/96
Sabrina	Para	$53,669,845	12/15/95
Mystery Men	Univ	$10,017,865	8/6/99

Career Trajectory

Geoffrey Rush Rank 198 Bankability 42

Real Name Geoffrey Rush
D.O.B. 7/6/51
Place of Birth Toowoomba, Queensland, Australia
Contact (A) Fred Specktor, CAA

Willingness to Travel/Promote	Professionalism	Career Mgmt	Talent
64	77	70	79

INSIDE DIRT

He's beginning to be able to carry a movie—an art-house movie.

◆ I think *The House on Haunted Hill* was a mistake for him. But he's an excellent actor.

◆ He's not a leading man. His *Shine* Oscar was for playing a character part.

◆ He let us share his limo whenever we wanted at the Moscow Film festival. He did all the interviews requested of him. He takes his newfound celebrity in stride. An all-around great guy.

◆ In Australia he's always been known as a tremendous comedian. Thank god *Shakespeare in Love* showed his talents in that department. He should do a lot more comedy.

Star Power

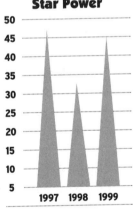

50
45
40
35
30
25
20
15
10
5

1997 1998 1999

Box Office Bait

MOVIE	STUDIO	N.AMERICAN GROSS	RELEASE
Shakespeare in Love	Miramax	$100,241,322	12/11/98
Shine	FL	$35,888,564	11/22/96
Elizabeth	GRAM	$30,012,990	11/6/98
Les Miserables	Sony	$14,096,321	5/1/98
Mystery Men	Univ	$10,017,865	8/6/99

Career Trajectory

Ian McKellen

Rank 199 **Bankability 42**

Real Name	Ian Murray McKellen
D.O.B.	5/25/39
Place of Birth	Burnley, Lancashire, England
Contact	(A) Chris Andrews, ICM

Willingness to Travel/Promote 62 **Professionalism** 87 **Career Mgmt** 73 **Talent** 90

INSIDE DIRT

He saved his film career with *Gods and Monsters*.

♦ He was destined to be this generation's John Gielgud, where his best work would have been on stage. Just in the nick of time came *Gods and Monsters,* and people realized how great he was.

♦ His name still doesn't bring in financing. It was impossible to sell *Gods and Monsters* before it got its Oscar nominations.

♦ The fact that he was nominated for playing a gay part was extraordinary.

♦ A wonderful, wonderful character actor.

♦ He and Rupert Everett are role models as successful gay actors.

♦ In *Apt Pupil,* Brad Renfro looked frightened by Sir Ian's sheer acting ability.

♦ He took Monica Lewinsky to the British premiere of *Gods and Monsters.* That's one way to keep you on Hollywood's call sheets.

Star Power

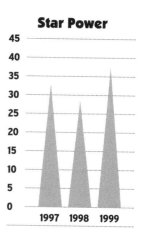

A bar chart showing values for 1997, 1998, and 1999, with the y-axis ranging from 0 to 45.

Box Office Bait

MOVIE	STUDIO	N.AMERICAN GROSS	RELEASE
Last Action Hero	Columbia	$50,016,394	6/18/93
The Shadow	Univ	$31,951,990	7/1/94
I'll Do Anything	Columbia	$10,424,645	2/4/94
Apt Pupil	Sony	$8,814,516	10/23/98
Scandal	Miramax	$8,800,000	4/28/89

Career Trajectory

Steven Seagal

Rank 200 **Bankability 41**

Real Name	Steven Seagal
D.O.B.	4/10/52
Place of Birth	Lansing, Michigan, USA
Contact	(A) Jason Barrett, ICM

Willingness to Travel/Promote	Professionalism	Career Mgmt	Talent
35	26	52	20

INSIDE DIRT

It's a miracle that Steven Seagal is even on this list.

♦ He and Van Damme will be making straight-to-video movies the rest of their lives.

♦ He is the self-proclaimed authority on every subject known to man. He knows everybody's job better than they do.

♦ Like Stallone, the greater his success, the worse directors he has chosen to work with, because he wants to take over the director's job.

♦ Internationally, women never liked him.

♦ Our production got all these mysterious bills for his medication. We wrote them off as first-aid kits.

♦ I don't think he's particularly difficult to work with.

♦ His career is beyond the after-burner stage—it's on the fumes. And by the way, that's a Goodyear Blimp coming toward you—oh, no, it's not! It's Steven Seagal!

Star Power

65
60
55
50
45
40
35
30
25
20

1997 1998 1999

Box Office Bait

MOVIE	STUDIO	N.AMERICAN GROSS	RELEASE
Under Siege	WB	$83,511,316	10/9/92
Executive Decision	WB	$56,679,192	3/15/96
Under Siege 2: Dark Territory	WB	$50,022,097	7/14/95
Hard to Kill	WB	$47,381,386	2/9/90
Marked for Death	Fox	$43,120,554	10/5/90

Career Trajectory

Appendix A

Star Lists

The Bottom of the Heap

(Stars who just missed the list)

1. Tobey Maguire
2. Robert Carlyle
3. Matthew Broderick
4. Courteney Cox
5. Penelope Cruz
6. Matthew Perry
7. Edward Burns
8. Kathy Bates
9. Gillian Anderson
10. Joan Cusack
11. Emmanuelle Beart
12. Mel Brooks
13. Gabriel Byrne
14. James Coburn
15. Jeff Daniels
16. Faye Dunaway
17. Laura Dern
18. Patricia Arquette
19. Joe Pesci
20. Ryan Philippe

Top Women Stars

	Name	Bankability
1.	Julia Roberts	100
2.	Meg Ryan	93
3.	Michelle Pfeiffer	81
4.	Gwyneth Paltrow	80
5.	Cameron Diaz	79
6.	Catherine Zeta-Jones	79
7.	Nicole Kidman	78
8.	Jodie Foster	76
9.	Sandra Bullock	74
10.	Sharon Stone	73
11.	Meryl Streep	70
12.	Ashley Judd	68
13.	Annette Bening	67
14.	Sigourney Weaver	66
15.	Demi Moore	66
16.	Kim Basinger	65
17.	Drew Barrymore	64
18.	Kate Winslet	64
19.	Winona Ryder	63
20.	Cate Blanchett	63
21.	Goldie Hawn	62
22.	Barbra Streisand	62
23.	Julianne Moore	61
24.	Helen Hunt	61
25.	Jennifer Lopez	60
26.	Glenn Close	60
27.	Natalie Portman	60
28.	Rene Russo	60
29.	Charlize Theron	60
30.	Emma Thompson	59
31.	Uma Thurman	59

Out of a possible 100 points

Top African-American Stars

	Name	Bankability
1.	Will Smith	90
2.	Denzel Washington	83
3.	Eddie Murphy	82
4.	Wesley Snipes	74
5.	Samuel L. Jackson	63
6.	Whitney Houston	58
7.	Morgan Freeman	54
8.	Chris Rock	53
9.	Cuba Gooding, Jr.	49
10.	Danny Glover	48
11.	Laurence Fishburne	46
12.	Chris Tucker	45
13.	Angela Bassett	45
14.	Whoopi Goldberg	44
15.	Michael Jordan	43
16.	Martin Lawrence	43
17.	Oprah Winfrey	43
18.	Halle Berry	42
19.	Janet Jackson	38
20.	Ice Cube	38
21.	Sidney Poitier	36
22.	Spike Lee	34
23.	Michael Clarke Duncan	33
24.	Ving Rhames	31
25.	Queen Latifah	30
26.	Forest Whitaker	29
27.	Jamie Foxx	29
28.	Don Cheadle	29
29.	Charles S. Dutton	28
30.	Damon Wayans	27

Out of a possible 100 points

Top Latino Stars

Name	Bankability
Cameron Diaz	79
Antonio Banderas	69
Jennifer Lopez	60
Salma Hayek	52
Freddie Prinze, Jr.	51
Andy Garcia	42
Penelope Cruz	41
Rosie Perez	31
Ruben Blades	24
Hector Elizondo	24
Jimmy Smits	23
Edward James Olmos	19
Julie Carmen	19
Sonia Braga	18
John Leguizamo	17
Anthony Quinn	17
Trini Alvarado	16
Maria Conchita Alonso	15
Lorenzo Lamas	15
Wilson Cruz	14
Esai Morales	12
Richard "Cheech" Marin	11

Out of a possible 100 points

Top Asian Stars

Name	Bankability
Jackie Chan	70
Chow Yun-Fat	46
Jet Li	44
Michelle Yeoh	30
Tia Carrere	28
Joan Chen	28
Gong Li	24
Lou Diamond Philips	23
Jason Scott Lee	19
Rae Dawn Chong	19
Jason Lee	16
Maggie Cheung	14
Gary Tagawa	13
John Lone	13
Bai Ling	13
Margaret Cho	13
B. D. Wong	10
Pat "Nariyuk"; "Pat" Norita	10
Ming-Na Wen	6
Soon Tek Oh	4

Out of a possible 100 points

The Top Ten Directors

1. Steven Spielberg   100
2. James Cameron   97
3. George Lucas   94
4. Roland Emmerich   91
5. Sam Mendes   90
6. Oliver Stone   89
7. Wolfgang Petersen   89
8. Ridley Scott   87
9. Martin Scorsese   86
10. Robert Zemeckis   85

Appendix B

Voices from the Scene

What demands does an actor make of a producer? Never-ending. They're like black holes to China—there's no light that comes out of them.

—Producer

I don't get too close to stars. I don't like to become friends when I'm working with them. They're too narcissistic. There's no nurturing from stars. There's nothing given back to you, except glamor. That's part of their quality. You have to respect it.

—Manager

Most people assume actors are stupid. I always assume they have something to say.

—Director

Without the glamor and the celebrities, producing a film is like building a dog food factory. It's just this much lumber and that many electricians.

—Financial Executive

In the end, working for (the star) was just exhausting—the screaming, the coverups and the image-making. The reason I left? It was like riding a mechanical bull. The reason you get thrown from the bull isn't because of the bull, but because you're too tired to hold on.

—Studio Executive

Other people might say what a nice guy an actor is on a set. But that's usually such bullshit. Do you mean *really* nice? If most actors come out of their trailer and don't spit fire and yell, "Where the fuck is my chair?", then crew people will say, "Oh, he's great to work with."

—Crewmember

She was horrible. The first day she stayed in her trailer and was late three hours to the set. The second day, three hours. She was late on the third day so as the producer I read over my SAG book and there this little-known clause called the Recalcitrant Actors clause. That makes actors responsible for the overages and insurance expenses they incur. So I called the Guild and I invoked it! Within 20 minutes there were 12 union reps that came down to the set and got her out of her trailer.

—Producer

A lot of stars aren't crazy. They're like kids. They're only crazy when you let them be crazy.

—Director

Actors are investments. From a guarantor's perspective, it's not our obligation or right to judge the excess or the absurdity of what goes on. If it's in the budget, then you accept the behavior of that culture. Nothing more to say.

—Film Bonder

We rave about an actor when they're just doing their job, because we're used to the jerks. Many of them are doing it just for the money. They're not doing it for the movie.

—Crewmember

I'm not going to mention names, but I have had a number of actors I've tried to make movies with, who needed urine samples. I don't think we need to go there.

—Director/Producer

There are too many movie stars in Hollywood and not enough real actors.

—Director

These actors are making so much money and it's our job to be a slave and make sure everything is really pleasant for them. And that's what pisses me off about the whole system. They get hissy and demanding. It's the kind of behavior you wouldn't accept in any other human being who wasn't making so much money.

—Crewmember

Hollywood's no more catty or difficult than theater or the advertising business. There's nothing different about Hollywood, except how much people get paid.

—Writer/Producer

The truth is, the greater the star you become, the more and more unfamiliar the word "no" becomes to you. It's all about how to deal with that.

—Production Executive

It's all about psychology. If you approach somebody like a big movie star, then they'll take that rope and tug on it. They'll become that movie star, they'll make all those demands.

—Script Woman

Sure, crews become interchangeable for a star. A movie has up to two hundred people in its cast and crew, and a star can often shoot five movies a year. That's potentially 1,000 people each year they have to remember the name for. Who could do that?

—Production Coordinator

He was in the office screaming at these studio guys, "I'll never work with you fuckheads again!" He was ballistic. Then a year later this same director is actually hired by the same studio people. So I asked him, what about "never working" with them again? And he said, "Well, that was when I thought they'd never ask."

—Producer

I tried to get her out of the makeup trailer for fifteen minutes. But she was in the middle of telling this story to everyone about how she had fucked this guy and how she was so high and so drunk that she fell on her face and broke her nose—or was it his nose? And I was pushing the button down on my walkie-talkie so everyone on the set could hear it.

—Crewmember

If an actor's a jerk to the crew, believe me they'll be a jerk back.

—Producer

The thing that kills me is that these stars are so desperate to be acknowledged and worshipped and loved that they would do it all for free if they had to. We pay them $20 million and they'd do it for fuckin' free. That's the kick in the ass.

—Star's Executive

I'm retiring to write my memoirs. I get to rant on D-boys and D-girls and say what I *really* think about this town. It's called *I'll Breathe Through the Pain: Confessions of a Hollywood Bottom.*

—Hollywood Executive

Star Index